Staircases or Treadmills?

Staircases or Treadmills?

*Labor Market Intermediaries
and Economic Opportunity
in a Changing Economy*

Chris Benner • Laura Leete • Manuel Pastor

Russell Sage Foundation • New York

The Russell Sage Foundation

The Russell Sage Foundation, one of the oldest of America's general purpose foundations, was established in 1907 by Mrs. Margaret Olivia Sage for "the improvement of social and living conditions in the United States." The Foundation seeks to fulfill this mandate by fostering the development and dissemination of knowledge about the country's political, social, and economic problems. While the Foundation endeavors to assure the accuracy and objectivity of each book it publishes, the conclusions and interpretations in Russell Sage Foundation publications are those of the authors and not of the Foundation, its Trustees, or its staff. Publication by Russell Sage, therefore, does not imply Foundation endorsement.

Library of Congress Cataloging-in-Publication Data

Benner, Chris.
   Staircases or treadmills? Labor market intermediaries and economic opportunity in a changing economy / by Chris Benner, Laura Leete and Manuel Pastor.
      p. cm.
   Includes bibliographical references.
   ISBN-13: 978-0-87154-169-7
   ISBN-10: 0-87154-169-6
   1. Employment agencies. 2. Labor market—United States. 3. Labor supply—United States. I. Leete, Laura. II. Pastor, Manuel. 1956– III. Title.
   HD5861.B46 2007
   331.12′80973—dc22

                                                                                    2006033288

Text design by Genna Patacsil.

RUSSELL SAGE FOUNDATION
112 East 64th Street, New York, New York 10021
10 9 8 7 6 5 4 3 2 1

Contents

About the Authors

CHRIS BENNER is an assistant professor of geography at the Pennsylvania State University.

LAURA LEETE is Fred H. Paulus Director of Public Policy Research and associate professor of economics and public policy at Willamette University.

MANUEL PASTOR is professor of geography and American studies and ethnicity at the University of Southern California.

The authors had five collaborators:
Annette Bernhardt, deputy director of the Poverty Program at the Brennan Center for Justice at New York University School of Law; **Bob Brownstein,** policy and research director of Working Partnerships USA in San Jose, California; **Laura Dresser,** research director of the Center on Wisconsin Strategy, University of Wisconsin at Madison; **Justin Scoggins,** assistant research specialist at the Center for Justice, Tolerance, and Community at the University of California at Santa Cruz; and **Sarah Zimmerman,** director of research and government affairs at the Service Employees International Union (SEIU), Local 1000, Sacramento, California.

Foreword

The idea for the research project that forms the basis of this book first emerged out of the efforts of Working Partnerships USA (WPUSA) in Silicon Valley, and the Center on Wisconsin Strategy (COWS) in Wisconsin. Both organizations have experimented with building labor market intermediaries as part of a broader strategy of promoting improved wages, better working conditions, and "high-road" economic strategies. Now that the research has been completed, we have been asked by the authors to say something about the organizational background to the study it reports, and the implications of its finding for future work. What inspired our interest in worker-friendly labor market intermediaries in the first place, and how did they fit into broader organizational goals? What did we hope to learn from this comparative study? What do we take from its conclusions? In this foreword, we offer some answers to these questions.

Why were we interested in intermediaries? The answer is straightforward. It is not news that the old institutions of the American labor market are no longer working for most workers. For a generation now, in sharp contrast both to America's past and other countries today, U.S. worker compensation has fallen behind productivity growth. Deregulation, union decline, and corporate and workplace restructuring have defeated expectations of job security or advancement for many. Unprecedented inequalities have opened in labor markets, and a growing share of workers are stuck in dead-end jobs within them. Policy response to these developments has been feeble, when not actually making them worse. Pretty clearly, the distinctive American employer-based welfare state is dead or dying, and suitable institutions and policies have not replaced it.

Since their beginnings a decade or more ago, COWS and WPUSA have been centrally concerned with these problems and in modeling regional policy and institutional solutions to them. Simply put, we built the worker-friendly intermediaries that we did—at COWS, the Wisconsin Regional Training Partnership (WRTP), and at WPUSA, the Working Partnership Staffing Services Firm (WPSS), and Temp Worker Membership Association—because we thought they might be part of such solutions.

By way of background, our two organizations are clearly different in institutional structure and area of most intense field experiment: respectively, with COWS based at the University of Wisconsin and doing most of its early field work in Milwaukee, and WPUSA affiliated with San Jose's South Bay Central Labor Council and focusing on Silicon Valley. But both organizations share a comparable "think-and-do-tank" mix of applied research and institutional experimentation. They are also committed to promoting "high-road" strategies of firm and regional competitiveness—that is, strategies centered on adding value and reducing waste in regional economies, and equitably capturing the benefits of doing both, with the aid of more competent and accountable public institutions—as against the "low-road" alternative of simply reducing firm costs by reducing labor costs, regulatory standards, and tax burden for public goods. Both organizations also concentrate their efforts in metropolitan regions, which comprise most of the national economy. Of great interest and promise to us, their greater population and firm density, built infrastructure and potential financial base for more abundant public goods, and better prospects for popular democratic organization also make metropolitan regions natural platforms for building the high road.

In the years before this study, in both metro Milwaukee and metro San Jose, we had seen sharp increases in wage inequality, job dislocation, and, especially at the bottom of the labor market, decreased access to career advancement opportunity. In an evolving labor market, we also found tremendous confusion among both workers and employers about existing, needed, and desirable levels and kinds of workforce skills, and the means of their efficient supply. For low-roading employers content to sweat labor, this skill question was distinctly secondary. But for workers seeking something better, and for employers seeking to upgrade their operations in face of new competitive pressures, it suggested an opportunity for improving living standards. WRTP and WPSS were built to develop that opportunity.

An ideal (or close to ideal) labor market for individual workers would be one that, however fluid its application of human capital, had steadily rising levels of demand for varied skills, was transparent to participants in its entry requirements and terms of skill advancement, and enabled and rewarded that advancement for all. Existing labor markets, of course, are very far from this ideal. Skill demand is uneven and less than transparent, opportunities to meet it are unfairly distributed among workers, and skill acquisition is commonly not rewarded. But we thought that the new institutions we were building could get us closer.

These did indeed engage in what the study here calls market-meeting, -molding, and -making functions. Part of their work ("meeting") was about solving coordination problems that the market was not solving on its own by providing better information about job opportunities and their skill requirements and making better connections between job seekers and providers. A larger part of their work ("molding") was about improving current or prospective job quality and opportunities for advancement by developing clearer entry-level skill standards and regional skill-based career ladders, as well as allied compensation systems, to replace the firm- and job-based ones of old. More fundamentally still ("making"), they aimed at restructuring the regional labor market by developing sectoral upgrading throughout its key sectors and equipping workers, firms, and public institutions with capacity to meet the more stringent performance demands that such practice implied.

As evident from these endeavors, we saw our intermediary efforts as part of a larger policy and institutional agenda. As often summarized, that agenda was to close off the low road, help pave the high road, and enable workers and firms stuck on the first to roll along the second. Intermediaries were critical to the second and third parts of this strategy, but that still left the conflict-laden first. Unlike more hopeful observers of American labor markets, we saw little evidence that increased competition would inevitably lead to skill-upgrading or higher compensation. The low-road option, however disastrous socially, was clearly a live option. And its pursuit by some firms made high-roading more difficult for others by eating away at their markets and weakening their political will. It had to be discouraged.

From the start, then, our specific intermediary efforts rested in a strategy of both carrots (assistance to firms of all kinds) and sticks (higher standards on firm performance) and of new sorts of cooperation and conflict between labor and firms. This mix was at first confusing to many of our eventual partners in the efforts. Labor was skeptical that we could get beyond mere adversarialism without selling out—that is, that we could work so closely with firms without compromising our commitments to workers—or doubtful that any cooperation could survive the emergence of conflict. Business was skeptical that we had anything to offer them but conflict, and nervous that the cooperation we promised was just a "camel's nose" for recruiting their workers into unions. Public sector institutions were skeptical that private sector actors would actually improve their performance, not just engage in rent-seeking. Firms were also suspicious of each other's motives. The same was true of labor and community.

Despite these problems, obviously, the experiments went forward. We leave it to readers to judge their respective success. The volume that follows documents that they delivered concrete gains to large numbers of workers, helped firms upgrade, and effectively fed broader policy advocacy. We are partial, of course, but for us that makes them at least a qualified success. In any case, that record and this rationale are probably enough to explain why we tried them in the first place and why readers might be interested in learning more.

What did we hope to learn from this research? We wanted to understand, in very different labor markets, the pervasiveness of the trends we were responding to. We wanted to understand how workers felt about existing labor market institutions, and how other intermediaries were performing. We were in general less concerned than the authors with the common use of other types of LMI's, but we were very interested in their qualitative variation. And most of all, we wanted to identify opportunities and barriers to improving the performance of intermediaries like the ones we were associated with—either by improving their own operation or knitting them into a new system of regional labor market institutions.

And, finally, what do we make of the conclusions of this study? *Staircases or Treadmills?* finds in part a high incidence of intermediaries; as a class, little positive impact by them on work, with actual negative effect by temp agencies; but positive outcomes from a limited number of "best practice" intermediaries, including our own. None of these conclusions particularly surprises us. Given the amount of confusion in American labor markets at present, it is natural that a large number of organizations will arise and overclaim their address of worker problems. And some, like the temp agencies to which WPUSA tried to build an employer rival, will actively exploit worker vulnerability. That explicitly labor-friendly efforts do significant good is also unsurprising. The real question is how to get more of the last category of intermediaries, or their functional equivalent, in better designed regional labor market systems.

Here we think the authors' suggestions—more professional management, the encouragement of worker-owned alternatives, clearer standards on performance, better coordination between private and public intermediaries—all make sense. We should learn from good intermediaries, deliberately support their work, integrate them in public systems in the pursuit of public ends, and encourage further experiment and learning by them.

But in truth, to get the full contribution of worker-friendly intermediaries, we do not think there is a substitute for higher public standards on firms themselves, more deliberate public efforts at sectoral upgrading, and a much greater commitment to preparing adult workers for the higher demands from firms that would result—a deliberate public effort to take the high road. Along with the policies just mentioned, that means greater economic protections for workers—a higher social wage of health insurance, retirement security, and access to lifelong training; a renewed commitment to full employment; a restored right to form their own associations in the economy (unions)—especially as they are asked to take on new risks and contribute more to economic governance. It means removing from our tax codes, land use law, and much else current subsidies to the low-roading alternative, and encouraging regional cooperation on the high-road one. It means recognizing the gains to workers of reducing waste in their own consumption (as in inefficient use of energy) as well as firm production, and discouraging social dumping internationally (in our international trade and financial rules) as well as at home.

We think of the relation of helping intermediaries and such meliorative policies in positive- not zero-sum terms. The intermediaries that we developed grew up in the shadow of, and out of necessity created by, essentially bad public policy. Better policy will not obviate the need for local institutions, armed with local knowledge and accountable to the public interest, to make that policy work. Indeed, it will enable their real strengths and contribution to be seen. But however much we welcome them, we do not see good intermediaries as a substitute for such policy, but as their complement.

Amy Dean, Working Partnerships USA
Joel Rogers, Center on Wisconsin Strategy

Acknowledgments

The research project that forms the basis of this book emerged out of the policy and advocacy efforts of Working Partnerships USA in San Jose, California, and the Center on Wisconsin Strategy at the University of Wisconsin at Madison. Both organizations are "think-and-do tanks" dedicated to conducting research and pursuing strategies that can improve social well-being and economic performance nationally and in their respective regions. We are deeply grateful to the founders of the two organizations, Joel Rogers and Amy Dean, and to their staffs for their institutional support, intellectual advice, and inspiration.

We owe a special thanks to our collaborators, Annette Bernhardt and Laura Dresser from the Center on Wisconsin Strategy and Bob Brownstein and Sarah Zimmerman from Working Partnerships USA. All four were centrally involved in the project, helping to develop the original research proposal and participating in the project in various ways. Laura Dresser coordinated the Milwaukee component of the research project. She was involved in every aspect of the research design and implementation: helping to design the survey, overseeing the University of Wisconsin Survey Center in conducting the survey, designing our qualitative research methodology, and overseeing and conducting portions of the qualitative research in Milwaukee. Annette Bernhardt was also involved in every aspect of the research design and implementation and played a particularly critical role in designing and analyzing the results of our quantitative survey. She played a vital role in developing our qualitative research design and conducting the case study profiles in Milwaukee. Sarah Zimmerman played an essential role in developing our qualitative research design and in conducting and analyzing our intermediary profiles in Silicon Valley. Bob Brownstein was centrally involved in the original research proposal, helped analyze our research findings—particularly those related to the qualitative research—and played an important role in helping us think through the policy implications of our findings.

At several points throughout the project, all seven of us met to review our findings and discuss our analysis, either in person for multi-day meetings or via video conference for shorter discussions. Bernhardt, Brownstein, Dresser, and Zimmerman were co-authors of the original report of our research that forms the basis of this book. By common agreement among the seven of us, the three of us who became co-authors of the book took the responsibility to revise that report for publication. The final book is substantially revised from the earlier report. Nonetheless, the book simply would not have been possible without the involvement of these four collaborators. Their intellectual contributions and hard work are reflected throughout the entire book. This was truly a collective effort, and we are deeply grateful for all their contributions.

We also owe a special thanks to Justin Scoggins of the Center for Justice, Tolerance, and Community at the University of California at Santa Cruz. Justin played a critical role in helping to develop and test our measure of social connectedness and co-authored portions of chapter 6 and the data appendix.

This book would not have been possible without substantial financial support from the Ford, Rockefeller, and Russell Sage Foundations, for which we are very grateful. We also thank the Institute for Labor and Employment of the University of California for additional funding used to obtain and process California's unemployment insurance system wage record data.

In the course of undertaking this research, we received extraordinary assistance and support from numerous staff members and colleagues. We received valuable research assistance from Rachel Rosner of the Center for Justice, Tolerance, and Community at the University of California at Santa Cruz; Matt Zeidenberg and Pablo Mitnik at the Center for Wisconsin Strategy (COWS) at the University of Wisconsin at Madison; and Louise Auerhahn and Sarah Muller at Working Partnerships USA. Erin Hatton, COWS research assistant, was an integral member of the Milwaukee team, doing fieldwork and profiles of intermediaries and contributing to the survey design. Allisa Jones at the Willamette University Public Policy Research Center provided wonderful assistance with formatting final reports and documents. We would like to thank Lina Guzman, Kelly Elver, and other staff members of the University of Wisconsin Survey Center for their patience and perseverance in helping us complete a challenging survey project.

We are also deeply grateful to the many colleagues who have offered valuable comments, insights, and reviews of our work. From the very beginning of the project, we received invaluable advice from our foundation program officers and research advisory board: Eileen Appelbaum, Susan Christopherson, John Colburn, Amy Dean, Mara Manus, Katherine McFate, Eric Parker, Michael Reich, Joel Rogers, Eric Wanner, and Ed Yelin. We also are grateful for the valuable feedback and policy advice from Donald Cohen, Maureen Conway, Richard Freeman, Robert Giloth, Steve Herzenberg, Chancy Lennon, Nancy Mills, Paul Osterman, Jamie Peck, Hal Plotkin, Jerry Rubin, Cathy Ruckelshaus, Nik Theodore, and Orson Watson. In addition, we would like to thank two anonymous reviewers for their detailed, insightful, and thoughtful comments on our draft manuscript.

Chris Benner
Laura Leete
Manuel Pastor

Chapter One

Mobility and Economic Opportunity: The Role of Intermediaries

Many Americans work in low-wage jobs at some point in their lives. For many of them, low-paid work is only a temporary situation and they are able to move over time to higher-paid positions with better career opportunities. A substantial number of people, however, remain in low-paid jobs for long periods of time. Indeed, some seem to be caught in an endless cycle of moving from one low-paid job to another, all with poor working conditions, few benefits, and limited opportunities for advancement. Why do some people seem to be stuck in low-wage work while others eventually are able to take advantage of better economic opportunities?

In trying to answer this question, most researchers focus on two things: who you are and where you work. An individual's educational and personal background, skills and work experience, motivation and personality, race, gender, and age, all clearly shape the kinds of work that person can do, his or her value to employers, ties to certain kinds of work opportunities, and opportunities for advancement. Similarly, characteristics of where individuals work—the size, competitiveness, organizational structure, and human resource practices of their employer, the industry they are in, their location— clearly shape wage levels, career advancement opportunities, and vulnerability to layoffs. Together, people's personal characteristics and the nature of their workplaces go a long way toward explaining their economic success or failure in the labor market.

In recent years, however, many researchers and policymakers concerned with career advancement have been paying increasing attention not just to the characteristics of workers and employers but also to the third-party organizations that help match people looking for work with employers looking for employees. The impact of some of these third-party organizations on advancement opportunities may be increased by the additional assistance they provide, including training, management assistance, technical support, and career services. Such organizations are not a new phenomenon: public-sector employment services for unemployed workers, union hiring halls in the building trades, and for-profit temporary placement agencies have existed for a long time. The number and variety of organizations involved in job-matching activities, however, seem to have increased significantly since the 1980s. Moreover, at least some of these organizations seem to be playing more important roles in shaping labor flows and even in restructuring the quality and quantity of jobs in U.S. labor markets. Researchers have responded by trying to understand what makes these job-matching services effective or not, while more and more policymakers have been promoting better "workforce intermediaries" as a strategy for improving job advancement opportunities for disadvantaged workers.

How do these third-party labor market intermediaries (LMIs) affect labor market outcomes? In particular, to what extent do LMIs affect opportunities for disadvantaged workers, and to what extent can a focus on improving LMIs themselves help disadvantaged workers find better jobs and build better careers? These are the questions that motivated this study.

In this book, we address these questions by combining qualitative and quantitative research to study the overall impact of a comprehensive set of intermediaries in two regional labor markets: Milwaukee, Wisconsin, and California's Silicon Valley. These regions were selected initially because we suspected that they would provide a significant opportunity to contrast the organization of work and labor markets in the so-called old and new economies. Yet, as we will see, there were as many commonalities as differences between the two regions. Furthermore, our research period, ranging from the mid-1990s to 2002, spanned both a period of very tight labor markets and the first year of an economic downturn, allowing us to investigate some aspects of the effects of absolute unemployment levels on LMI activities. Because of these cross-regional and temporal elements, we thus believe that our findings may be applicable in many different regional labor markets and conditions.

Our research found that LMIs are widespread in these two regional labor markets: more than one-quarter of all workers in both regions have held a job in the previous three years that they got through an LMI. Furthermore, while unemployed and disadvantaged workers are somewhat more likely to use intermediaries, we found evidence of intermediary use across the labor market, and among both the unemployed and employed. We found little evidence, however, that most of these organizations do much to improve economic opportunities for the workers who use them. We also found that the most widely used types of LMIs are those that provide the fewest services to workers. Given the high prevalence of LMIs, we think that efforts to develop better LMIs could have an impact on labor market outcomes. Our research suggests, however, that a key policy effort for those concerned about the experience of lower-wage workers should be not only improving LMIs but also steering people to better LMIs.

This introductory chapter attempts to set the stage for what follows. We begin with a more detailed characterization of the labor market and the policy changes that have led to an increased attention to the role of intermediaries in shaping labor flows and the structure of labor market opportunities. Then, in reviewing previous research on intermediaries, we develop a conceptual framework for our analysis of them, characterizing the wide variety of organizations involved in intermediary activity by the functions they play, the interests they serve, and the strategies they employ. We conclude the chapter by briefly outlining our empirical research and describing the structure of the rest of the book.

Why Are Labor Market Intermediaries Important?

The cover article of *Fortune* magazine on September 19, 1994, declared "The End of the Job." In an information age of shifting work tasks and online networked relationships, the author William Bridges argues, jobs are simply a "social artifact" more appropriate for an industrial era of factories and stable routine tasks. Work still needs to be done, he noted, but it is being organized in different ways that require workers to be more flexible, adaptable to change, and ready to move rapidly between different organizational contexts (see also Bridges 1994). This theme was echoed a half-decade later in *Newsweek*'s February 1, 1999, cover story,

"Your Next Job." This article—which offers a new slogan for today's working class, "Workers of the world, untie"—argues that in the "new economy," if workers can acquire the right skills, get connected, and embrace risk by moving to new opportunities, the potential rewards are substantial.

These articles reflect a widely held perception that we are in a "new economy," a global, information-driven economy that is fundamentally different from our old industrial economy. In this new economy, the stable, lifetime job of the industrial era has allegedly disappeared, and workers now need simply to adjust to flexible, rapidly changing, and volatile workplaces. The popularly held vision of these changes probably exaggerates the scale of the economic transformation that is occurring; binary oppositions between old and new, industrial and informational, tend to overemphasize differences while neglecting important continuities in the economy, in the way work is organized, and in the structures of economic opportunity in the labor market, particularly for disadvantaged workers. Nonetheless, over the last three decades there have been changes in the U.S. economy that have affected the level of stability or volatility that workers can expect in the labor market. Rapid technological development, changing corporate structures and management practices, the deregulation of key industries, the decline of unions, and intensified international competition have all contributed to greater uncertainty and unpredictability in labor markets. Many older workers have experienced disruptive job losses and middle-age career changes. Workers entering the labor force can expect to hold fewer steady jobs, to not often find themselves on a within-company upward career trajectory, and to receive less on-the-job training. Many workers in contemporary labor markets face greater volatility than in the past and are more likely to move from job to job, whether voluntarily or involuntarily, over their lifetime.

The most obvious indicator of greater volatility in the labor market is the dramatic spread of temporary employment. During the last period of economic expansion, from March 1991 to March 2001, while total nonfarm employment grew by 22 percent, employment in temporary help services grew by 123 percent.[1] Though temporary help firms still account for less than 3 percent of total employment, during this period they were responsible for nearly 10 percent of net job growth. Between 1979 and 1995, employment in temporary help firms grew 11 percent annually, five times faster than the average for all nonagricultural employment (Autor 2003).

Data on job tenure also provide evidence of declining job stability, though not as dramatic a change as in temporary employment. There has

Table 1.1   Median Years of Tenure with Current Employer,
by Age and Sex, 1983–2002

	1983	1987	1991	1996	1998	2000	2002
Men							
20 to 24 years	1.5	1.3	1.4	1.2	1.2	1.2	1.4
25 to 34 years	3.2	3.1	3.1	3.0	2.8	2.7	2.8
35 to 44 years	7.3	7.0	6.5	6.1	5.5	5.4	5.0
45 to 54 years	12.8	11.8	11.2	10.1	9.4	9.5	9.1
55 to 64 years	15.3	14.5	13.4	10.5	11.2	10.2	10.2
Women							
20 to 24 years	1.5	1.3	1.3	1.2	1.1	1.0	1.1
25 to 34 years	2.8	2.6	2.7	2.7	2.5	2.5	2.5
35 to 44 years	4.1	4.4	4.5	4.8	4.5	4.3	4.2
45 to 54 years	6.3	6.8	6.7	7.0	7.2	7.3	6.5
55 to 64 years	9.8	9.7	9.9	10.0	9.6	9.9	9.5

Source: U.S. Department of Labor, Bureau of Labor Statistics, "Employee Tenure" (news
release), available at: http://www.bls.gov/news.release/tenure.toc.htm

been some disagreement over the empirical findings, because of both data
inconsistencies and the difficulty of distinguishing changes in employment
systems from demographic changes in the labor force that also affect job
tenure.[2] For instance, as more women have entered the labor force of the last
thirty years, pursued careers, and taken less time out for child-rearing, their
average tenure in the workforce has clearly gone up. One way of distinguishing changes in employment systems from demographic shifts is by focusing
just on changes in tenure for men, since their labor force participation levels have not changed as much as is the case with women (though focusing
on men does not take into account many other factors, such as changing
racial composition and the impact of growing immigration). For men at all
age levels and all education levels, job tenure has been declining since the
1980s. The median tenure for men age forty-five to fifty-four, for instance,
declined to 9.1 years in 2002, down from 11.2 at the beginning of the 1990s
and 12.8 in 1983. For men age fifty-four to sixty-four, the median tenure in
2002 was 10.2 years, down from 13.4 years in 1991 and 15.3 years in 1983
(see table 1.1).

Changes in job stability are even more apparent when we look not just at cross-sectional data on tenure but also at longitudinal data on the work experience of comparable cohorts for the recent period compared to the past. Studying the first sixteen years of work experience for two different cohorts of non-Hispanic white men from the National Longitudinal Survey (NLS), for instance, Annette Bernhardt and her colleagues (2001) find that a recent cohort (who entered the labor market in 1979) were 34 percent more likely to experience job changes than a cohort who entered the labor market in 1966. Even in traditionally stable industries, the odds of a job separation for the recent cohort were 30 percent higher. By their early thirties, the recent cohort was 21 percent less likely to hold tenures of seven years or longer, compared to the original cohort (see Bernhardt et al. 2001).

Perhaps more important than increased turnover, however, are people's changing expectations of their employment contract. Many analysts argue that employers are providing significantly fewer expectations of job security (Rousseau 1995). The rules, procedures, expectations, and norms regarding the employment relationship within firms seem to be changing, and employers are making fewer commitments to internal advancement opportunities and protection against layoffs (Osterman 1999, ch. 4). The employment relationship seems to have become a more open-ended negotiation based in large part on market power (Cappelli 1999). Firms are more willing to lay off employees for reasons other than declining sales, such as restructuring, and they are also more likely to lay off people in white-collar and management positions, not just blue-collar and service workers.

It is important not to overemphasize the scale of these changes, especially as they relate to opportunities for disadvantaged workers. As David Neumark (2000) argues, the evidence shows that the bonds between workers and firms have been weakened, but not entirely broken. Furthermore, many service and low-wage workers have always had low levels of job security and volatile employment conditions, even when many blue- and white-collar workers in core sectors of the economy held stable long-term employment. Nonetheless, job security in core sectors of the economy has eroded to some extent, and the model of a long-term stable career in a single company, which shaped economic growth and labor market policies in the post–World War II period, no longer represents the dominant employment system in this country. More importantly for the purposes of this book, with job searches on the rise and internal mechanisms for career advancement on the decline, these changes in labor markets and employment systems have created new opportunities for third-party organizations to play intermediary roles in the U.S. labor market.

Private-sector intermediaries have been most prominent in taking advantage of these opportunities, as is clearly evident in the dramatic growth in the temporary help services industry; this industry, however, is not the only kind of private-sector intermediary. Headhunters and permanent job placement firms have also become important, at least in professional and managerial sectors of the labor market. Web-based job search sites, including general job sites (for example, monster.com and hotjobs.com) and sites that specialize by industry or occupation (such as Dice.com and prgjobs.com in the information technology industry), have also become important intermediaries, though few provide more than basic information resources (Autor 2001; Crispin and Mehler 1999). Intermediary activity is not limited, however, to the private sector. Many public agencies, nonprofit organizations, educational institutions, and unions have also expanded their efforts to act as labor market intermediaries in recent years.

For federally funded workforce development programs, the interest in expanding intermediary activities has emerged along with a shift in emphasis from helping disadvantaged workers find entry-level jobs to helping a broader spectrum of people advance to better jobs. There are a variety of reasons for this policy shift. One factor was the experience with the "work-first" approach to welfare reform: many recipients were able to find jobs but remained stuck in low-paid work (Albelda 2001; Anderson, Halter, and Gryzlak, 2004; Bok and Simmons 2002). In addition, various evaluations of workforce development programs in the 1980s and 1990s demonstrated at best only modest wage increases for many users of these programs (Bloom et al. 1997; Grubb 1995; U.S. Department of Labor 1995; GAO 1994). At the core of these analyses of the weaknesses of such programs was the argument that they need to have stronger ties with employers, particularly those that provide better advancement opportunities. Thus, the Workforce Investment Act of 1998 produced a significant restructuring of these programs to make them more accountable and more responsive to the needs of employers, not just disadvantaged workers, and to encourage them to provide services relevant to a broader spectrum of employers and workers, not just those in the lower tiers of the labor market (Barnow and King 2005).

These changes in federal policy during the 1990s that emphasized the value of intermediary activities in the labor market were also being mirrored by local workforce development initiatives around the country. Many nonprofit organizations, along with a smaller number of business associations, community colleges, labor unions, and public-sector workforce agencies, began experimenting with building workforce partnerships or networks that linked economic and workforce development goals; provided a range of services, not just job placement; integrated multiple sources of funding (such as public, private, foundation, and fee-for-service); and invested in the longer-term career advancement of the workers they served. These initiatives have come to be known as "workforce intermediaries," and they are increasingly seen as representing "best practice" in the workforce development field (Fischer 2005; Giloth 2004; Harrison and Weiss 1998; Pindus et al. 2004).

Another source of interest in labor market intermediary activity has come from unions and the labor movement. Unionization levels have declined significantly since the 1960s: today less than 10 percent of the private-sector labor force is unionized. There are a variety of reasons for this decline, and the debate within the labor movement about what to do about it is intense. One important strand of analysis argues that industrial unionism—at least the form of industrial unionism that came to dominate the U.S. labor movement after the New Deal era—has become increasingly ineffective in representing workers' needs in the changing U.S. economy (Heckscher 1996; Turner, Katz, and Hurd 2001). Industrial unionism, as opposed to craft unionism, operates from an explicit assumption of long-term stable employment with a single large employer that controls the conditions of employment. Industrial unions in the United States have tended to focus on bargaining over issues of compensation and work practices, leaving to company management the larger, more strategic issues of corporate investment, technological development, and market competition. This structure of representation worked fairly well in large manufacturing industries under relatively stable competitive conditions. In the current economy, with its high levels of volatility, uncertainty, and complex networking and outsourcing production arrangements, representation based on a single work site or single employer is less effective in protecting workers' interests. For workers who move frequently from employer to employer or those whose working conditions are not primarily determined by a single employer (such as temporary workers and many workers in subcontracting relationships), there are few opportunities in the current industrial relations system for adequate representation (Friedman 1994).

In response, unions have been experimenting with a range of innovative ways to become involved in issues of labor supply, labor quality, placement, and career advancement. These initiatives are carried out through alliances with employers, community groups, and other unions, and they focus on strengthening internal career ladders as well as creating new external career ladders within industries and across industries, expanding labor involvement in job matching, and designing and delivering training (AFL-CIO Working for America Institute 2000). These initiatives create intermediaries between workers and employers that deal with a range of work- and employment-related issues (Parker and Rogers 2001). In many ways these initiatives are similar to the structure of construction trade unions, whose hiring halls and apprenticeship training programs have been common for many years. In industries where project-based employment is the norm, such as in the television and movie production industry, an active intermediary role for unions is accepted practice (Gray and Seeber 1996). The emergence of these initiatives in other industries, however, indicates the growing belief among many union leaders that standard industrial-model unionism is no longer adequate for addressing the labor market concerns of a wide range of the American workforce. The result is a growing role for unions as intermediaries in the labor market (Wolf-Powers 2003).

Thus, it is clear that for-profit intermediaries have become much more prominent in the labor market and that various unions, nonprofit organizations, community colleges, and public-sector agencies have become more engaged in intermediary activities as well. These initiatives represent a wide range of organizations, however, with a diverse set of goals. All intermediaries are, to some extent, brokers between workers and employers, but employers' reasons for engaging with, say, a temporary help agency are entirely different from their reasons for engaging with a union or nonprofit-based intermediary. Does it make sense, then, to analyze such a diverse set of activities under a single analytical category? Is it possible to make a meaningful comparison between a temporary help agency and a union or nonprofit-based intermediary, and if so, how?

Many previous studies of intermediaries have avoided these questions by focusing on specific types or subsets of intermediaries. Thus, the literature on temporary help agencies is substantial, and there have been important debates on their role in shaping economic opportunity and the structure of labor markets (Autor 1999, 2003; Autor, Levy, and Murnane 1999; Erickcek and

Houseman 1997; Gonos 1997; Houseman, Kalleberg, and Erickcek 2001; Kalleberg 2000; Neuwirth 2004; Parker 1994; Rogers 2000; Segal and Sullivan 1997b). There is a growing literature on intermediaries that focus on disadvantaged workers, particularly those rooted in specific industry sectors (Fitzgerald 2006; PEERS 2003). Case studies of particular intermediaries have provided valuable insights into "best practice"—the detailed and subtle factors that shape the effectiveness of particular initiatives (Benner 2003c; Osterman and Lautsch 1996).

Going beyond individual intermediaries or types of intermediaries to understand the very diversity of the organizations that provide intermediary services in the labor market and their broader impact provides important insights that are not possible from taking a narrower view. Perhaps the most important goal of taking this broader view is to gain a clearer understanding of how widespread this intermediary activity is in contemporary labor markets. To date, no study has tried to document the extent to which all the different kinds of intermediaries are used and their importance in shaping labor market outcomes. In addition, studying all intermediaries in a particular regional labor market provides important insights into the differences between them, such as which workers and employers use which intermediaries and why. Finally, from a policy perspective, an understanding of whether lessons from the activities of one set of intermediaries can be applied to other intermediaries is valuable in efforts to improve the functioning of intermediaries overall. All such efforts, however, require a clear understanding of what should be considered an intermediary, how best to understand the services that intermediaries provide, and how best to analyze their overall role in the labor market.

What Is a Labor Market Intermediary? An Organizational Approach

We start by defining labor market intermediaries as organizations—public, private, nonprofit, or membership-based—that help broker the employment relationship through some combination of job matching, training, and career support services. Our focus on specific organizations is narrower than some other approaches, which define labor market intermediaries as including "the set of informal conventions, public and private institutions, as well as public laws and regulations, that links individuals and communities with market economies" (Carnevale and Desrochers 2004, 170). Such a broad approach to understanding labor market mediation can be useful, but we are more focused on the extent to which particular *organizations,* providing discrete services to workers and firms, are having an impact on labor market outcomes.

For us, the sine qua non for an intermediary is job matching. Thus, we exclude many organizations that do only training, including community colleges, except to the extent that they have particular programs that provide direct training-to-job placements. Nor do we include private-sector contract training companies, which function only as the outsourced supplier of training services. By contrast, we do include temporary agencies that steer job-seekers to employment, whether or not they provide training or are concerned with workers' career advancement. We also include agencies that provide career support services, including those that seek to transform work and the labor market in ways that might benefit workers, but only if they provide active job placements. This excludes many unions and other advocacy groups—such as interfaith alliances for a living wage and community organizations pushing for local hiring requirements—that are not involved in mediating the hiring decision.[3]

What sort of agencies do fall within our definition of a labor market intermediary? LMIs could range from organized day-labor sites to headhunter firms that place top-level executives, but our emphasis on larger institutions and our interest in the experience of lower-income workers help narrow the field considerably. In our empirical work, we included public agencies that provide welfare-to-work services; private firms that place workers in temporary or temporary-to-permanent positions; unions that utilize a hiring hall model; community colleges with programs for training and immediate placement of displaced workers; nonprofit institutions that focus on assisting a particular population, such as recent immigrants, with particular job search challenges; and professional associations that help new technicians garner skills and employment.[4]

Although job placement is a key feature of LMIs, most of these organizations (but not all) have moved past simple job matching in recent years. Federal and state employment services, for example, have improved their labor market information and referral systems through the development of one-stop career centers. Many temporary agencies have moved beyond simple placement to provide a range of direct human resource management services to employers. In the context of welfare reform, nonprofits have recognized that tracking new workers beyond the first job is critical to permanent success. Seeking to address the issues of people and places left behind, community-based organizations and community development corporations have increasingly focused not just on job brokering but also on workforce development partnerships (Harrison and

Table 1.2   An Organizational Typology of Labor
Market Intermediaries

Organization Type	Examples
For-profit sector	Temporary agencies, headhunters, and for-profit training providers
Nonprofit or community-based	Nonprofit employment training and placement services for disadvantaged workers
Membership-based	Union-based initiatives and membership-based professional associations
Education-based	Community colleges
Public-sector	One-stop career centers, private industry councils (PICs), and welfare-to-work agencies

Source: Authors' compilation.

Weiss 1998; Pastor et al. 2000; Wilson 1996). Noting the decline in union density, labor-based institutions have been experimenting with a wide range of new intermediary initiatives, including efforts to directly take on the circumstances of temporary workers.

Given this impressive and widening range of functions, how should we conceptualize the work of LMIs? One simple categorization would be by sector or organization, the implicit breakdown used thus far (see table 1.2). There are, of course, important distinctions between the public, private, and nonprofit sectors, especially since the financial base of an intermediary can impose a set of constraints on which services are provided and for whom. In addition, organizational structure largely determines the types and range of the different constituencies who interact with the intermediary and thus may shape their mandates or missions in important ways—as with community colleges and federally funded training programs, or union-based initiatives that are responsive to the needs of the labor movement. Moreover, these organizational markers are commonly known and accepted. This was important for the survey we conducted, since distinctions between the for-profit, nonprofit, and public sectors were more familiar to our respondents as they thought through their own use of intermediary services.

At the same time, such organizational distinctions do not entirely capture differences or represent the complexity of existing arrangements. Within the welfare reform process, for example, we find public-sector agencies contracting placement and follow-up services to private firms and nonprofit agencies. Community colleges may be making job connections, but they are often using federal funding by subcontracting with the public agencies responsible for aiding displaced workers. Nonprofit organizations, and even unions, are experimenting with creating for-profit entities, both to diversify sources of funds and to build credibility in the private sector (Carré et al. 2003). Workforce intermediaries often represent complex partnerships of public agencies, business and business associations, nonprofit organizations, and community colleges that are not easily captured in a simple organizational typology.

Similarly, a simple organizational distinction does not capture the breadth and depth of the services provided by different intermediaries. More broadly, such a distinction does not capture the extent to which intermediaries may change the structures of economic opportunity, rather than just provide services to individual workers and firms. Trying to understand this broader impact is important, since at least some intermediaries explicitly try to play a more active role in shaping the quality and quantity of jobs rather than simply taking existing supply and demand from employers and workers as given. Private temporary agencies, for example, are increasingly providing a variety of personnel and work-flow management services on top of their recruitment and placement services, thus directly affecting wage levels and labor productivity. Similarly, some workforce intermediaries, especially those organized on a sectoral basis, try to link their placement and training services with technological assistance, marketing, access to capital, and other economic development services designed to improve the competitiveness of the firms they serve, thus improving the employment and advancement opportunities for the workers they assist.

To understand the full range of outcomes for both individual workers and the market as a whole, it is necessary to develop a more complex typology that includes a fuller range of functions and considers both the relationships formed and the direct interests represented in various arrangements. The first step is to develop a deeper analysis of the market space occupied by LMIs.

A Broader View of Labor Market Intermediaries

LMIs, especially in their job-brokering role, arise in part from the imperfect information and information asymmetry that are ubiquitous in labor markets. On the employer side, it is difficult to ascertain worker quality on the basis of limited data.[5] Since a full assessment can be an expensive and time-consuming task, there is a clear rationale for LMI use: organizations that focus on assessment and placement can develop economies of scale and specialized skills that allow them to provide a better and cheaper service than employers can do for themselves in-house. Certain kinds of LMIs also offer an opportunity to minimize the cost of error: because the employer of record is often the LMI and the employment contract is explicitly or implicitly not permanent, employers can more easily let an employee go (Bartik 2001). This is particularly true of temporary agencies, but many nontemp agencies adopt this practice as well by making explicitly interim placements.

On the worker side, imperfect information and information asymmetry underlie the costs associated with discovering available employment and signaling to employers one's skills and reliability. Many workers solve this dual problem by using social networks—that is, gaining job information and trusted referrals from friends and relatives (Fernandez and Weinberg 1997; Granovetter 1995). Others find that their networks are not up to the task, particularly when they live in conditions of concentrated poverty that constrain their social circle (Jargowsky 1997; Pastor and Adams 1996). Indeed, one reason those concerned with low-income individuals are increasingly interested in LMIs is exactly for their potential to help those job-seekers who have weaker or less effective social networks secure employment (Harrison and Weiss 1998; Johnson, Bienenstock, and Farrell 1999; Massey and Shibuya 1995; Pastor and Marcelli 2000).

These information problems in the labor market not only help explain the existence of LMIs but also offer at least three reasons why there appears to be a secular increase in intermediaries. The first is simply the decline in worker tenure over time (Bernhardt et al. 2001): with job switching more common, the number of potential uses of LMIs is up. Second, as technological change leads to increasingly complex job requirements, the amount of information needed to match workers to jobs has probably been ratcheted up, and both the value of signals and the cost of a poor match have gone up as well (Benner 2003b). Third, some have suggested that social capital is generally on the decline (Putnam 2000), and if so, job-getting social networks are likely to be collateral damage; in this event, LMIs (and other institutions like Internet job services) would fill the role of a partial substitute.[6]

The increase in intermediary use is also connected to shifting employment systems and the changing economy, as discussed earlier. It is important to recognize, however, that changing employment systems are driven in part by changing market conditions and in part by specific employer strategies. Firms have certainly faced new forms of global competition, new technological conditions, and an atmosphere of deregulation, all of which tend to create variations in product demand (Scott 1998). Thus, to the extent that firms have downsized—or reduced their long-term commitment to their core labor force while increasing their use of a buffer workforce through outsourcing, subcontracting, and contingent or temporary work—it can be argued that this strategy is driven by strong market incentives and the need to promote labor flexibility in the face of increased economic risk. We think, however, that it is wrong to attribute firm and labor force reorganization entirely to these market factors; as David Gordon (1996) eloquently argues in *Fat and Mean,* firms have taken advantage of external pressures to induce shifts in the balance of power between employers and employee. After all, a buffer labor force is usually less expensive in terms of both salaries and benefits, and the heightened insecurity felt by all employees can lower wage costs. In this view, the redefinition of work and the reconstitution of the labor experience are partly aspects of the perennial struggles between capital and labor (see also Osterman 1999).

Why do the relative weights of market versus organizational (firm) factors matter? From one point of view, the increase in labor market intermediaries is connected to the rise of a new set of markets. That is, as external conditions increasingly force firms to differentiate between core and temporary employees, two things happen: workers become more likely to move between jobs, and firms experience upward pressures on their hiring costs as a share of total budget. These consequences give rise to a demand for job brokers who can meet employee needs and provide the specialized service of delivering lower-cost interviews and screening functions to firms with a churning labor force. Although outcomes for workers may be better or worse depending on the degree of training offered, the quality of employment networks, and the like, the judgment of LMI quality in this case would be largely focused on how well an agency "meets" the market by efficiently and effectively responding to the demands of workers and employers.

Suppose, however, that LMIs are actively involved in "making" the market—that is, restructuring the labor market on both the supply and demand sides. Consider, for example, the increasingly common case of temporary agencies being contracted to run whole aspects of the personnel process for some section of a company's labor force. The initial impetus for a company to outsource this function to a temporary agency may have been an external pressure

Figure 1.1   The Relational Structure of Intermediaries

		Relationship To Employers	
		Weak	Strong
Relationship to Workers	Weak	• "Job bank" data-bases • Some welfare-to-work programs	• Temporary agencies • Contract-based training organizations • Day labor contractors
	Strong	• Professional and membership organizations • Community colleges	• Union hiring halls • Intensive community-based organizations that have employer commitments • Media unions

Source: Authors' compilation.

to reduce costs and a belief that the temporary agency could provide the service more efficiently, while allowing the client firm to focus on functions more central to its competitive success. The impetus may also have come, however, from a desire to defuse unionization efforts, to avoid the legal liability of being the employer of record, or simply to lower costs by lowering wages. Either way, the direct intervention of the temporary firm in the work site of its client firm alters relations within the firm because it goes beyond simply doing a better job of articulating job-seekers and employers in the market.

Thus, market imperfections and economic changes have given new importance to organizations that can match workers and employers and offer the more extended training and restructuring services described here. These organizations also emerge in the context of complex power relationships between workers and employers, and different organizations focus on the interests of workers and employers to varying extents. Since job brokering and training roles can be played by private, nonprofit, or state agencies, some have argued that another basis for categorization or differentiation would be the *depth of the relationship* that the intermediary has on each side of the brokering process (see figure 1.1). On the worker side, a weak relationship might consist of a visit to an employment center or website or taking a onetime course on résumé writing. By contrast, a strong relationship might involve a more intensive and probably longer-term interaction with the intermediary—for human capital development or access to health benefits and professional networks. The same logic could be used on the employer side. A weak relationship might consist of simply listing one's job openings with a placement agency. A strong relationship might entail repeated use of a temporary agency or a commitment by the employer to hire workers from the intermediary. Of course, intermediaries may also have multiple programs and therefore organizationally may fall into more than one cell.

Why is this relational approach useful? Recall the concerns that motivate this project: understanding and improving opportunities for career development, employment stability, and upward mobility for those at the bottom end of the labor market. In this regard, while the strong-employer/weak-worker relationships of many temporary agencies may provide some employment continuity for contingent workers, the nature of these ties to firms can also facilitate a two-tier wage and job structure. Thus, one possible policy strategy would be to encourage further development of "strong-strong" institutions or to disseminate information on superior practices to LMIs in order to steer them toward better worker outcomes. Research on unions in media industries, for example, shows how "strong-strong" ties in an industry rich in social capital, networks, and skill requirements can facilitate winning outcomes for both sides of the labor market (Christopherson and Storper 1989; Gray and Seeber 1996).

Putting It Together: Interests, Scope, and Relations

It is useful, but still somewhat incomplete, to conceptualize LMI activities according to the type of organization and the depth or strength of relations between actors. In our view, it is also critical to explicitly add the dimensions of interest and the scope of activity. Three possible sets of interests would be employers' desire to improve profitability, workers' desire to maximize income, and communities' desire to utilize the labor market to promote local economic development. As for scope, we add to the usual functions of LMIs—making placements and providing training—the additional function of "making markets," that is, contributing to the transformation of labor demand itself.[7] (These functions are discussed in more detail in chapter 3.)

How does this framework play out analytically? Although ultimately multiple interests must be met—workers want jobs, firms want employees, and intermediaries are one bridge—it may be helpful to see LMIs as oriented to one or another set of primary interests. LMIs that view their primary client as the employer may seek to enhance profitability by filling positions quickly and not internalizing significant costs of training. In this process, however, they may also make markets by pushing for simplifying the work process and lowering requirements, partly in order to facilitate their own brokering but also to serve employer needs. This basic outline is consistent with the profile of many temporary agencies.

Employee-focused LMIs, on the other hand, see workers as their primary client; their aim is to use the hiring process to improve employee outcomes, including in part by increasing workers' bargaining power in the labor market and with particular employers. A classic example is the union hiring hall, which can be enforced by bargaining and the threat of strikes (as with longshoremen) or by maintaining a monopoly on skills valued by employers (as with the building trades).

Community-based organizations, as Bennett Harrison and Marcus Weiss (1998) remind us, have also gotten into the LMI business, particularly with innovative training and placement programs like Project Quest in San Antonio, Texas. Many of these programs are easily classified as employee-oriented, but even as they target their efforts at those on the bottom end of the labor market, their ultimate objective is to translate the gains to particular geographic communities. Moreover, such efforts have also generally been wrapped in the language and practice of community development and have sometimes borrowed broad business retention goals from that framework; witness, for example, Cleveland's Westside Industrial Retention and Expansion Network, founded by three community development corporations to support industrial clusters that could provide employment for residents of lower-income communities (Indergaard 1997). Thus, recognizing that intermediaries may have a community orientation in addition to an employee orientation seems warranted.

It is important, however, to stress one cloudy facet of this prism of interests: LMIs are more successful to the extent that they serve multiple interests. Thus, even an agency primarily oriented to one set of actors must solve problems faced by another set of actors. A ready example is a temporary agency that focuses primarily on employers' needs but must also offer help to workers by quickly placing them in jobs and working toward longer-term job matches for them. Likewise, community college programs may see their primary clients as students, but to work effectively for these clients they must be viewed by employers as a key resource.

Securing acceptance from employers poses a special challenge for worker- and community-oriented programs. They are able to meet this challenge most effectively, we argue, when they solve a key problem that employers may face. Even union hiring halls, which one would suppose to be anathema to employers because of their control over wages, can reduce search costs for firms and ensure the quality of work executed by craft workers, particularly when the union also takes on training to guarantee a certain quality. Labor and community-driven workforce development strategies can also help solve industrywide problems that employers may face. If an industry has high levels of turnover, for instance, individual employers may be reluctant to invest in the training of their own workforce for fear they will lose the value of that human capital investment to competing firms. This problem can be solved by an external agency organizing collective commitments to train for nonfirm-specific skills, thereby lifting up the general level of investment in workforce training in the industry as a whole (Herzenberg, Alic, and Wial 1998; Parker and Rogers 2001). Such solutions sometimes allow employee- and community-oriented intermediaries to exercise greater influence over the demand side of the labor market, potentially increasing wage levels and benefits.

Putting together the relational, interest, and scope frameworks may offer analytical clarity and policy change. Our qualitative and quantitative work suggests that those LMIs that hold the most promise for improving outcomes for disadvantaged workers are those that hold worker and community interests as central, maintain strong relations with both workers and employers, and seek to expand their scope of operations to improve the structure of work, thus altering the demand side.

The Content and Structure of the Book

As our analysis makes clear, we were not simply interested in a quantitative assessment of the distribution of intermediaries in the labor market, though this was an important and central part of the analysis. Instead, we wanted to engage in a deeper analysis of the operation of intermediaries throughout regional labor markets, the structure of their relationships with workers and employers, the impact of these different relationships on the activities of workers and firms, and ultimately the impact of these relationships on labor market opportunities for disadvantaged workers. Thus, we collected three types of data, using both qualitative and quantitative methodologies, which together provide a far-reaching overview of the role of LMIs in the regional economies we studied (see the appendix for a detailed discussion of the methodology).

First, we used existing public data sources to analyze the similarities and differences in labor market and demographic patterns in Milwaukee and Silicon Valley. Our selection of Milwaukee and Silicon Valley as comparative regions for analysis was based on a hypothesis that there would be important differences between the scale and types of activities of intermediaries in these two regions, whose economies could be thought of as proto-typical "old industrial" and "new informational." Since we had a particular interest in the relationship between the use of intermediaries and volatility in labor market conditions, we also conducted a detailed analysis of the patterns of volatility as evidenced in unemployment insurance wage record data for California and Wisconsin for the years 1992 through 1999—the period immediately prior to our survey and field research. The analysis of this data and of the similarities and differences in labor market conditions in the two regions is presented in chapter 2. Although we found important differences between the two regions, particularly in industrial structure and demographic characteristics, the differences in volatility in labor market conditions were not as profound as we might have expected.

Our second major data-gathering exercise was a qualitative study of labor market intermediaries in Silicon Valley and Milwaukee. This began with a series of five focus groups with representatives of intermediaries in each region to probe how participants conceptualized their intermediary work, how they related to both workers and employers, and how they related to other organizations in the region providing intermediary services. These focus groups helped us select 23 "typical" intermediaries that we studied in-depth in both regions by conducting 146 lengthy interviews (one to two hours each) with intermediary staff and both their worker and employer clients. This research helped us understand the broad landscape of intermediaries in each region and the factors shaping their activities. The in-depth case studies also allowed us to reach a deeper and more nuanced understanding of the specific services provided by intermediaries in both regions, the challenges they faced in marketing and providing those services to their clients, and the reasons why workers and employers used particular intermediaries.

Our analysis of this qualitative research is presented in chapter 3. In addition to presenting a picture of the overall landscape of intermediary activity in each region, we categorize those activities as follows: (1) services that are part of the basic job-matching process, which we term *market-meeting*, since they take the preferences and characteristics of both workers and employers in the labor market as given; (2) services, such as training, industry research, and facilitating networking opportunities, that we term *market-molding*, since they try to influence workers' characteristics and aspirations or the economic trajectories of individual firms and regional industries; and (3) *market-making* activities, which seem to play a more critical role in structuring the jobs themselves, such as by providing incumbent worker training or acting as the employer of record following placement services.

Finally, incorporating many of the insights gained in our qualitative research, we developed a detailed survey designed to analyze workers' use of intermediaries and their impact on labor market outcomes. The survey, which we administered by phone between August 2001 and June 2002, received 1,346 responses (659 in Milwaukee and 689 in Silicon Valley) from individuals between the ages of twenty-five and sixty-five who had worked sometime in the past three years, including both users and non-users of LMIs. Our analysis of this survey is presented in chapters 4, 5, and 6.

Chapter 4 focuses on the incidence and type of intermediary use, workers' reasons for using intermediaries, and the services and satisfaction workers got from intermediaries, with a special emphasis on the experiences of disadvantaged workers in the two regions. We show that intermediary use was widespread: 29.8 percent of workers in Milwaukee and 26.3 percent of workers in Silicon Valley had held a job in the previous three years that they obtained through an LMI (our broadest measure of intermediary use). The proportion of workers who used different types of intermediaries was remarkably similar across both regions, with private placement agencies providing roughly half of all intermediary placements in all of our measures of intermediary use. Furthermore, while disadvantaged workers were more likely to use intermediaries than other workers, we show that more advantaged workers (whether measured by income, education, or race), made significant use of LMIs in the labor market as well. We show that workers used intermediaries not just to find jobs when they were unemployed but also to find better jobs. Finally, we show that the most widespread type of intermediary, the private-sector temporary agency, also provides the fewest number of services to workers. This is reflected in workers' generally lower levels of satisfaction with the assistance provided by these intermediaries, including the quality of the jobs in which they were placed.

Chapter 5 examines the impact of intermediaries in more detail, looking at job outcomes based on occupation, industry, wages, and benefits. We compare outcomes based on whether or not workers used an LMI and which kind of LMI they used, as well as how these outcomes differed for disadvantaged workers. Although there are many important subtleties to the interpretations, our survey finds that in both regions temporary agency use was consistently associated with lower hourly wages and less access to both employer-provided pensions and health insurance. This holds true even after controlling for detailed worker and job characteristics and after separating the effect of temp agencies from temporary job placements per se.

Moreover, because of the nature of the survey, these are not just contemporaneous effects, and thus temp use may not be beneficial to labor market outcomes for disadvantaged workers. Significantly, we find few other clear relationships, in both regions, between outcomes and the use of other types of labor market intermediaries, such as professional associations, community and vocational colleges, unions, and nonprofit or government agencies. This lack of apparent relationship may be due to either too few observations in these groups or inadequate precision in defining these categories. Of course, a few very well structured programs can make a difference for many disadvantaged workers, and particular disadvantaged workers may benefit from using many different types of intermediaries, a pattern revealed in our qualitative analysis. But the broad organizational categories we used in the survey were unable to distinguish such impacts. This finding is different from the more optimistic picture of the long-term effects of temp use offered by Fredrik Andersson, Harry Holzer, and Julia Lane (2005). To try to explain this anomaly, we spent some time reworking our data to more closely parallel theirs. This helped us resolve the apparent inconsistency: it seems that, in the medium term, temp use may increase the number of hours worked but lower hourly wages, with the net welfare effect a judgment to be rendered by researchers, policymakers, and clients.

Finally, we explore in chapter 6 how individuals sort into the different LMIs. Paying particular attention to the role of social networks, we explore the idea that since most people find jobs through their social networks, LMI use may be negatively related to the strength of social capital. We thus construct a measure for social capital from people's responses to the survey and analyze how this relates to intermediary use. Our central finding is that labor market participants with higher levels of social capital were indeed less likely to be LMI users. Similarly, when distinguishing among different types of LMI use, we find that people with higher social capital were less likely to use the temporary agencies that yielded the problematic outcomes we document and were more likely to use other, "higher-quality" LMIs.

As the first study to try to measure systematically the incidence and impact of all types of intermediaries within regional labor markets, our findings must be treated as suggestive rather than conclusive. But these findings, particularly about the widespread use of intermediaries, do reinforce the need for further research on intermediaries, and they have important implications for future research and policy initiatives. We discuss these in chapter 7, where we highlight a further set of questions related to the incidence and impact of labor market intermediaries rooted in geographic differences and the ways in which industrial structure and demographic dynamics shape intermediary use. We also highlight a set of questions related to the effectiveness of intermediaries in influencing the worker outcomes unearthed by our study, focusing in particular on the connections between social networks and intermediary use and on the features that shape "best practice" in placement activities. We conclude the chapter with a brief discussion of the implications for labor market policy, especially the importance of developing intermediary policies, including ways to steer workers toward better intermediaries and to improve the dissemination of best practices across and between different types of intermediaries.

Chapter Two

The Old and New Economies:
A Comparison of Milwaukee and Silicon Valley

Most workers, especially those in the lower tiers of the labor market, search for employment opportunities within the area accessible by daily commute. Similarly, employers search for employees to fill job openings primarily from within regional labor markets. Clearly there are exceptions to this, at both the upper and lower ends of the labor market, and some intermediaries may recruit on a national or even international scale (for example, headhunters for skilled positions or labor brokers for seasonal or migrant farmworkers). Nonetheless, most job matching happens within regional labor markets. As a result, the characteristics of most intermediaries, including the local offices of multinational temporary help agencies, are fundamentally shaped by the economic sectors, demographics, and institutional processes of the regional labor markets in which they operate.

Our selection of Milwaukee and Silicon Valley as the two regions to compare in our analysis was based on a supposition that there would be important differences between these two regions in the scale and type of intermediary activities. We saw Silicon Valley as the prototypical "new economy" region, driven by rapid innovation, technological change, and global competition, with open labor markets in which large sectors of the workforce move frequently from job to job (Benner 2002; Saxenian 1994). We saw Milwaukee, on the other hand, as a prototypical "old economy" region, comparable to many cities in the Midwest and Northeast that experienced a painful period of economic restructuring during the crisis in the dominant industrial manufacturing sectors in the 1980s yet showed signs of economic vitality in the 1990s (Center on Wisconsin Strategy 2002).

The purpose of this chapter is to describe the general context of our study, highlighting the nature of the labor markets and providing a broad overview of the intermediaries in these two regions. Our discussion is divided into three sections. We first present an analysis of the labor market in each region, including demographic characteristics of the population, trends in employment and unemployment, the sectoral composition of employment, wage trends, occupational structure, and occupational wage levels. We then turn to an examination of labor market volatility in both regions. Here we look at indicators of job stability, number of jobs held, job duration, and income mobility. Finally, we provide an overview of the landscape of public, private, and membership-based intermediaries in each region.

In all three arenas, we find significant differences between the two regions that we might expect to affect the nature of intermediary activity. Broadly, these differences support the characterization of Silicon Valley as a region with higher levels of volatility and more rapid change. And as we will see in subsequent chapters, these regional differences are reflected in differences in intermediary use, although sometimes in unexpected ways. However, Milwaukee has also experienced "new economy"–style change and volatility, albeit expressed through the restructuring of older traditional industries. Despite different economic and demographic dynamics in each region, we uncover many similarities in the operations of labor market intermediaries. This suggests that many of the conclusions we draw from this study may be applicable in other regions as well.

The Labor Force and Industrial Structure of Milwaukee and Silicon Valley

Demographics

The total populations of our two regions (as measured by the Milwaukee and San Jose metropolitan statistical areas [MSAs]) are roughly similar, though Silicon Valley grew much faster in the 1990s. Silicon Valley also has a somewhat younger distribution of the working-age population, and the population has a significantly higher level of educational achievement: table 2.1 shows that in 2000 more than

Table 2.1   Demographic Characteristics of Milwaukee and Silicon Valley, 1990 and 2000

	Milwaukee		Silicon Valley	
	1990	2000	1990	2000
Total population	1,432,149	1,500,741	1,504,400	1,709,500
Gender				
Male	48.1%	48.5%	50.7%	50.9%
Female	51.9	51.5	49.3	49.1
Age				
19 or younger	29.2	29.1	27.3	27.3
20 to 24	7.2	6.3	8.5	6.7
25 to 34	17.8	13.8	21.2	17.8
35 to 44	15.2	16.3	16.2	17.6
45 to 59	14.1	18.2	14.8	17.6
60 or older	16.8	16.2	12.1	13.0
Education				
Completed high school		88.0		91.4
Bachelor's degree or higher		27.6		42.4
Race				
White	81.0	74.4	58.2	44.2
Black	13.6	16.1	3.5	3.1
Hispanic	3.6	6.3	21.0	24.0
Asian	1.3	2.4	17.4	27.3
Immigration				
Foreign-born	3.9	5.4	23.2	34.0

Source: 1990: Department of Finance, data files; 2000: U.S. Census Bureau, Census 2000 of Population and Housing, summary file 1. Produced by the California State Census Data Center.

42 percent of the population of Silicon Valley had completed a four-year degree, compared to only 28 percent in Milwaukee (data from the 2000 U.S. census).

There are also significant racial, ethnic, and immigrant differences between the two populations. In the Milwaukee MSA, 74 percent of the population is white, and African Americans are still the dominant nonwhite group, accounting for 16 percent of the total population in 2000. The Hispanic population nearly doubled over the course of the 1990s but still made up only 6 percent of the population in 2000. In Silicon Valley, by contrast, no single race makes up a majority of the population: non-Hispanic whites accounted for 44 percent of the population in 2000, and Hispanics and Asians each constituted roughly one-quarter of the total population. It is important to note that the Asian population in Silicon Valley includes people of many disparate ethnicities and nationalities, with significantly different labor market experiences. People of Indian, Chinese, and Japanese origin in the Valley typically are in the upper tiers of the regional labor market, while Vietnamese, Filipinos, and many Korean workers are in lower-paid occupations. The importance of international immigration to Silicon Valley's workforce is clearly evident in the percentage of the Silicon Valley population who are foreign-born: 34 percent in 2000 (and 23 percent in 1990), compared to only 5 percent in the Milwaukee MSA (and 4 percent in 1990).

The two regions also differ significantly in the residential patterns of different racial groups. Though ethnic pockets do exist in Silicon Valley, by and large it has a more complex and integrated spatial structure than Milwaukee, where the African American population is more geographically isolated than are people of color in Silicon Valley. One indicator of this is the index of dissimilarity, which for blacks and whites in Milwaukee was 82.2 in 2000, indicating that 82.2 percent of all African Americans would have had to change census tracts in order for each census tract to have the same racial composition as the MSA as a whole (see table 2.2). For Silicon Valley, the dissimilarity index is 40.5 for blacks and whites and 51.6 for Hispanics and whites, indicating considerably less residential segregation. As we will see, these different patterns of segregation are probably an important part of the different patterns of labor market intermediary use we see in the two regions.

Employment and Unemployment

Both of these labor markets expanded during the 1990s, though again, Silicon Valley grew significantly faster than the Milwaukee MSA (27 percent and

Table 2.2   Index of Dissimilarity, Milwaukee and San Jose, 1980 and 2000

	Milwaukee-Waukesha		San Jose	
	1980	2000	1980	2000
White with black	83.9	82.2	48.9	40.5
White with Hispanic	55.2	59.6	45.7	51.6
White with Asian	30.9	41.3	32.4	41.7
Black with Hispanic	75.3	78.0	33.8	33.2
Black with Asian	79.4	64.2	31.5	31.2
Hispanic with Asian	55.9	52.4	36.9	44.5

Source: Calculations from 2000 U.S. census data.

15 percent, respectively, between 1989 and 2000). There have been bumps for both regions, however, along the way. Figure 2.1 shows the historical levels of unemployment in each region from 1989 to 2000. Both regions entered the 1990s emerging from serious economic challenges in the 1980s; Milwaukee in particular faced a crisis in its core metalworking industries that resulted in unemployment exceeding 9 percent through most of 1983 and 1984. After a brief recovery in the late 1980s, both regions were then hit by the national recession of the early 1990s; this time Silicon Valley was especially affected by the decline in military spending that followed the end of the cold war. By the latter half of the 1990s, however, both regions were on steady growth paths, with Silicon Valley experiencing an unprecedented boom that eventually resulted in an unemployment rate of only 2.5 percent in December 2000. Subsequently, however, the technology-led economic slowdown of the second half of 2000 led to significant employment loss in Silicon Valley, and monthly unemployment rates peaked at over 9 percent in 2003. Milwaukee's economic trajectory is quite similar: the MSA posted unemployment as low as 2.6 percent in December 1999, but by June 2003, its unemployment rate had peaked at 7.0 percent.

The Sectoral Composition of Employment

Looking at the sectoral composition of employment in both regions reveals some interesting similarities and differences, and these patterns may call into question the characterization of Milwaukee as "old economy" and Silicon Valley

Figure 2.1   Unemployment Rates for Milwaukee and Silicon Valley,
1989 to 2000

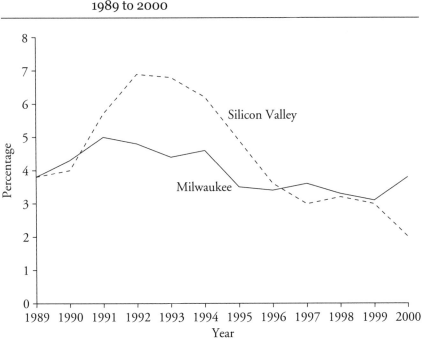

Source: Authors' compilation from Wisconsin Department of Workforce Development and
California Employment Development Department data.

as "new economy," particularly at a broad level. Despite Milwaukee's reputation
as an industrial manufacturing city, a higher percentage of the Silicon Valley
workforce is employed in manufacturing industries than in Milwaukee.
Manufacturing accounted for 25.2 percent of total employment in Silicon
Valley in 2000 (down from 32.2 percent in 1989), compared to 20.7 percent
of all employment in Milwaukee (down from 24.5 percent in 1989). Both regions
saw significant growth in service industries during the 1990s, with 21.1 percent
growth in Milwaukee between 1989 and 2000 and 38.1 percent growth in
Silicon Valley. By the end of the decade, more than one-third of those employed
in both regions were in service industries (36.5 and 35.4 percent, respectively)
(see table 2.3).

Yet behind this aggregate picture lie important differences at a more detailed
industry level. Manufacturing in Silicon Valley is dominated by the computer,

Table 2.3 Industry Employment, Milwaukee and Silicon Valley, 1989 and 2000 (One-Digit SICs)

Industry	1989		2000		Percentage Change 1989–2000	
	Milwaukee	Silicon Valley	Milwaukee	Silicon Valley	Milwaukee	Silicon Valley
Agriculture, forestry, and fishing	0.4%	0.6%	0.7%	0.5%	53.8%	−12.8%
Construction	3.6	3.6	4.2	4.7	16.5	31.8
Manufacturing	24.5	32.2	20.7	25.2	−15.3	−21.7
Transportation, communications, and utilities	5.8	2.6	5.4	2.8	−7.8	6.9
Wholesale trade	6.1	6.6	6.0	5.5	−1.4	−16.7
Retail trade	17.8	14.3	15.9	13.5	−10.8	−5.4
Finance, insurance, and real estate	7.2	3.8	6.8	3.1	−4.8	−17.4
Services	30.1	25.6	36.5	35.4	21.1	38.1
Public administration	4.5	10.7	3.9	9.2	−13.0	−13.9
Total employment	715,692	814,200	822,023	1,030,500	14.9	26.6

Source: Milwaukee: Information received by request from Wisconsin Department of Workforce Development. Silicon Valley: information received from California Employment Development Department (EDD); official estimates of employment by industry released by the EDD, 2000.
Note: Mining is excluded because of very small cells.

semiconductor, electrical components, and measuring and controlling instruments industries—all part of the region's information technology industries. In contrast, Milwaukee's manufacturing employment is still dominated by blue-collar positions in the more traditional metalworking industries. Milwaukee's more diversified manufacturing base extends beyond industrial and commercial machinery to include significant concentrations in fabricated metal products, electronic components, printing and publishing, food and kindred products, and instruments. Similarly, in the category of service industries, Silicon Valley's employment is heavily concentrated in business services (which includes software) and engineering, accounting, research, and management services. By contrast, Milwaukee shows a stronger presence of traditional service industries such as health, educational, and social services. To some extent, then, the "new" versus "old" economy comparison between Silicon Valley and Milwaukee continues to hold (see table 2.4), although, as we note later, both economies are characterized by the extensive use of labor market intermediaries.

Wages

Workers in Silicon Valley generally earn more than workers in Milwaukee. Median hourly wages in 2000 were $18.82 in Silicon Valley but only $14.00 in Milwaukee; for both regions, these figures represent a rebound from stagnating and even declining real wages in the 1980s and early 1990s. Figure 2.2 gives a closer account of wage trends over time, showing changes in wage deciles across the past two decades. The regional differences are striking. During the 1980s, Milwaukee experienced strong and widespread declines in real wages, with workers in the bottom decile losing 17.2 percent and those at the median losing 9.6 percent. In contrast, in Silicon Valley the story was one of stagnation: only workers in the top third of the wage distribution saw any real wage increases. In Milwaukee, declining wages in the 1980s corresponded with the decline of the manufacturing sector over the decade. As throughout the industrial Midwest, Milwaukee residents, especially black central-city residents, were hit hard by deindustrialization. The negative wage trend tracks with other social indicators over the decade.

The 1990s brought a remarkable turnaround, especially after the recession at the start of the decade. In Milwaukee, the economic boom of the late 1990s served to make up for some of the ground that had been lost in the 1980s, especially at the bottom of the distribution. Some gains were probably attributable

Table 2.4   Detailed Industry Employment, Milwaukee and Santa Clara
County ("Silicon Valley"), 2000 (Two-Digit SICs)

Industry	Milwaukee	Santa Clara County
Agriculture, forestry, and fishing		
Agricultural production: crops	9.4%	33.3%
Agricultural production: livestock and animal specialties	0.8	2.1
Agricultural services	89.8	64.0
Construction		
Building construction: general contactors and operative builders	19.9	20.0
Heavy construction other than contractors	7.6	4.7
Construction: special trade contractors	72.4	75.3
Manufacturing		
Food and kindred products	7.2	1.5
Textile mill products	0.2	0.0
Apparel and other finished products made from fabrics	0.9	0.2
Lumber and wood products, except furniture	0.8	0.4
Furniture and fixtures	1.0	0.5
Paper and allied products	3.2	0.7
Printing, publishing, and allied industries	12.3	2.9
Chemicals and allied products	3.2	2.2
Petroleum refining and related industries	0.1	0.1
Rubber and miscellaneous plastics products	4.8	0.9
Leather and leather products	0.7	0.0
Stone, clay, glass, and concrete products	1.3	1.1
Primary metal industries	4.5	0.6
Fabricated metal products, except machinery and transportation equipment	11.6	3.4
Industrial and commercial machinery and computer equipment	22.1	27.1
Electronic and other electrical equipment and components, except computer equipment	12.4	36.8

Table 2.4   Detailed Industry Employment, Milwaukee and Santa Clara County ("Silicon Valley"), 2000 (Two-Digit SICs) *(Continued)*

Industry	Milwaukee	Santa Clara County
Transportation equipment	4.9	4.3
Measuring, analyzing, and controlling instruments; photographic, medical, and optical goods; watches and clocks	6.7	16.9
Miscellaneous manufacturing industries	2.1	0.2
Transportation, communications, electric, gas, and sanitary services		
Local and suburban transit and interurban highway passenger transportation	11.1	7.9
Motor freight transportation and warehousing	26.2	22.5
United States postal service	13.5	
Water transportation	16.2	17.2
Transportation services	8.0	9.8
Communications	12.8	28.7
Electric, gas, and sanitary services	12.1	13.4
Wholesale trade		
Wholesale trade: durable goods	67.5	82.7
Wholesale trade: nondurable goods	32.5	17.3
Retail trade		
Building materials, hardware, garden supply, and mobile home dealers	4.7	3.6
General merchandise stores	11.9	9.4
Food stores	13.8	12.0
Automotive dealers and gasoline service stations	10.2	8.6
Apparel and accessory stores	4.6	5.6
Home furniture, furnishings, and equipment stores	4.9	9.4
Eating and drinking places	36.1	37.7
Miscellaneous retail	13.9	13.7
Finance, insurance, and real estate		
Depository institutions	27.0	25.4

(continued)

Table 2.4   Detailed Industry Employment, Milwaukee and Santa Clara
County ("Silicon Valley"), 2000 (Two-Digit SICs)
(Continued)

Industry	Milwaukee	Santa Clara County
Nondepository credit institutions	5.9	8.8
Security and commodity brokers, dealers, exchanges, and services	8.7	8.7
Insurance carriers	29.2	9.5
Insurance agents, brokers, and service	10.1	7.9
Real estate	13.9	35.6
Holding and other investment offices	5.2	4.0
Services		
Hotels, rooming houses, camps, and other lodging places	2.0	2.4
Personal services	2.8	1.7
Business services	25.8	46.3
Automotive repair, services, and parking	2.5	2.4
Miscellaneous repair services	0.6	0.7
Motion pictures	0.6	0.7
Amusement and recreation services	3.6	3.2
Health services	26.2	13.8
Legal services	2.3	2.6
Educational services	15.5	6.2
Social services	9.3	4.0
Museums, art galleries, and botanical and zoological gardens	0.1	0.1
Membership organizations	2.6	1.9
Engineering, accounting, research, management, and related services	5.4	13.2
Private households	0.5	0.8
NEC	0.1	0.2
Public administration		
Executive, legislative, and general government, except finance	82.2	21.5
Justice, public order, and safety	5.2	33.5

Table 2.4   Detailed Industry Employment, Milwaukee and Santa Clara
County ("Silicon Valley"), 2000 (Two-Digit SICs)
(Continued)

Industry	Milwaukee	Santa Clara County
Public finance, taxation, and monetary policy	1.7	5.6
Administration of human resource programs	3.2	3.6
Administration of environmental quality and housing programs	1.0	3.3
Administration of economic programs	3.9	10.5
National security and international affairs	2.6	4.1
Nonclassifiable establishments	0.0	0.4

Source: From Covered Employment and Wages (ES-202) data provided by Wisconsin Department of Workforce Development and California Employment Development Department.
Note: Mining is not shown because of very small cells.

to the strength of manufacturing in the late 1990s and the fact that retirements in the industry provided a source of jobs for new entrants. In Silicon Valley, it was the top of the distribution that gained the most, while the declining or stagnating wages in the bottom two deciles of the wage distribution indicated a significant increase in economic inequality in the region.

Occupations

How do these aggregate wage patterns play out in particular occupations? Table 2.5 shows the 1999 occupational structure in Milwaukee and Silicon Valley, as well as the median hourly wage in each occupation. Two significant features emerge from this table. First, the occupational structure in in Silicon Valley includes a higher percentage of occupations requiring more education. Thus, for example, employment in computer and mathematical occupations accounted for 7.7 percent of the workforce in Silicon Valley, compared to only 1.6 percent in Milwaukee, while employment in architecture and engineering occupations accounted for 6.4 percent of employment in Silicon Valley, compared to only 2.1 percent in Milwaukee. In the other direction, Milwaukee had a higher proportion of workers in production occupations (14.8 percent versus 10.8 percent), in office and administrative support (18.8 percent versus 15.4 percent), and in health care occupations (4.5 percent versus 2.9 percent).

Figure 2.2   Change in Wage Percentiles, 1979 to 1989 and 1989 to 2000

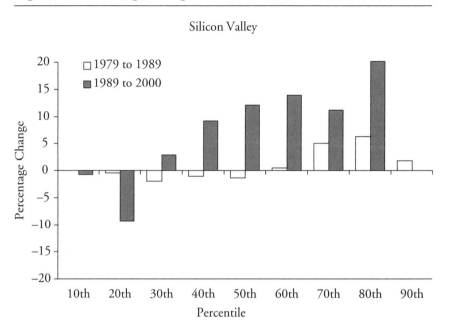

Silicon Valley

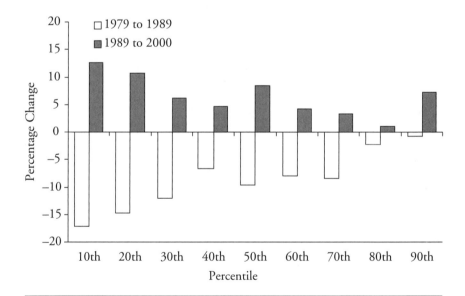

Milwaukee

Source: Authors' compilation from U.S. Census Current Population Survey data.

Table 2.5 Occupational Employment and Wages, Milwaukee and Silicon Valley, 1999

	Milwaukee		Silicon Valley	
Occupation Category	Percentage	Median Hourly Wage	Percentage	Median Hourly Wage	Percentage Difference
Management	6.3	$28.91	7.2	$41.65	44
Business and financial operations	3.4	20.39	4.1	23.70	16
Computer and mathematical	1.6	21.23	7.7	32.85	55
Architecture and engineering	2.1	22.79	6.4	30.28	33
Life, physical, and social science	0.7	17.70	1.0	24.71	40
Community and social services	0.9	14.03	0.5	15.51	11
Legal	0.8	32.00	1.2	45.92	44
Education, training, and library	4.8	15.73	4.7	19.53	24
Arts, design, entertainment, sports, and media	1.1	14.97	1.0	20.38	36
Health care practitioners and technical	4.5	18.99	2.9	25.42	34
Health care support	2.5	9.74	1.2	10.62	9

(continued)

Table 2.5   Occupational Employment and Wages, Milwaukee and Silicon Valley, 1999 *(Continued)*

Occupation Category	Milwaukee		Silicon Valley		
	Percentage	Median Hourly Wage	Percentage	Median Hourly Wage	Percentage Difference
Protective service	2.0	16.24	2.1	11.00	−32
Food preparation and serving related	7.3	7.05	7.6	7.34	4
Building and grounds cleaning and maintenance	3.2	8.33	3.4	8.91	7
Personal care and service	2.2	7.92	1.4	9.67	22
Sales and related	9.0	9.93	8.7	12.26	23
Office and administrative support	18.8	11.50	15.4	14.30	24
Farming, fishing, and forestry	0.1	10.43	0.2	6.44	−38
Construction and extraction	3.6	20.86	3.9	21.07	1
Installation, maintenance, and repair	3.5	16.91	3.1	18.68	10
Production	14.8	12.59	10.8	12.38	−2
Transportation and material moving	6.9	10.45	5.6	10.88	4

Source: U.S. Department of Labor, Bureau of Labor Statistics, "1999 Metropolitan Area Occupational Employment and Wage Estimates, Milwaukee-Waukesha, WI PMSA," and "1999 Metropolitan Area Occupational Employment and Wage Estimates, San Jose, CA PMSA," available at: http://www.bls.gov/oes/1999/oes_5080.htm and http://www.bls.gov/oes/1999/oes_7400.htm.

Second, in almost all occupations, median wages in Silicon Valley were higher than they are in Milwaukee. In general, this simply reflects the overall regional wage difference. But note that the Silicon Valley wage premium was particularly pronounced in higher-skilled, highly paid occupations and largely disappeared in many lower-paid occupations. Thus, for example, the median wage in computer occupations was $32.85 in Silicon Valley, a full 55 percent higher than the $21.23 median wage in Milwaukee. In contrast, the median wage in production occupations was actually 2 percent lower in Silicon Valley than in Milwaukee ($12.38 versus $12.59). Given that the cost of living is significantly higher in Silicon Valley (and that this affects all points in the income distribution), this differential suggests that low-wage workers are likely to face more difficulties in Silicon Valley than in Milwaukee.

Labor Market Volatility

Data from the state unemployment insurance (UI) systems allow us to examine some measures of labor market volatility in both regions. These data (discussed in detail in the appendix) provide information on each job held by each worker in each quarter for all covered employment. The available information includes a worker's quarterly earnings and the employer's industry and location. Data for all establishments in California and Wisconsin were available to us for the years 1992 through 1999, as were data for single-site establishments located in Santa Clara County and the Milwaukee metropolitan area. Although single-site employer data are not ideal, they provide the only regionally specific information available within a state. In an extensive analysis of the single- versus multi-establishment data discussed in the appendix, we conclude that the single-site data are sufficiently representative of all establishments to be of interest. We use these items to examine measures of job stability and upward income mobility in California and Wisconsin (and in Silicon Valley and in Milwaukee), both in aggregate and at various levels of industry disaggregation.[1]

Job Stability

As measured by the percentage of jobs that lasted from one quarter to the next, over the period 1992 to 1999 job stability was somewhat higher in Wisconsin than in California, and higher among single-site establishments in Milwaukee than among such establishments in Silicon Valley (see figure 2.3). In 1999 in Wisconsin, for example, 84 percent of jobs persisted from one quarter to the

Figure 2.3   Job Stability: Jobs That Continued from One Quarter to the Next, California and Wisconsin, 1992 to 1999

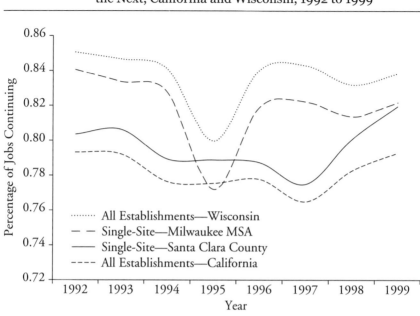

Source: Authors' compilations from Covered Employment and Wages (ES-202) data provided by the states of California and Wisconsin.

next, compared to 79 percent in California. Similarly, among single-site establishments, job stability in Milwaukee was typically two to four percentage points higher than in Santa Clara County from 1992 to 1998. Differences in this measure might reflect in part the overall level of job creation in the economy (if more jobs are being created, more workers move from one job to another), or they may be indicative of differences in the demographic structure of the labor force (older workers will stay on a job longer than younger workers). Regardless of the root of any differences in job stability, however, lower job stability is likely to indicate more labor market churning, which in turn is likely to give rise to more demand for labor market intermediation.

   This pattern of greater job stability in Milwaukee and Wisconsin is also seen at a more detailed industry level, though there is considerable variation from industry to industry. As can be seen in figures 2.4 and 2.5, variations in job stability by industry are similar at both the regional and state levels. For example, in 1997 (the last year for which we could disaggregate data by

Figure 2.4   California–Wisconsin Selected Industries Comparison: Jobs Continuing from One Quarter to the Next, 1997

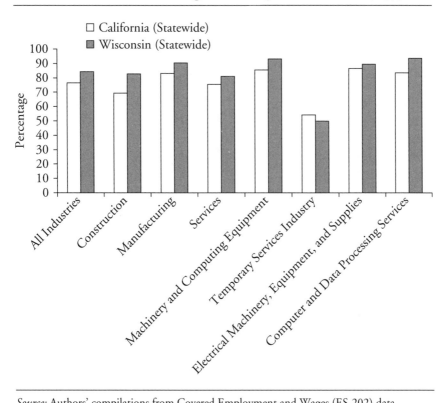

Source: Authors' compilations from Covered Employment and Wages (ES-202) data provided by the states of California and Wisconsin.

industry in both states), the job stability measures for Santa Clara County (for single-site establishments) ranged from 51 percent in the temporary services industry to 88 percent in public administration. Similarly, in Milwaukee job stability ranged from 47 percent in temporary services to 94 percent in hospitals and 95 percent in mining. Across nearly all industries, at both the regional and state levels, jobs in Wisconsin and Milwaukee were persistently two to four percentage points more stable than jobs in California and Santa Clara County.

Interestingly, the one exception to this rule is in the temporary help services industry. Statewide and regionally, job stability is higher in temporary services in California than in Wisconsin (and higher in Santa Clara County than in the

Figure 2.5   Milwaukee–Silicon Valley Selected Industries Comparison:
Jobs Continuing from One Quarter to the Next, Single-Site
Establishments, 1997

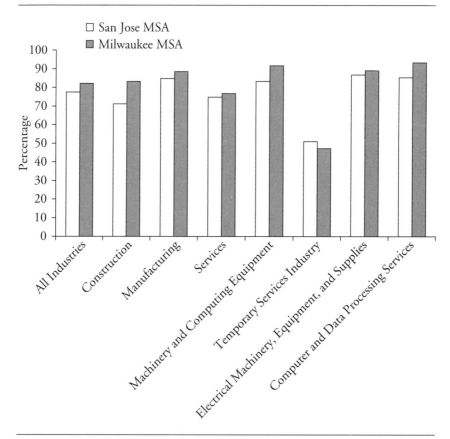

Source: Authors' compilations from Covered Employment and Wages (ES-202) data
provided by the states of California and Wisconsin.

Milwaukee MSA). For example, in 1997, 54 percent of temporary help jobs
in California, and 51 percent of temporary help jobs in Silicon Valley, persisted
from one quarter to the next, compared to 50 percent and 47 percent in
Wisconsin and Milwaukee, respectively. The reasons for this difference are not
possible to discern from the UI data. It is possible that it has its roots in a different industry or occupational composition of the temporary job placements in
each state; alternatively, this difference could represent a higher institutional-
ization of temporary work in Silicon Valley.

Number of Jobs Held and Job Duration

Two other measures closely linked to job stability are the number of jobs held and mean job duration. These measures show a somewhat contradictory picture of job stability in each region. We measure the number of jobs held for all those who were employed sometime in 1997 as the number of different employers they had during the period 1995 to 1997.[2] We estimate a mean of 2.2 jobs in California and 2.4 jobs in Wisconsin. By these measures, the higher number of jobs held in Wisconsin than in California seems to belie the previously discussed finding of greater job stability in Wisconsin. There are a number of possible explanations. One explanation might be a difference between the two states in the rate at which people held multiple jobs: perhaps more workers in Wisconsin held more than one job. Another explanation might be a difference in experiences of unemployment: perhaps more residents of California experienced periods of nonemployment during this time. A third explanation might be tied to different patterns of labor market churning: perhaps even though fewer jobs ended from quarter to quarter in Milwaukee, the people who did leave their jobs moved from job to job more frequently. Finally, it should be noted that these data do not correct for the differences in the demographic data in the two states. If more-educated workers held their jobs longer, then longer job durations in California would be expected.

We discuss the details and methods of our own labor market survey in subsequent chapters, but it is worth noting here that the mean numbers of jobs estimated with the UI data are comparable in magnitude to those estimated from our survey. Over the 1999 to 2001 period, our survey yields estimated means of 1.9 and 1.7 jobs held by survey respondents in Silicon Valley and Milwaukee, respectively.[3]

Turning to measures of job duration, we construct two alternative measures. First we measure the average duration of job spells that began in the second quarter of 1992, following them through the fourth quarter of 1997 (with a maximum possible duration of twenty-three quarters). The mean duration in Wisconsin (2.7 quarters) was slightly higher than in California (2.5 quarters), but Silicon Valley and the Milwaukee region showed the reverse pattern (with mean job durations of 2.8 and 2.6 quarters, respectively). Table 2.6 shows the mean job durations by industry; these exhibit considerable differences between the two regions. We also measured job duration retrospectively as the number of quarters that a job had lasted, for all jobs held during the fourth quarter of

Table 2.6   Average Job Length: Number of Quarters in an Employer Spell for Spells Beginning in the Second Quarter of 1992 (Duration Calculated Through the Fourth Quarter of 1997)

	California	Wisconsin
All industries	2.5	2.7
One-digit industries		
Agricultural production: crops	1.7	2.1
Mining	3.0	2.9
Construction	2.2	2.5
Manufacturing	3.1	3.0
Transportation and public utilities	3.0	3.1
Wholesale trade	3.0	3.1
Retail trade	2.7	2.7
Finance, insurance, and real estate	3.3	3.7
Services	2.5	2.4
Public administration	3.3	2.4
Environmental quality and housing	2.9	2.8
Unclassified establishments	1.7	2.2
Selected two-digit industries		
Construction (SIC 152–179)	2.2	2.5
Machinery and computing equipment (SIC 351–359)	3.6	3.5
Temporary services industry (SIC 7363)	1.8	1.7
Electrical machinery, equipment, and supplies (SIC 361–369)	3.7	—
Communications (SIC 481–489)	3.0	—
Computer and data processing services (SIC 737)	3.7	—
Metal industry (SIC 331–349)	—	3.1
Transportation (SIC 401–478)	—	3.1
Hospitals (SIC 806)	—	4.4
Single-site establishments: Santa Clara County, California, and Milwaukee, Waukesha, Ozaukee, and Washington counties, Wisconsin		

Table 2.6   Average Job Length: Number of Quarters in an Employer
Spell for Spells Beginning in the Second Quarter of 1992
(Duration Calculated Through the Fourth Quarter of 1997)
(Continued)

	California	Wisconsin
All industries	2.8	2.6
One-digit industries		
Agricultural production: crops	2.1	2.3
Mining	2.6	2.6
Construction	2.3	2.5
Manufacturing	3.7	3.2
Transportation and public utilities	2.9	3.1
Wholesale trade	3.4	3.1
Retail trade	2.6	2.7
Finance, insurance, and real estate	3.0	3.6
Services	2.7	2.3
Public administration	3.0	2.4
Environmental quality and housing	3.3	2.3
Unclassified establishments	1.8	1.2
Selected two-digit industries		
Construction (SIC 152–179)	2.3	2.6
Machinery and computing equipment (SIC 351–359)	4.0	3.7
Temporary services industry (SIC 7363)	1.9	1.6
Electrical machinery, equipment, and supplies (SIC 361–369)	3.9	—
Communications (SIC 481–489)	3.7	—
Computer and data processing services (SIC 737)	4.0	—
Metal industry (SIC 331–349)	—	3.0
Transportation (SIC 401–478)	—	3.1
Hospitals (SIC 806)	—	4.9

Source: Authors' compilations from Covered Employment and Wages (ES-202) data provided by the states of California and Washington.

1997. (Measuring back to the first quarter of 1992 allows for a possible maximum of twenty-four quarters.) By this measure, the mean duration in California is considerably lower, at 7.2 quarters, as compared with 10.0 quarters in Wisconsin.[4] These figures are quite comparable to measurements from our Survey of Labor Market Intermediary Use (see chapter 4); we calculate comparable durations of 7.9 and 10.2 quarters for Silicon Valley and Milwaukee, respectively.[5]

Thus, the UI data appear to largely confirm the magnitude of comparable measures calculated from our survey of the Silicon Valley and Milwaukee regions, and it appears that job stability is lower in California and Silicon Valley than in Wisconsin and Milwaukee by several measures: percentage of jobs that persist from one quarter to the next, length of new jobs started, and duration of currently held jobs. One measure, however, the number of jobs held, is marginally higher in Wisconsin than in California. Thus, the overall picture that emerges is of only somewhat higher levels of labor market volatility in California, with both regions showing some significant levels of job changing.

An Overview of Intermediary Institutions in Each Region

As a final point of comparison between our two regions, we now turn to a brief examination of the public, private, and membership-based institutions that shape labor market intermediary development in each region.

Public-Sector Intermediaries

In both regions, a wide variety of state and federally funded programs provide training and placement services. There is one major source of job training funds: federal training programs aimed at economically disadvantaged workers (including adult, youth, and older workers) and dislocated workers who have recently been laid off from their work.[6] A second significant source of funding comes from various welfare assistance and welfare-to-work programs. A third set of training programs has been developed as the result of specifically identified problems or targeted communities, such as programs to assist workers displaced by the North American Free Trade Agreement (NAFTA) or programs for military veterans (who often face particular barriers to employment). A fourth major source of funds is specific to California: the Employment Training Panel is a program that was founded in 1982 to provide training funds to employers to upgrade the skills of their incumbent workforce.

The result of these various funding streams is a wide range of training programs that often have little relationship to each other. The Workforce Investment Act (WIA) of 1998, in part through its provisions requiring the creation of one-stop career centers, was an attempt to integrate these various services into a more cohesive system. During our study, however, WIA was only in its initial stages of implementation, and thus the workforce development system in each region could still quite accurately be described as "a non-system with a bewildering variety of purposes, services, and funding" (Grubb 1996, 9).

The Publicly Funded System in Silicon Valley

At the beginning of our study, Silicon Valley had two private industry councils (PICs) that oversaw federally funded workforce development training in the region. Both of the PICs had their origins in the Joint Training Partnership Act (JTPA) of 1983, and both evolved into workforce investment boards (WIBs) under the provisions of the Workforce Investment Act of 1998. The North Valley (NOVA) PIC/WIB covers the northern part of Santa Clara County, with the Silicon Valley PIC/WIB covering San Jose, Milpitas, and southern Santa Clara County. The Silicon Valley PIC/WIB is larger both in terms of funding and in terms of its service area, which covers the central and southern portions of Santa Clara County, including the city of San Jose. It is larger because the area it represents includes more poor neighborhoods and thus a larger population that is eligible for publicly funded training. NOVA, in contrast, is located in an area with fewer disadvantaged workers and is more directly shaped by the dynamics in the high-tech industry. It is in an area that was at the heart of the emerging semiconductor industry in the 1960s and has been the core of high-tech innovation since. Partly as a result, the NOVA PIC/WIB is more developed in its role as an intermediary in the labor market and has been highly innovative in developing its programs and funding base.

Silicon Valley has a substantial network of nonprofit and community-based organizations involved in workforce development and training. Nonprofit or community-based initiatives receive the bulk of their training and workforce development funding from public sources. They are seen by these funding programs as a service delivery vehicle for public-sector training funds that might otherwise be directly administered by the public-sector agencies. For example, the NOVA and Silicon Valley WIBs contract out about 75 percent of their funds to other agencies to implement the training. Because nonprofits and community-based organizations can be more grounded in the social networks of poor communities, they are often more effective than many standard government training programs.

The community colleges in Silicon Valley have also played a crucial role in providing training for the region's workforce. Much of the training provided through the community college system, of course, is for people who are just moving into the labor market. For those moving from high school into community colleges and getting the training needed to enter the labor market for the first time, community colleges are best analyzed as part of the basic education system. However, for people who are returning to community colleges for training and possible placement at a later point in their career, community colleges play a crucial role as a labor market intermediary. This role has become more significant in recent years and is expected to become even more so in the coming years. In addition, all of the community colleges in the area have further expanded their role as labor market intermediaries by establishing contract training and economic development assistance departments to provide customized training and assistance to local firms. There are three community college districts in Santa Clara County, with a total of six campuses that vary in size and serve students from a range of different ethnic backgrounds (see table 2.7).

The Publicly Funded System in Milwaukee

As in Silicon Valley, the institutional arrangements, funding sources, and various actors in Milwaukee's regional labor market are complex. The major institutions that are focused on low-wage labor markets and connecting central-city residents to jobs include the Milwaukee Area Technical College (MATC), the Milwaukee private industry council, five different private providers and administrators of the state's welfare reform program, and a myriad of community groups, neighborhood organizations, and other community-based organizations that incorporate job access, training, and advancement into their programs.

With more than sixty thousand students in classes each year (85 percent of those attending part-time) and an annual budget of $200 million, MATC is a large provider of work-related training for workers and firms in the region. Many of these students are disadvantaged workers from the central city; in 1999 more than ten thousand central-city workers were enrolled in MATC programs. MATC runs substantial work-based learning programs for local firms as well. More than forty local "workplace education centers" are set up on work sites but are staffed by MATC instructors. Each year more than twenty-five-hundred workers attend training and workshops in those centers.

Table 2.7 Community College Districts in Silicon Valley

	Foothill–De Anza Community College District	West Valley–Mission Community College District	San Jose–Evergreen Community College District
Student body			
Number of students	40,700	25,000	20,000
Race-ethnicity			
Caucasian	40.0%	63.4%	16.0%
Asian	27.0	9.3	46.0
Hispanic	11.0	12.1	26.0
African American	4.0	2.4	6.0
Other or nonspecified	13.0	—	—
Campuses	Foothill College (Los Altos Hills); De Anza College (Cupertino)	West Valley College (Saratoga); Mission College (Santa Clara)	San Jose City College (San Jose); Evergreen Valley College (San Jose)
Economic development programs	Occupational Training Institute; Center for Applied Competitive Technologies; Business and Industry Institute	Community education; corporate training; California Procurement Training and Assistance Center; Alternative Transportation Solutions; Silicon Valley Small Business Development Center; Workplace Learning Resource Center	Institute for Business Performance

Source: Authors' compilation.

Training ranges from advanced process skills to basic education in English as a second language (ESL) and math. The focus of the training program is to provide the workforce with basic and applied workplace skills. MATC works with the Wisconsin Regional Training Partnership and other local partners in promoting the program and its benefits to area employers. Other technical colleges in the region serve the suburban counties and generally do not focus so directly on disadvantaged workers. However, some of the suburban technical colleges have developed strong linkages with firms in their area. Perhaps most notable here is Waukesha County Technical College, which has developed a strong printing program.

The federal Workforce Investment Act and other sources of money fund the Milwaukee PIC to support job search, case management, and training services for disadvantaged and displaced workers in the region. With an annual budget of close to $15 million in the late 1990s (the total budget includes funds for youth programming as well), the Milwaukee PIC disbursed funds to a wide variety of support and training organizations, and in the mid-1990s it played a role in bringing together the region's first two one-stop career centers. During the period of our research, the Milwaukee PIC was also implementing changes associated with the passage of the WIA, which included developing some new programs and implementing new rules around certified training provision and individual training accounts.

Implementation of Wisconsin Works (W2), Wisconsin's welfare reform program, also brought substantial changes to the landscape of Milwaukee's labor market institutions. In Milwaukee County, W2 was administered by four private agencies (one for-profit and three nonprofit). Each W2 provider managed a one-stop career center for a specific neighborhood in the city. W2 providers also worked directly with the region's staffing services and temp agencies to connect workers to jobs; as a result, temp agencies located offices close to each one of the region's W2 career centers. As with other industries, W2 providers have developed strong relationships with temp agencies in order to secure job placements for clients. Likewise, W2 agencies have forged ties with neighborhood groups, churches, and other smaller organizations in order to offer a broad range of services to clients.

Private-Sector Intermediaries

Temporary help agencies are the most important and widespread type of intermediary in each labor market. Employment in employment services firms (including firms classified as both a temporary help agency and a placement services firm) grew rapidly in both regions throughout the 1990s. In Milwaukee, employment in employment services (NAICS 5613) grew by 95 percent between 1990 and 2000, rising from 2.2 percent of total employment to 3.8 percent. In Silicon Valley, the growth was even more dramatic: employment in the industry grew 127 percent in the decade and increased from 2.3 percent to 4.1 percent of total employment (see table 2.8).

The recessions in early 1991 and again in 2001 had a significant impact on the employment services industry, which is a highly cyclical industry. (This impact was especially evident in Silicon Valley, where employment in the industry fell by more than 50 percent between 2000 and 2002.) Yet it is clear that, over time, the employment services industry in both regions is becoming a significantly larger source of employment.

There are broad similarities between the two regions in the employment services industry, but a deeper analysis shows some intriguing differences. On average, firms in the employment services industry in Silicon Valley are larger and pay significantly more than their counterparts in Milwaukee. In 2000 in Silicon Valley, for instance, the average firm in the industry employed 124 people and paid an average salary of $29,924 a year. In Milwaukee the average firm size was only 72 people, and the average salary was only $17,901 (see table 2.9).[7] A deeper look at establishment size provides even more indicators of key differences between the employment services industry in both regions. It is not simply that firms in Silicon Valley were larger than those in Milwaukee, but that Silicon Valley seemed to have a somewhat more bifurcated industry structure, with a higher percentage of both very small and very large firms. For instance, 30 percent of all employment services firms in Silicon Valley employed only one to four people, compared to 26 percent of firms in Milwaukee, while 5 percent of firms in Silicon Valley employed more than five hundred people and 2 percent employed more than one thousand, compared to only 2 percent in Milwaukee that were larger than five hundred employees, and none larger than one thousand (see table 2.10).

These statistics help identify a key difference between the employment services industry in the two regions—a difference that is evident in our survey and qualitative research as well. In Milwaukee, the temporary help industry is focused on the lower tiers of the labor market. In Silicon Valley, in contrast, this is true for only a portion of the industry; another portion focuses on placing more-skilled personnel, most frequently in the region's information technology

Table 2.8 Growth in the Employment Services Industry, Milwaukee and Silicon Valley, 1990 to 2004

| Year | Milwaukee MSA | | | | | San Jose MSA | | | | |
| | Employment Services | | | Total Nonfarm | | Employment Services | | | Total Nonfarm | |
	Number	Index	Percentage of Total	Number	Index	Number	Index	Percentage of Total	Number	Index
1990	16,800	100	2.2%	757,500	100	18,800	100	2.3%	822,900	100
1991	13,600	81	1.8	749,900	99	17,500	93	2.1	814,000	99
1992	16,900	101	2.2	760,100	100	18,100	96	2.3	800,300	97
1993	19,600	117	2.5	772,700	102	19,100	102	2.4	805,300	98
1994	23,200	138	2.9	788,800	104	22,800	121	2.8	808,900	98
1995	24,400	145	3.0	804,000	106	30,300	161	3.6	841,500	102
1996	23,600	140	2.9	812,900	107	34,300	182	3.9	890,500	108
1997	26,300	157	3.2	827,800	109	38,000	202	4.0	938,300	114
1998	28,500	170	3.4	846,000	112	39,100	208	4.0	968,300	118
1999	33,100	197	3.8	862,100	114	38,800	206	3.9	983,800	120
2000	32,800	195	3.8	867,900	115	42,700	227	4.1	1,043,000	127
2001	26,300	157	3.1	856,900	113	27,700	147	2.7	1,016,500	124
2002	24,100	143	2.9	839,500	111	19,600	104	2.1	915,800	111
2003	23,000	137	2.8	830,400	110	22,000	117	2.5	868,800	106
2004	28,100	167	3.4	832,300	110	25,200	134	2.9	859,900	104

Source: U.S. Department of Labor, Bureau of Labor Statistics, "Current Employment Statistics."

Table 2.9   The Employment Services Industry in Milwaukee and
Silicon Valley, 1998 to 2002

	Number of Firms	Number of Employees Week of March 12	Average Employment Per Firm	Total First-Quarter Payroll	Estimated Equivalent Average Annual Pay[a]
Santa Clara County					
1998	364	44,260	122	$285,746	$25,824
2000	409	50,765	124	379,770	29,924
2002	345	20,335	59	193,063	37,976
Milwaukee-Waukesha					
1998	316	26,486	84	100,759	15,217
2000	369	26,694	72	119,463	17,901
2002	370	21,669	59	110,268	20,355

Source: U.S. Census, County Business Patterns, various years. Available at:
www.census.gov/epcd/cbp/view/cbpview.html.
[a]Equals total first-quarter payroll times 4, divided by number of employees week of March 12.

industry. Thus, we see significant numbers of small niche firms that specialize in placing skilled computer programmers, web designers, and other high-tech workers. We also see many of the larger multinational firms in Silicon Valley developing specific services for their highly skilled worker clientele alongside more traditional services to the lower tiers of the labor market.

Membership-Based Intermediaries

Both Milwaukee and Silicon Valley have unionization rates above the national average, though levels of unionization in Milwaukee are significantly higher than in Silicon Valley. In 2000 in Milwaukee, 68.2 percent of public-sector employees and 13.8 percent of the private sector were union members (see figure 2.6). In the San Francisco Bay Area, 53.7 percent of public-sector employees and 10.8 percent of private-sector employees were unionized.[8] Unionization rates in the public sector have risen significantly in both regions since the mid-1980s, while private-sector unionization rates have continued to fall.

In Milwaukee, unions have traditionally been strong in the region's man-ufacturing industries. The economic restructuring of the 1980s helped spur

Table 2.10   Employment Services Firms by Size, Milwaukee and San Jose, 2000

| | Total Number of Establishments | Number of Establishments by Employment Size Class/Percentage of Total | | | | | | | | |
		1 to 4	5 to 9	10 to 19	20 to 49	50 to 99	100 to 249	250 to 499	500 to 999	1,000 Or More
Milwaukee	369	96/26%	31/8%	36/10%	57/15%	68/18%	56/15%	18/5%	7/2%	0/0%
San Jose	409	122/30%	33/8%	36/9%	48/12%	56/14%	67/16%	26/6%	12/3%	9/2%

Source: U.S. Census Bureau: County Business Patterns (available at: http://www.census.gov/epcd/cpb/view/cbpview.html).

Figure 2.6   Private- and Public-Sector Union Membership Rates in Milwaukee, Wisconsin, and the San Francisco Bay Area, California, 1986 to 2000

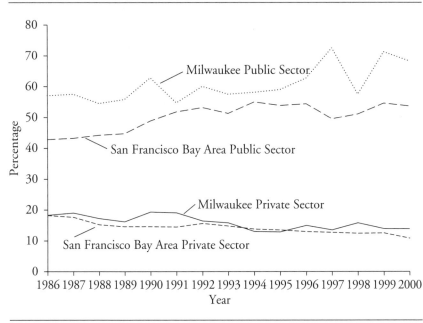

Source: Authors' compilation.

these unions, along with the Milwaukee County Labor Council, to become more directly involved in workforce and economic development issues. One result was the creation of the Wisconsin Regional Training Partnership, a multi-firm and multi-union workforce intermediary that has become nationally recognized for the effectiveness of its work. The partnership by 2002 involved over seventy companies and unions in a range of industries, including many services industries as well as manufacturing industries. Also in the 1990s, the Milwaukee County Labor Council began to forge new partnerships with community leaders, which led to the creation of the Milwaukee Jobs Initiative (MJI). This initiative, which includes leadership from labor, business, and community organizations, has connected nearly fifteen hundred central-city residents with jobs in the region, and the project has helped influence and redirect workforce and economic development policy in the region.

In Silicon Valley, even though overall unionization rates are lower than in Milwaukee and the region's high-tech employers are almost entirely non-union, unions are still quite strong in many traditional sectors, such as transportation, hotel, retail food, and construction, and they have significant strength in the public sector and the building trades. Since the early 1990s, the Central Labor Council has played a significant role in revitalizing labor activities in the area and has been innovative in exploring intermediary opportunities in the region, including the creation of the Temporary Workers Employment Project, designed as a more worker-oriented placement firm than the traditional temporary agency (Brownstein 2000).

Silicon Valley also has dozens, if not hundreds, of professional associations and similar user groups that sometimes play an intermediary role in occupations related to the region's information technology industries. Many of the occupations represented by these associations could more accurately be thought of as "semiprofessions," such as technical writers, system administrators, database developers, and web designers. These midlevel workers in the information technology industries all face rapidly changing technology, skill requirements, and employment conditions in regional labor markets. To help their members deal with these labor market conditions, many of these associations focus on networking and identifying new job opportunities. To do this, these associations must build closer ties with employers than is customary for traditional professional associations (whose members are often self-employed), and often they must also provide placement services for their members (Benner 2002, 2003a).

Summary

This chapter has provided an overview of the economic and institutional context in which labor market intermediaries operate in the two regions that are the focus of this study. In many regards, Silicon Valley and Milwaukee are quite distinct—their economic histories and current educational and demographic compositions are quite different. Both economies are strongly rooted in manufacturing, but their particular manufacturing specialties are quite different, as are the compositions of their service sectors. Interestingly, however, they share some distinct commonalities. Both regions have large service sectors that provide a significant portion of regional employment, and both have rapidly growing temporary help service industries. The differences between the regions in levels of volatility, though somewhat higher in Silicon Valley, are on the order of a few percentage points, not orders of magnitude.

In considering measures of volatility in the labor market, we find that there is more job changing in Silicon Valley and that jobs are shorter-lived there than in Milwaukee. The "new economy" characteristics of Silicon Valley would lead many to expect this difference. The area is home to a computer and electronics industry in which new firms are continuously being created and existing firms are rapidly growing. This labor market churning is associated with higher wage levels and wage growth in upper tiers of the labor market in Silicon Valley. At lower tiers, however, wages in Silicon Valley are more similar to Milwaukee and have stagnated in the 1990s. This is the context in which we examine workers' use of labor market intermediaries in the two regions.

Chapter Three

Meeting, Molding, and Making Markets: How Intermediaries Shape Labor Flows

The central question that drove the research for this book was this: how do labor market intermediaries affect labor market outcomes for disadvantaged workers? Answering this question requires knowing both how prevalent LMIs are in the labor market and how they affect labor market processes. To understand how prevalent they are, we knew we had to survey workers themselves and ask whether they have used intermediaries, why they may have used them and how often, what kinds of services they have received, and the quality of the jobs they have obtained through intermediaries. In the following three chapters, we report on these factors, which formed the core of our survey of workers.

To understand how intermediaries affect labor market processes, however, we knew we could not limit our study to a survey of workers but also needed to look at the services and activities of intermediaries themselves in more depth. Even before we could develop appropriate questions to include in our survey, we needed a better understanding of the similarities and differences between the wide range of organizations that serve as intermediaries in the labor market and in the various services they provide. In addition, we sought to answer a range of questions about the role of intermediaries in the labor market: Why do different intermediaries provide the different services they provide? What are the challenges they face in trying to provide these services, and how have they addressed those challenges? How do different intermediaries find particular types of job-seekers and employers, and conversely, how do workers and employers find particular types of intermediaries? What is the nature of the relationships that intermediaries build with workers and employers? Why do intermediaries work with the particular workers and employers that they do? How do intermediaries affect the characteristics and behaviors of workers and employers?

Other studies that attempt to answer such questions have focused on particular intermediaries or types of intermediaries. Thus, we have a growing number of studies focusing on temporary help agencies (Autor 1999, 2003; Autor et al. 1999; Erickcek and Houseman 1997; Gonos 1997; Houseman et al. 2001; Kalleberg 2000; Neuwirth 2004; Parker 1994; Rogers 2000; Segal and Sullivan 1997b), public-sector employment programs (Bloom et al. 1997; Grubb 1996), union hiring halls (Fick 1987; Thieblot 2002; Well 2005), and even community college placement programs (Grubb et al. 1997; Grubb et al. 1996). In recent years, we have also seen a growing number of studies of best-practice intermediaries that focus in-depth on particular individual intermediaries (Osterman and Lautsch 1996; Parker and Rogers 2001), intermediaries that are organized on a sectoral basis (Aspen Institute 2002; Pindus et al. 2004; Elliot et al. 2001), or new intermediaries that are experimenting with different organizational structures and services (Carré et al. 2003).

These studies have all provided valuable insights into how different intermediaries or types of intermediaries operate, but there remain important gaps in our understanding of the role of intermediaries in contemporary labor markets. Rather than studying individual intermediaries or types of intermediaries, we wanted to analyze the variety of intermediary organizations as a set of institutions that are all providing a core job-matching function that seems to be more important in contemporary labor markets than in the past. We wanted to understand the variety of forces that have led these different institutions to engage in intermediary activities and the factors shaping how they have developed those activities over time. We also wanted to understand how different intermediaries are integrated into regional labor markets and respond to changes on both the supply and demand sides of the labor market, and how this integration shapes labor market outcomes for disadvantaged workers. Most of all, we wanted to better understand the institutional, social, and market landscape against which our survey would be conducted, combining qualitative insights with the quantitative data we wished to analyze.

To study such a diverse set of institutions and the variety of forces shaping their intermediary practices, we had to go beyond a survey of workers' experience to conduct in-depth research on intermediaries themselves; for this work, we chose qualitative or case study research methods. This decision stemmed in part from the fact that there is no universal list or database of organizations engaged in intermediary activities that we could use to administer a survey; even if we could have generated such a list, it seemed doubtful that we could develop a standardized list of questions that would be equally effective in helping us understand the operations of organizations as diverse as, say, temporary help agencies and unions. More importantly, however, our understanding of how these organizations operate needed to be informed by *their* perceptions of the labor market and labor market changes. What did they think was important in being an intermediary? What did they perceive as important for serving both employers and workers?

We began our research by forming a series of five focus groups (three in Silicon Valley and two in Milwaukee) with thirty-seven representatives (twenty-three in Silicon Valley and fourteen in Milwaukee) from a wide range of intermediaries in each region. These focus groups probed how the participants conceptualized their intermediary work, what services they provided and why, how they approached recruiting both employers and workers, and how they related to other organizations in the region that also provided intermediary services. These focus groups helped us gain a broad overview of the landscape of intermediaries in each region and the factors shaping their activities. We also used these focus groups to select a smaller number of intermediaries to focus on in more depth. Our goal was not to identify exemplary intermediaries, but rather to find "typical" intermediaries that might help us better understand the day-to-day processes, experiences, and activities in which intermediaries engage. We selected twenty-three cases (seven that had participated in the focus groups and sixteen new cases) for in-depth study. At least two cases in each region were in one of these five categories: temporary agencies, community-based or nonprofit organizations, community or technical colleges, membership-based organizations (such as unions and professional associations), and public agencies (such as welfare-to-work agencies and private industry councils). We conducted in-depth, one- to two-hour interviews with the staff of each intermediary (typically two or three staff members). We also interviewed the staff of at least two employers that were connected to the intermediary and two workers who had received training or placement from the intermediary. A total of 146 interviews were conducted in the two regions. We used a common protocol to guide the interviews, but the in-depth nature of the interviews also allowed us to explore aspects of each intermediary's operations or perceptions that were particularly interesting or revealing (for details on our qualitative methodology, see the appendix).

Some of the intermediaries we studied agreed to be publicly identified, and where appropriate, we refer to them in the text. Some other intermediaries and all of the employers and workers we interviewed requested anonymity, and we thus refer to them in more generic terms. Even where we discuss particular intermediaries, however, our emphasis is not on describing their particular practices but on identifying the forces that shape their activities so as to gain insight into intermediaries as a set of institutions.

In presenting the findings of our research, we have found it most useful to classify the activities of intermediaries into three broad categories that describe a spectrum along which those activities shape fundamental characteristics and dynamics of the labor market. At one end of the spectrum is a set of job-matching activities that comprise outreach, assessment, placement, and various support services. We term these activities *market-meeting*, since they largely take the characteristics of jobs in the labor market as given and simply match workers with employers to fill those jobs. By definition, all of the intermediaries we studied have some set of activities in this category, but the specific nature of those activities differs significantly between intermediaries.

At the opposite end of the spectrum are intermediary activities that affect, to varying degrees, the quality and distribution of jobs in the labor market, such as incumbent worker training, acting as the legal employer, contractual bargaining around work organization and working conditions, and various advocacy activities. We term these activities *market-making*, since intermediaries play a critical role in structuring the character of jobs themselves.

In the middle of the spectrum are a range of activities—such as providing pre-employment and vocational training, building and disseminating information on industry trends or occupational progressions, and facilitating networking opportunities for both workers and employers—that we term *market-molding*. These activities do not directly change the underlying characteristics of jobs, but they may go beyond short-term match-making and improve career opportunities for workers over time or shape the economic trajectories of individual firms and regional industries.

In the discussion that follows, we look first at market-meeting and market-molding activities and begin by describing in more detail the activities in each category. Since our primary concern is with how intermediaries affect disadvantaged workers, we also describe what we learned from our respondents about the most effective ways to help disadvantaged workers and the factors they saw as important in shaping the ability of different intermediaries to reach those "best practices," including the obstacles faced by different types of intermediaries in trying to achieve those practices. In the area of market-meeting activities, "best practice" meant not simply placing disadvantaged workers in any job, but placing people in the *best possible* job given their particular skills, experience, interests, and life circumstances, while also providing the support they needed to be successful in that job. In the area of market-molding activities, "best practice" meant taking a longer-term perspective, that is, looking at how various intermediary activities shaped career advancement opportunities for disadvantaged workers.

Following this discussion of market-meeting and market-molding activities, we turn our attention to market-making activities. Here our discussion is not structured around best practices per se, but instead around the processes or mechanisms by which intermediaries have an impact on the quality of jobs, including HR practices, productivity, and work organization. Only a small number of intermediaries have this kind of far-reaching impact on the labor market, and their impact can be both positive and negative, depending on the intermediary and the values of those judging the intervention. We conclude the chapter by shifting the lens from the *activities* of intermediaries to a discussion of *types* of intermediaries, exploring the opportunities and constraints faced by the different types of intermediaries, as well as the overall landscape of intermediaries.

Market-Meeting: Simply Finding Jobs or Finding Good Jobs?

The activity common to all intermediaries we studied was job matching—linking workers interested in new jobs with employers seeking to hire new employees. Yet this apparently simple task involves a complexity of different activities that require a range of types of expertise and experience. On the supply side of the labor market, intermediaries differ significantly in the extent to which they specialize in particular population groups, how they identify and reach job-seekers, how they assess job-seekers' skill sets and interests, and how they match them with potential employers. On the demand side of the labor market, intermediaries differ significantly in the extent to which they specialize in particular industries, how they find and build relationships with different employers, how they assess employers' needs, and how they make a match with appropriate job-seekers. Intermediaries also differ in how deeply involved they are in the match-making process, the extent to which they intervene to ensure the success of the match, and how they learn from successful or unsuccessful matches.

It is possible to classify this whole range of job-matching activities into four key subareas:

- Outreach to workers and employers
- Assessment of worker capacities and employment possibilities
- On-the-job assistance
- Support services

We examine each of these subareas in turn and discuss the factors that shape the effectiveness of these activities in improving employment opportunities for disadvantaged workers.

Outreach to Workers and Employers

Obviously the first step in making a placement is to recruit both job-seekers and employers in search of new employees. If intermediaries are going to provide improved employment opportunities for disadvantaged workers, they have to be working with disadvantaged workers, either directly or through networks of contacts. To provide opportunities for good placement, however, it was clear from our interviews that intermediaries thought it essential to *not be limited to serving disadvantaged workers only.* Intermediaries that worked primarily with disadvantaged workers, particularly nonprofit organizations and public-sector agencies, described their frustration at all too frequently being able to place people only in relatively low-paid and dead-end jobs. Without a significant number of more highly qualified workers in their pool, they faced the significant stigma of being viewed by many employers as irrelevant for their workforce needs or as simply sources of relatively "poor-quality" workers; often, they said, employers engaged with them only when labor markets were extremely tight, or out of a sense of social obligation. These intermediaries consistently identified the ability to establish relationships at higher levels of the labor market, either directly or through networks of relationships, as an important requirement for making the best match of experience, skills, and desires and providing better employment opportunities for disadvantaged workers.

Even if intermediaries do not have a pool of more qualified workers they are trying to place, it is important for the quality of their placements that they reach out to "better" firms—better in terms of wages, worker treatment, or prospects for advancement. This may seem obvious, but again, it can be difficult in practice, especially for public agencies and nonprofit organizations. For many years public agencies have been responding primarily to the demands of the most desperate employers, which are often the only ones interested in hiring the population these agencies work with. Typically it is only during periods of very low unemployment that public agencies have a chance to reach higher into the labor market and work with better employers that may not have even known about their services in the past.

In many ways, outreach on both sides of the labor market is essentially a marketing project, and thus the importance of marketing skills was a consistent theme across all our focus groups and in interviews across all types of intermediaries. The for-profit agencies, citing the importance of marketing in meeting the competitive pressures they faced, seemed the most in tune with marketing needs and also had the greatest marketing capacity. In tight labor market conditions like those that still prevailed in the fall of 2000, when our interviews were primarily conducted, competition for workers and firms can become quite fierce; the for-profit agencies in our study were investing lots of time and energy in identifying potential workers and exploring new marketing techniques, from building personal ties with a wide range of community-based organizations to dropping flyers in parking lots. Under these conditions, many private-sector intermediaries were very interested in the most disadvantaged sectors of the labor market and willing to work closely with nonprofits and public agencies to find such workers. Staff we interviewed in both the public-sector agencies and the nonprofit intermediaries claimed that as many as 30 percent of their placements were made directly through for-profit temporary agencies. That links between private- and public-sector intermediaries were extensive was also reinforced by the temporary agencies we interviewed. For example, one private temporary agency in Milwaukee claimed to have recruiting contacts with a network of 170 community-based organizations, including churches, welfare-to-work agencies, and job centers, that produced over 30 percent of the job-seekers they ultimately placed.

For-profit agencies have another advantage over nonprofit and public-sector agencies in marketing their services: they are completely unconstrained in *how* they market to workers. They do not have to meet eligibility criteria or complex requirements put in place by various public and private funding sources. Public-sector agencies, particularly nonprofit employment services providers and the welfare-to-work programs, described the constraints of working only with the people eligible for their services. Most of those we interviewed felt that this restriction was justified in that it ensured that scarce resources were invested in those most in need. They also felt that working closely with the disadvantaged helped them develop significant expertise in understanding the particular problems and social conditions of this sector of the population. Nonetheless, this focus limited their role as labor market intermediaries to low-wage sectors of the labor market and made it harder to build relationships with employers at higher levels. Some public and nonprofit LMIs tried to build relationships with specific HR managers and other recruiters in large firms with a range of employment opportunities, so as to leverage those relationships into good placements for their job-seeking clients. More typically, however, they described their relationships with employers as limited to receiving job listings from a wide array of them; as a result of these shallow relationships, they had only limited knowledge with which to evaluate the quality of the employment opportunities.

A nonprofit intermediary in Silicon Valley presents a particularly clear example of the limitations faced by nonprofit and public agencies. The organization had worked with a Croatian refugee who was referred to it through a church-based refugee relocation program funded by the federal government. The refugee came with significant experience in the printing business, first in Croatia and later in Bosnia and Germany, and received some assistance from the organization in the form of English-language training and basic printing training, which familiarized him with some of the differences between U.S. printing equipment and the equipment with which he had previously worked. The only jobs to which the nonprofit LMI was able to refer him through its recruiting networks, however, were low-paying positions far below his capacities. He ultimately found a more appropriate job through his own efforts. While the nonprofit had relationships with small employers that were looking for entry-level people with basic skills in offset printing, it had no relationships with the larger, more technologically sophisticated firms that might have provided better employment opportunities in the field, despite the fact that the nonprofit advertised training in the printing industry as a particular expertise.

Among the membership-based intermediaries we interviewed, membership was typically built on a particular industry or occupation, and thus their outreach was limited to employers in that industry and to workers with the interest or skills to find employment in that occupation. This occupational/industry focus, however, allowed these organizations to develop relationships with both workers and employers in the industry that were clearly deeper than the relationships described by the nonprofit and public agencies. At the core of their membership base were people already employed and typically skilled enough in their positions that employers were prepared to pay them higher wages. Thus, whether they were unions or professional associations, membership-based intermediaries described much more limited interaction with disadvantaged workers than the private and public-sector intermediaries we interviewed. Nonetheless, our union-based interviewees also gave specific examples of people from truly disadvantaged backgrounds who had obtained good jobs in part through the successful assistance of the intermediary activities of the union. The Wisconsin Regional Training Partnership (WRTP) in Milwaukee, for example, began as a union-initiated labor-management partnership but subsequently got involved in training and placement specifically for disadvantaged workers, with major foundation funding and in cooperation with the Milwaukee Area Technical College. This alliance provided direct access for disadvantaged workers to good unionized jobs in the region's metalworking, electronics, plastics, and related industries.

The importance of such network relationships was also clear in our interviews with community college–based intermediaries. Our focus here was not on the standard courses and educational activities of community colleges, but instead on the specific divisions or programs within the community colleges that played a more direct role in the labor market. This included contract training programs that provided customized training for specific employers and a small placement and support services program at one of the community colleges in Silicon Valley designed to help disadvantaged workers take advantage of training resources at the college and find good jobs. Overall, the outreach efforts of these programs were the most limited of all the intermediaries we profiled. Intermediary staff members did cite the value of leveraging the extensive educational resources of the community college in building ties with employers—a perspective that was reinforced in the employer interviews—and the success of their programs was clearly tied to the success of their marketing to employers. Recruitment of workers, however, either was not a program goal (as in the case of the contract training programs) or was pursued only through networks of relationships with other intermediaries in the labor market.

Assessment

Finding workers and firms is only the first step in the job placement process. Intermediaries market themselves on their ability to make effective connections between supply and demand. Effective connections depend on accurate assessment of both the capacities and interests of workers and the specific needs and working environments of employers. The issue of "fit" emerged frequently in our interviews, in terms of both the culture of the firm and the personal characteristics of workers. For the people we interviewed, skills alone were not enough to make good connections, and as a result, they relied on more informal methods of trying to ensure that the connections they initiated were appropriate ones.[1] It was apparent that the depth of the relationships between the intermediary and the workers and employers played an important role in these assessments and that such relationships were strengthened by length of contact and diversity of opportunities for interactions.

How do intermediaries build strong relationships with both workers and employers? The membership-based intermediaries we profiled typically achieved this through a combination of contractual relationships and skill development. A construction union in Silicon Valley, for example, not only had strong ties with its membership base (which might be expected of a membership-based organization) but also had particularly strong relationships with employers. The business officer for the union estimated that 80 percent of the contractors who hired union members had started out as workers and union members themselves and only later moved into being contractors. Thus, he argued, they had a deep appreciation for the placement and training services the union provided and the value of working with the union for their business performance. The union also ran a multimillion-dollar training center that provided both workers and contractors with sophisticated skills and the updated technical knowledge required for building complex and technically sophisticated facilities in the region's high-tech industries. Many employers and their client firms in the high-tech industry taught courses in this center, providing ongoing opportunities for the union to understand the rapidly changing skill requirements and employment needs in the industry.

The private staffing agencies that we profiled seemed to achieve these deeper relationships primarily by working with specific employers over long periods of time, which allowed them a greater opportunity to thoroughly understand the culture of the firm and the worker characteristics it preferred. In both regions, staffing agencies had developed ongoing relationships with large firms and used those long-term relationships to improve their services to the firm. This was especially true for staffing firms that moved on-site, where the employers we interviewed confirmed that these agencies clearly understood their particular needs. In some cases, these on-site relationships had evolved to the point where the temporary firms were treated essentially as a profit unit within the client firm, with the manager of the on-site temporary agency responsible not simply for placing appropriate workers but for monitoring the performance and output of workers on the temporary agency payroll, reporting those results to the client firm, and jointly working out systems for improving the productivity of workers on the temporary agency's payroll. In these cases, the staffing agencies had deep relationships with their employer clients and a subtle understanding of the types of workers their clients were looking for.

Most of the intermediaries we profiled, however, had limited relationships with employers, in part because of the small numbers of workers any single intermediary had placed in a particular firm or occupation. Employers were understandably unwilling to invest a significant amount of time in building a relationship with a single LMI unless it could provide large numbers of people or reliably deliver workers with particular skill sets. Thus, most intermediaries we profiled were limited to simply taking job listings from employers in a scattershot approach and did not have the resources to get deeply engaged in their particular needs and working conditions. For example, one employer in Silicon Valley, an international car rental company, estimated that after conducting background checks, administering basic skills tests, and conducting interviews, they were able to hire only about 10 percent of the people referred to them from any single intermediary. Since building a deeper relationship with any single LMI would not only be difficult, given time constraints, but also unlikely to result in an adequate number of people to hire, this employer spread its recruiting networks as wide as possible.

Most intermediary relationships with workers were also weak, even among the nonprofit and community-based organizations. These relationships were often driven primarily by short-term placement based on minimal assessment of workers' needs. Those intermediaries that did provide training (an issue examined in more detail later) seemed to form somewhat stronger ties with workers over the course of the training period. Frequently, however, that relationship remained limited to the period of training, which rarely lasted longer than six months.

On-the-Job Assistance

For workers to be successful in a new job, they must perform well. Ideally, employers provide all the support and assistance required to ensure that their employees can function effectively at the job site and wages are sufficient to take care of any personal problems that might interfere with work. In reality, however, disadvantaged workers frequently encounter obstacles to performing well on the job. Difficulties in communication, unfamiliarity with a new work environment, personality clashes, power relations, concerns about working conditions, work responsibilities, or transportation and child care are not always easily handled directly between employer and employee.

On-the-job assistance was the most obvious gap in the services provided by the intermediaries we profiled. For the public-sector and nonprofit intermediaries, on-the-job postplacement support was limited to follow-up phone calls at those intervals required by their funding sources (for example, at 30 days, at 90 days, at 180 days, or at one year) to verify continued employment. Some public-sector intermediaries in these follow-up phone calls did ask workers about particular problems they might be facing and tried to help them solve those problems. The Santa Clara County Social Services Agency went somewhat further in providing a hotline called Job Keeper, which was designed as a resource for people to use when they ran into problems on the job and needed assistance. Providing a hotline, however, is a passive approach that requires some significant initiative on the part of disadvantaged workers and provides little help in anticipating and avoiding problems on the job before they occur.

One promising effort to provide on-the-job support we encountered, primarily among membership-based intermediaries, was the development of mentoring relations between new and incumbent workers. The construction union in San Jose provides a clear example of this strategy: each apprentice was always placed with a journeyman-level member who was responsible for the apprentice's performance on the job and provided regular evaluations. This pairing lasted for the full five years of the apprenticeship program, though it was most critical in the first few years. Another example is the Wisconsin Regional Training Partnership, whose staff worked directly with firms and unions to build shop-floor support for new workers. Such support proved critical in an industry where new entrants were likely to differ from the dominant workforce not only in race and gender but also in age. Mentors provided new workers in manufacturing with the sort of support that a relative might have provided in the past. The success of mentors was notable in the Milwaukee Jobs Initiative retention rates, which exceeded 70 percent even at six and nine months. Silicon Valley Webgrrls, the professional association we profiled, provides another membership-based example: this online listserv provided newcomers with access to literally hundreds of other members in other workplaces throughout the region. The daily interactions on this list reflected both the technical and personal support that this community of mostly women in web design occupations could give each other in dealing with the challenges of their jobs (Benner 2003c).

It is important to note that follow-up support occurs in the private sector as well, not just in public-sector or membership-based intermediaries. One Silicon Valley agency we profiled was a for-profit temporary agency with the mission of serving disadvantaged workers. The agency had developed a strategic system for supporting workers on the job. Staff members visited the work site on a weekly basis, meeting with the workers they had placed, discussing workplace problems, and helping to avert problems before they occurred. The agency also attempted to develop mentoring relationships by encouraging clients and mentors to attend weekly on-site workshops that offered practical support and career development assistance. In addition, the agency had developed a partnership with a nonprofit career guidance center that provided its clients with information, counseling, and career advice.

Support Services

The other critical area of assistance that disadvantaged workers frequently require is access to forms of support that may not be directly related to their performance on the job but that fundamentally affect their success in employment. This support can include everything from access to stable and accessible child care and assistance with transportation to treatment for substance abuse and counseling for other personal challenges (such as abusive relationships). Intermediaries rarely provide these services themselves. In Silicon Valley, the typical source for these types of support is the Santa Clara County

Social Services Agency, and so the relationship between the intermediary and the county social service system is critical. In Milwaukee, the one-stop job centers, which administer the state's welfare reform program, are the best source for this assistance.

In our interviews with workers in each region, we often heard dissatisfaction with access to these services. In Silicon Valley, the problem was typically *not* lack of knowledge about the services that were available. In fact, in anticipation of welfare reform, Santa Clara County created a broad, community-based advisory board in 1995 that includes nearly all of the major employment training and placement services in the county; this board meets on a monthly basis to discuss the strengths and weaknesses of current trends in social service provision and to develop mechanisms for improved service delivery, primarily by advertising those services, both through service providers and through appropriate media channels. The primary complaints we heard about county social services, however, were related to income eligibility requirements that were so low, given the cost of living in the area, that people became ineligible for services before fully getting on their feet. In one poignant example, a Salvadoran immigrant who was a single mother found a job in a private foster care agency through the county's Employment Connection placement services. Prior to being hired, she had been receiving $620 a month in cash assistance, food stamps, and assistance with child care. In her new job, she took home about $1,000 a month, but because she lost both her cash assistance and her subsidy for child care when she took the job, she found herself in a worse financial situation.

In Milwaukee, where the cost of living is closer to the national average, the problem was slightly different. Although eligibility for programs, especially child care subsidies and medical assistance, reached higher up into the labor market, it was generally only workers who had had extensive contact with the W2 agencies who knew what was available. Many low-wage workers were not aware of services for which they might legitimately have applied. Most intermediaries did not provide these services, and as a result, provision of the services was frequently fragmented. In Milwaukee, the W2 agencies were knowledgeable regarding what was available and worked with clients to access services. However, both the stigma attached to the agencies and a general lack of information seemed to prevent other workers from accessing the services and support for which they were eligible. Workers in both regions who did manage to secure support had to maintain multiple relationships: with LMIs, with service providers, and, in California, with the county (to maintain eligibility, even if the county was not providing the service). It was a complex system that presented numerous challenges to people who were often already struggling with other personal difficulties.

Market-Molding: Labor Market Intermediaries and Career Mobility

Job placement—connecting a person with a specific employer—is the central activity of most labor market intermediaries. In many ways, their job placement activity reflects a simple effort to solve a short-term problem on the demand or supply side of the labor market—a firm needing a worker, or a prospective worker needing a job. Some of the activities that intermediaries engage in, however, go beyond simply meeting this short-term match-making role. Many intermediaries, particularly in the public and nonprofit sectors, focus on providing training for job-seekers. Some of this training is in simple job search skills and "job readiness"; such training is designed to help people who face barriers to employment gain general skills, such as English as a second language, time management, or basic numeracy and literacy skills. Some intermediaries go beyond this to provide basic vocational training, although, with the exception of community college offerings, this training is frequently short-term, lasting for six months or less. Many intermediaries are also now paying more attention to career paths. The community-based and public-sector LMIs we studied consistently expressed the goal of promoting career mobility as an important part of their mission. In tight labor markets, promoting career mobility becomes an explicit goal even for many for-profit staffing services as they find themselves competing intensely for the same limited pool of job-seekers. Community colleges, unions, and community-based agencies, as well as for-profit staffing services, are increasingly marketing their services as a long-term resource for workers and promoting career advancement. These long-term perspectives are not limited to workers: intermediaries are also building relationships with employers that help build networking opportunities.

We call these various activities "market-molding" because they go somewhat beyond the basic match-making role of intermediaries. They have the potential for changing flows of labor through the labor market and providing improved employment opportunities for disadvantaged workers over the long term. These activities do not necessarily have a major impact on the quality or quantity of jobs in the labor market, but they can help individuals achieve better results in the labor market.

We discuss four subareas of activities that fall into this category: basic pre-employment training; lifelong learning and more advanced training; building and disseminating information on industry trends and/or the potential for career ladders within and across firms; and facilitating networking opportunities for both workers and employers. As in the previous section, we examine each of these activity subareas in turn, presenting what we observed to be the factors that were most important for helping disadvantaged workers and the different types of intermediary efforts in engaging in those activities.

Basic Pre-Employment Training

Pre-employment training programs offer services specifically designed for workers who are particularly disadvantaged in the labor market because they lack certain characteristics and skills that are considered prerequisites for success in any workplace but are not linked to a particular occupation or vocational skill set. The most common of these training programs is the English as a second language (ESL) course for immigrants with limited English skills. ESL programs that focus on terms and language specific to particular occupations or vocations are called vocational ESL (VESL) programs. Other training programs focus on developing the "soft skills" needed by people with limited labor market attachment as they become adjusted, or readjusted, to workplaces. These skills can include anger management, work ethics, punctuality, appropriate dress, and the like, as well as orientation to job search strategies, including résumé-writing, presentation, and interviewing skills. These skills may seem less important than harder, more technical skills, but for disadvantaged workers, according to many of our informants, they are absolutely critical in getting and retaining work.

Public and nonprofit organizations were the only organizations we profiled that provided any explicit training in soft skills, though community colleges (including contract training programs in both regions) were also important providers of ESL and VESL classes. These organizations were the only ones with a specific mandate to work with the most disadvantaged sectors of the labor market, and developing these programs was an important part of the services they provided. Respondents stressed that soft-skills programs were most effective, however, when they were not stand-alone offerings but instead were integrated into other aspects of their services. The Center for Employment

Training (CET) in San Jose, for example, structured all-day vocational training programs for unemployed people with the expectation that they would follow the norms of a typical work environment, including punctuality, dress, presentation, and communication, and would be referred to other services and support if they were unable to develop and maintain this performance. This program helped people become accustomed to a work environment characterized by much greater attention and support, and less stress, than they would have encountered in the typical workplace. It also helped CET identify individuals with particular challenges that required additional support services.

Vocational Training

In cases where the technical skills of prospective workers do not match the requirements of firms, the obvious answer is vocational training. In the best-practices scenario, vocational training is linked with skills that are in high demand in the labor market, ideally in a situation where the training is linked with guaranteed job placement.

The LMIs with the greatest capacity for providing extensive training opportunities are obviously the community or technical colleges. The increasing integration of the community college system with employer human resource requirements helps ensure that these training programs are oriented more toward employers' needs and provide immediate employment opportunities for those getting training. One clear example is a semiconductor-related manufacturing technician program that is run as a joint initiative of two community colleges in Silicon Valley. The program—a two-year AS degree that was developed in close cooperation with a major semiconductor manufacturer in the area—provides a combination of general education requirements in electronics and a series of detailed courses in semiconductor manufacturing and the care and maintenance of the machinery involved. It was developed in the mid-1990s, when there was a clearly identified skill shortage in the area. At that time the semiconductor firm identified the importance of promoting training to fill critical skill shortages in the future.[2] In the first years of the program, this company hired every single graduate of the program. The extraordinary marketability of these skills, at least with this particular employer, declined during the Asian financial crisis of 1998. However, the labor market for these skills continued to be tight, and graduates seemed to have no problem in finding employment that typically paid (in 1999) a starting wage of $40,000 a year for workers with only a two-year community college degree.

The limitation of this particular program was that it did not provide services to assist workers who might be facing special barriers to employment or who needed additional social services. Such gaps can be addressed even in the context of a community college. For example, the Occupational Training Institute, a community college–linked training institute we examined in Silicon Valley, did not directly develop its own training programs but instead saw its role primarily as providing job placement services, career guidance, and social services to a range of workers from disadvantaged backgrounds. Because the institute was located on the community college campus, however, it also had a detailed knowledge of the variety of vocational training programs offered by the college. Furthermore, since it was in constant communication with employers about their placement efforts, it was also able to provide feedback to the college on new training programs it could be developing. The institute was thus able to push the college to develop training programs in skills such as surface mount technology (required in circuit-board manufacturing) and multimedia skills sooner than the college would have done otherwise.

Nonprofit LMIs provide another source of training, with financial support primarily from federal and state workforce development programs. Most of these programs are forced to respond to the eligibility and structural guidelines of funding agencies, rather than directly to the needs of local employers. Certainly, the goal of JTPA, and more recently WIA, is to provide training that meets employers' needs. But the limited long-term impacts of JTPA programs are documented in a number of studies (Bloom et al. 1997; Grubb 1996; Lafer 1994), and the jury is still out on WIA. Furthermore, it can be difficult for programs to deal with changing funding requirements and sources. For instance, in the 1980s when the Comprehensive Employment Training Act (CETA) was replaced by JTPA, the Occupational Training Institute, which had been dependent on CETA funding, lost nearly all of its funding and had to lay off all but three of its employees. Through the decade and a half of the JTPA program, the institute expanded its range of funding sources and was able to grow again, up to twenty-eight staff people and an annual budget of $2.4 million. Nonetheless, with the shift from JTPA to WIA, its annual funding for the first year declined by 50 percent, until it was able to receive a significant grant from the Silicon Valley WIB to provide second-tier support services at one of the new one-stop career centers under development in southern Santa Clara County.

The for-profit intermediaries we profiled focused their limited training activities on self-paced, computer-based tutorial programs for particular software packages, typically the dominant Microsoft Office software (Word, Excel, PowerPoint), and sometimes for database or desktop publishing programs. This training was usually provided at no cost and thus offered some opportunity to those workers who were self-motivated and already familiar with computers. Several studies of such training programs, however, have argued that they often serve as a screening device for staffing services firms, helping them to identify workers who are likely to be successful placements, while weeding out the more difficult-to-place workers (Autor 1999; Autor et al. 1999).

A program rooted in unions provides a good example of training that is integrated with job needs. The Wisconsin Regional Training Partnership in Milwaukee helps organize training initiatives in partnership with firms, unions, and the technical college. Member firms or their unions identify openings that need to be filled. Workers and supervisors specify the skills required to perform the jobs, and the technical college designs a customized training program. Community organizations, publicly funded welfare centers, and neighborhood groups refer eligible job-seekers to the program. Firms screen applicants in advance of the training, and the firm hires any successful graduate of the program. Customized training projects along these lines—partnerships between employers, training providers, and community agencies—have emerged to fill employment needs. The training partnership has helped to make these processes more systematic and to market the possibility of customized training to additional local firms. The success of these training programs is notable—between 2000 and 2002, more than five hundred workers successfully secured jobs through these partnerships, at an average wage of over $10 an hour.

Intimate Industry Knowledge and Career Progressions

To improve the career mobility of workers, LMIs must have an intimate knowledge of labor markets that goes beyond simply knowing about job openings. LMIs must have a detailed understanding of the skill and experience required by those job openings as well as the pay structures and opportunities for internal advancement associated with them. Furthermore, where internal labor markets are nonexistent or minimal, they must be able to identify cross-firm occupational progressions, along with the training, experience, and contacts required to make such cross-firm movements possible. As if this were not challenging enough, in industries or occupations experiencing rapid technological changes or rapidly changing skill requirements, LMIs must also be able to develop or understand employment opportunities in the future. Essentially, for an LMI to make advancement probable, it has to not only see a career path but also help build systems to allow for smooth progress along that path.

Intermediaries have a difficult time gaining sufficient access to employers to gather this level of detailed information on job requirements or industry dynamics. In the public and nonprofit sectors, the interests of LMIs are driven primarily by the needs and personal circumstances of their worker clients. Staff members usually have expertise primarily in social services and education, but little experience working in the private sector. Relationships with employers often appear to be quite weak and scattershot as LMIs attempt to cover a wide range of industries or occupations. Furthermore, they even tend to have short-term relationships with their worker clients and make few efforts to maintain long-term communication. Many of the people we interviewed saw this as a major drawback, since their clients' experiences in searching for work often helped give the LMIs a better sense of changing industry dynamics and skill needs in the labor market. One career counselor at a community college–linked training program in Silicon Valley, for instance, said that the information provided to him about job opportunities by dislocated workers (who tend to have higher education levels and more work experience than disadvantaged workers) helped him assess the types of opportunities to recommend to disadvantaged workers looking for entry-level positions. In the absence of ongoing relationships with worker clients at higher levels in the labor markets, or even with workers who have lower-level jobs but more work experience, many LMIs miss the opportunity to learn from their clients as those clients gain more knowledge and information about career opportunities.

In the private sector, some LMIs clearly had a closer relationship with employers. This was particularly true in the larger on-site relationships; in the most developed cases the manager of the on-site staffing services unit often was responsible for managing the people the LMI had placed, as if it were simply a profit unit within the client firm. Even smaller, more specialized temporary firms seemed much more able to build close relationships with particular clients. One small temp agency in Silicon Valley, for instance, focused its placements in the medical instruments industry and thereby secured a useful level of knowledge about the dynamics in that field. According to its president, this knowledge enabled the agency to fit a particular niche for its clients that the larger, less specialized agencies had a difficult time filling. He did feel, however, that this strategy was risky, since "putting all your eggs in one basket"[3] could make the company extremely vulnerable in an economic downturn. Thus, even private-sector LMIs tried to diversify their placements and as a result had limited access to detailed industry information. In our interviews, private-sector LMIs provided only minimal evidence that they thought seriously about industry dynamics and changes beyond those relevant in the short term for immediate placements.

Of the intermediaries we interviewed, those that had the best intimate knowledge of industry dynamics were those with a membership base. The construction union in San Jose, for example, was seen by employers and workers alike as the best source of knowledge on changing skill requirements and occupational dynamics in the high-tech plumbing arena. Integrating information from their employer contacts, members' perspectives, training providers, and formal coursework, this union appears to know its particular occupational niche, and the opportunities for career advancement within it, better than any of the other actors. It was able to develop this expertise by putting substantial resources into its training center, which was originally established in 1961 in response to the recognized need for training in the piping industry. The center is now a 56,000-square-foot facility, with 28 classrooms where both journeyman- and apprentice-level courses are taught; the annual budget of more than $3 million is funded entirely from deductions from members' paychecks. Instructors in the center are primarily people from the industry with firsthand knowledge of changing technologies and skill requirements. Nearly all members of the union, including the most experienced, continue to take courses in an effort to stay on top of changing technology and safety regulations. As a result, piping contractors recognize that if they want to work on projects for one of many technology firms in the region, they have no other option but to hire union plumbers.

Silicon Valley Webgrrls, a professional membership association we examined, provides another, non-union, example. Members share detailed information about trends in the Internet industry and web design skills. They also share information about the strengths and weaknesses of various training programs and short-term courses and give each other feedback on specific web pages, including evaluation of the artistic design and responses to specific technical questions about design options or links with back-end databases. This detailed sharing of information takes place at regular monthly meetings, but more importantly, it also takes place in daily online communication through an email listserv. In this way, workers with similar skills in similar occupations, but working at different work sites and for different employers, are able collectively to stay on top of changes in the industry (Benner 2003c).

Building Social Networks

The importance of social networks in finding employment is by now well established. Following Mark Granovetter's groundbreaking study in the 1970s, numerous researchers have documented the ways in which social networks assist people in their job-finding efforts (Granovetter 1995; Montgomery 1991; Pastor 1996; Wial 1991). Networks, however, may also provide information on advancement opportunities (and thus lead to better jobs), on changing dynamics in the firm, industry, or occupation (and thus allow workers to prepare for emerging realities), and on opportunities for skill development. Thus, helping workers to strengthen social networks, and particularly to build social networks that might improve employment outcomes, is critical for building career mobility. To be successful in this area, LMIs need to provide the opportunities for workers to interact with other workers, both those with similar interests and experiences and, even more critically, those with different experiences, who may provide bridging opportunities to better social networks (Harrison and Weiss 1998; Melendez and Harrison 1998; Spaulding 2005).

None of the staffing services agencies we interviewed discussed building networks for their workers as an active pursuit. In practice, their actions may have interjected workers into a broader network simply by placing them in firms with which they might not otherwise have become connected; the network in the workplace may have subsequently helped these workers to develop a career. But to the extent that workers build personal connections where they are placed and use those connections to help move into the firm and advance unassisted in the industry, the agency loses a placement. Sometimes a staffing services agency may benefit from its workers moving into better positions, since it can charge a higher markup fee. This tends to happen, however, with relatively highly paid computer programmers and other high-tech contractors, not with lower-paid workers. In any case, we did not run across a staffing services agency that tried explicitly to help workers improve their networking skills, and again, the incentive structure is such that a deemphasis on networking at a staffing services agency is entirely sensible.[4]

By contrast, some nonprofit and public LMIs do pay specific attention to building the social networks of clients. Nearly every nonprofit or public LMI that offers training spends some time on communication skills, and some of these training programs focus on communication for the purpose of building networks, connections, and knowledge of opportunities. Many organizations also offer job clubs, where workers may discuss a range of issues, including current opportunities. Many agencies see this as a highly effective way of boosting motivation as well as improving employment opportunities. They are still limited, however, by the socioeconomic circumstances of their clients. Thus, while they may be able to strengthen "bonding" networks, they have little success in strengthening the "bridging" networks that might help people find better employment opportunities (Briggs 1998).

Within their particular occupations, the membership-based LMIs seem to provide the best opportunities for building workers' social networks. The sense of belonging that can accompany being part of a membership-based organization provides an immediate connection to a whole community of people with similar labor market experiences. With membership cutting across all age and experience groups, including both newcomers and more experienced workers, the social networks that are built almost always have some bridging component to them. This is clear in the case of union apprenticeship programs, in which newcomers are linked with mentors with greater experience in the occupation. It is also true for the Silicon Valley Webgrrls, whose efforts to promote both in-person networking opportunities and a supportive online community help the people who are pursuing new and better employment opportunities through these networks.

Market-Making: Fundamentally Changing Labor Market Structures and Dynamics

"Market-meeting" and "market-molding" efforts can have a significant effect on individual workers' lives, but they implicitly take the jobs themselves, and the wages and benefits attached to them, as givens. For workers who have access only to jobs with low pay or poor benefits, this strategy has inherent limits in improving their welfare. Thus, we searched for intermediary efforts to alter the job structure itself in some way. Our aim was to determine what leads intermediaries to play a more interventionist role, and what kinds of impacts this has on job quality, whether positive or negative.

How do intermediaries directly affect the quality and characteristics of jobs? We discuss four mechanisms. First, some intermediaries engage in advocacy activities, pressuring employers to change job characteristics. Second, some offer incumbent worker training, working with employers to improve the skills and productivity of workers on the job. Third, some intermediaries enter into contractual relations with employers that give them the leverage to have an impact on job quality through that contractual relationship. Finally, some intermediaries become the employer of record and in that role take on increasing responsibility for the character of the jobs they oversee. We discuss each of these activities in turn.

Advocacy

Obviously, government regulations have a significant impact on overall job quality. Policies such as the minimum wage, the Fair Labor Standards Act, OSHA (Occupational Safety and Health Administration) regulations, and hiring and wage requirements within local economic development programs all have a direct impact on employment conditions. To varying degrees, all types of intermediaries attempt to influence such regulations. Historically, unions and other pro-worker allies have fought for governmental regulations to improve working conditions, and such organizations continue to push for increasing the minimum wage and changing labor law to facilitate workplace representation. Similarly, temporary agencies, whether directly or through their lobbying agencies, try to influence legislation affecting taxation, joint liability, and responsibility for health and safety conditions (Gonos 1997). Various associations of nonprofit intermediaries attempt to lobby Congress for more funding and for certain provisions in the workforce development programs and criteria that indirectly affect their work.

All of these activities aimed at influencing government policy and regulation were beyond the scope of this research project. Our focus instead was on ways that intermediaries influence employer behavior that are directly related to the intermediary's own activity. In the case of individual workers, this occurs when an LMI intervenes with an employer to argue that a certain employee should be paid more than the standard rate or what has been offered. In the case of broader working conditions, however, intermediaries rarely play a strong advocacy role with employers. One exception we examined was an effort by

Working Partnerships, a labor-affiliated think tank and advocacy organization in Silicon Valley, to build a code of conduct specifically for temporary help agencies. The code of conduct was part of a more comprehensive approach to addressing the problems temporary employees faced. That approach had three components: the creation of a best-practices temp agency in an effort to set high standards for the industry; the formation of a temporary workers' membership association to lobby for change, in part by setting base standards for the industry; and improved access to training for workers who were clients of the staffing service and the membership association, with a longer-term goal of creating recognizable skill ladders through standardized certifications.

The code of conduct was developed as part of the membership association and was used to lobby employers in their use of temporary help agencies. The code was designed to set a minimum wage and establish basic rights, including agency neutrality in union-organizing efforts, as well as to make explicit higher industry standards. Like living wage campaigns, the code of conduct campaign involved lobbying employers (including public agencies) to give preferential treatment to temporary agencies that signed and abided by it. However, the code of conduct concept never went very far, partly because temporary workers themselves found it too complex and preferred to push instead for a simpler "bill of rights" that focused on ten key areas for improvement in temporary work conditions. The Working Partnerships staffing services agency also realized that it needed to make conditions on firms slightly less stringent to ensure adoption. In the meantime, the think tank's policy attention shifted to reform of the unemployment insurance program in the state to allow temp workers more reasonable access.[5] Thus, outside of the context of union collective bargaining relationships (discussed later), and aside from any efforts LMIs may make to represent individual workers in their individual placements, direct advocacy on the part of intermediaries to change job quality seems limited.

Incumbent Worker Training and Advancement

Intermediaries rarely get directly involved in internal training for their client firms. Employers provide most of the formal training opportunities for existing workers, and their own internal work organization practices shape internal learning opportunities without significant intermediary involvement. In a limited number of cases, however, intermediaries have leveraged their strong ties to employers or substantial training resources to work directly with existing workers and employers to provide training, improve work practices, and promote advancement opportunities.

Community and technical colleges are in a strong position to offer a wide range of relevant courses in accessible formats to employers, and in both regions these colleges have developed contract training programs to work directly with employers. Community colleges with strong information and industry connections and the accessible delivery of a current curriculum are in the best position to help workers move up. In Milwaukee, for example, the technical college works directly with firms to offer everything from basic skills to advanced process training. Opportunities for advancement inside manufacturing plants become much more substantial when workplace training infrastructure has been established, rules on the use of that infrastructure (for example, pay for training) have been negotiated, and "peer mentors" who inform workers about training opportunities have been identified. Note, however, that the community college is not doing all of this alone. Deep relationships with firms and their unions are involved, and the Wisconsin Regional Training Partnership, another LMI outside the technical college system, has helped build those relationships.

The membership-based organizations that we studied all had some incumbent worker training component as well. The construction union training center in Silicon Valley described earlier is perhaps the most developed example. Other significant examples include another Silicon Valley union effort in the telecommunications industry to train people for new positions in computer networking and systems administration and a five-year apprenticeship program of the construction union we profiled in Milwaukee. In all cases, the skills training provided was narrow but deep—that is, it covered only a particular occupational trajectory but provided full training in that occupation.

Contractual Bargaining Relationships

Unions that also serve as intermediaries differ from other intermediaries in that they have a contractual relationship with a group of employers that is protected under the National Labor Relations Act. This contractual relationship gives them leverage to influence the quality of jobs. They wield this influence in part simply by bargaining over wages and benefits and in part through the leverage of collective power—being able to increase wages within an employer cluster, or even a regional industry cluster, to significantly higher degrees.

Such an influence falls more in the realm of traditional union organizing and bargaining than intermediation, and a large literature describes the ways in which unionization can affect the overall quality and quantity of jobs. Sometimes unionization arguably has positive effects on job quality, by creating incentives for employers to compete on quality rather than cost and to invest in improved workplace practices, training, and technological improvements rather than try to cut employee costs. Sometimes, however, unions may also have negative effects: the high wages or inflexible work rules they negotiate can contribute to firms' lack of competitiveness and eventual job loss.

These positive and negative effects are well documented (Freeman and Medoff 1984), but neither sort of effect relates directly to the intermediary activities of unions. We looked more closely at cases where the presence of a contractual relationship allowed unions to leverage their intermediary activities to affect work organization and job quality on an industrywide level. This was apparent in both the hiring hall context and sectoral partnerships, where the contractual relationship helps leverage employer behavior in ways that can improve job quality.

Hiring Halls   We looked at two construction unions in Milwaukee and San Jose that operate hiring halls. Hiring halls emerged in construction because of the short-term, project-oriented nature of the industry. Unions helped solve the difficult issues of training and coordination among the many parties involved in this industry by operating hiring halls with apprenticeship programs. The general structure of hiring halls is simple. Employers call the hiring hall to notify it of the number of workers they want to hire. The hall dispatcher then assigns union workers to the jobs, using a ranking system, typically based on seniority. Workers who have completed the apprenticeship and have four or more years of seniority are at the top of the list; apprentices and inexperienced workers are ranked at the bottom. For the skilled trade occupations, the apprenticeship training programs are very intensive—they include both classroom and on-the-job training as well as mentoring—and typically take four or five years to complete. There are variations of this structure among the different trades (historically there have been no apprenticeships for laborers), but the overall logic is the same.

A key component of the hiring hall/apprenticeship model is the role of employer associations, which have a long history in this industry. The employer groups bargain collectively with the unions, jointly fund the apprenticeship program, and contribute to joint health care and pension funds. Employers that use the union hiring hall often join the local association and usually have to commit to being a "closed shop," that is, to hire only union workers.

Job quality in the building trades is extremely high, especially for the skilled occupations. No doubt the work is hard, but it is definitely well compensated. Plumbers in San Jose start at about $16 an hour as apprentices and earn up to $42 an hour once they have completed the training; electricians in Milwaukee earn about $10 as an apprentice and $25 an hour when experienced. Health and pension benefits are generous and start immediately, in addition to sick leave, vacations, disability, and so on. Such pay scales may seem an expensive proposition for employers, but they have much to gain from this system: a steady supply of labor, an intensive and standardized training program, and pooled benefits funds. It is also important to note, particularly in the case of the construction union in Silicon Valley's high-tech industry, that quality is paramount: firms are willing to absorb high labor costs to ensure that the plumbing for sophisticated operations is within a very narrow fault range.

The value of hiring halls in the construction industry is well demonstrated, but there are real limits to its replicability in other industries. The model depends on high union density, de facto monopoly control over apprenticeships, the high skill requirements of some of the occupations, and the exemptions granted in public policy through the Taft-Hartley Act as well as other public levers such as project labor agreements and prevailing wage legislation. Given all the necessary components, it is unlikely that the full-fledged model would work in unregulated industries with weak unions and a minimal skill base. Any success in other sectors would require a significant amount of support from both public policy and union organizing, as well as new strategies for raising skill and service levels.

Even within their traditional sectors, hiring halls face challenges. In the past, the trades had almost complete union coverage in big markets and, as a result, considerable leverage in bargaining over job quality, but unionization levels have declined in recent years. There are signs of renewed vitality, however, in the hiring hall arrangement within construction. In both the electrician and plumber trades, skill requirements have been rising because of new regulations, technologies, and work materials. Even the less-skilled trades, such as laborers, are finding ways to increase skill requirements (for example, by offering certifications for the removal of asbestos and other hazardous material).

As a result, union leaders are recognizing that their apprenticeship programs can sometimes attract employers.

Sectoral Partnerships   It is also possible for unions to use their contractual relationships to leverage employers into sectoral partnerships that promote increased investment in the industry. An example of this is the Wisconsin Regional Training Partnership, the consortium of manufacturers, unions, and public-sector partners in the Milwaukee metropolitan area. It was founded in 1992 at a time when local manufacturing was suffering from stiff international competition, outdated machinery and production practices, and an aging workforce. Initially consisting of a dozen employers, and with unions playing a key role from the outset, the partnership included by 2002 more than seventy firms from the metalworking, electronics, plastics, and related industries (a significant share of the regional market) that employed more than sixty thousand workers represented by industrial and craft unions.

The goal of the partnership is to support the creation of high-performance workplaces and quality jobs in the region and ensure an adequate supply of trained workers to fill those jobs. At the core of the partnership is a series of channels for communication, planning, and implementation between employers and unions to solve common problems. Joint management-labor working groups focus on three issues: plant modernization and technology upgrading, a key need in this sector; training incumbent workers so as to facilitate modernization and internal promotion; and training new workers through a program to link inner-city residents to good jobs. Cementing this triad are workplace education centers, which are located at the work site of most of the member firms and are linked to technical colleges in the area. These centers provide skills upgrading and training to meet changes in production and technology, as well as basic education and GED preparation. Although public funds initially subsidized the workplace education centers, the member employers now jointly spend $20 million annually to sustain them.

The logic behind the Regional Training Partnership is to marshal as many resources as possible to push participating companies toward a high-performance, "mutual gains" model that sustains both the firms' profits and the workers' wages and careers. The logic is simple, at least in theory: provide collective training solutions to problems that single firms cannot afford or devise on their own, with the price tag or entrance fee for such solutions being good wages and benefits, job security, and career ladders for workers (for a full discussion of the incentive structure, see Neuenfeldt and Parker 1996).

What have been the effects? Taken together, WRTP members stabilized manufacturing employment in the Milwaukee metropolitan area, claiming to have contributed about six thousand additional industrial jobs between 1997 and 2002. Among member firms, furthermore, productivity increased, exceeding productivity growth in nonmember firms. Once-stagnant wages also increased, outpacing wage growth outside the partnership. Direct training reached some six thousand workers (one-quarter of whom were people of color) each year. Because entry-level job requirements among member firms were known and broadly shared, moreover, the partnership could obtain employment opportunities for those traditionally neglected in Milwaukee's labor market. Between 1999 and 2002, in fact, the partnership placed more than thirteen hundred "disadvantaged" central-city workers—including many former AFDC recipients—in jobs that more than doubled their earnings (from $9,000 to $23,000 annually), while providing health insurance and clear opportunities for further advancement.

The promise of the sectoral partnership model is that it can change the nature of the jobs being created. The drawback is that it is quite difficult to pull off. Such a partnership requires a critical mass of employers and unions in a given sector, as well as any number of public partners, such as community colleges, private industry councils, and community-based organizations. Coordinating among the many different players, as well as identifying the interests and potential contributions of each, is an enormous and ongoing challenge. There may also be inherent limits to the stick-and-carrot approach. For example, one manufacturer happily used the partnership's services to design a mentoring program for its new Latino workforce but resolutely stuck with its ten-year-long relationship with a temp agency for recruitment.

It may also be hard for such a partnership model to be applied in other sectors or regions. After all, one key aspect of the model is that it solves the collective action problems of employers. Such problems, like underinvestment in training because of resource constraints and the fear that workers will carry skills away with them, are more easily resolved, with widespread employer participation, when another firm's trained workers could become your own (and vice versa). This problem also indicates why regional scale is important. Since workers are generally rooted in a local labor market, it is easier to assume that increasing training efforts within the regional cluster will ensure that externalities are captured by the same regional cluster. How this could be expanded to clerical or temporary workers, however, or to a national scale, remains unclear.

Employer of Record

One of the services that temporary help agencies provide is being the employer of record. In this role, they take on not only the intermediary responsibility of finding the right matches for an employer's workforce needs but also all the legal responsibilities of being an employer, including those related to wages, working conditions, taxes, and adhering to labor legislation. Being the employer of record also gives them an additional leverage point for shaping the quality of the job and the character of the work performed. In both Milwaukee and Silicon Valley, we found that by acting as the employer of record intermediaries have an important and lasting impact on job quality and the organization of work, in both indirect and direct ways. First, as in all outsourcing arrangements, temp agencies play a central role in the externalization of work and employment that has become more common in recent years. Second, temp agencies are increasingly affecting firm structure in deeper and more direct ways by working as on-site consultants for firms on workplace redesign, outsourcing, and financial and legal decisions, as well as by taking over the operation of entire departments. In both cases, this can have both positive and negative impacts on job quality.

The most prevalent way in which temp agencies affect job quality is by tailoring their services to facilitate the reduction of core workforces and the utilization of external agencies to employ noncore workers. One agency in Milwaukee, for example, recruits, screens, and hires workers for a book binding company. The company argued that it needed a large external workforce because of the seasonal nature of its business. From the firm's perspective, the use of temporary labor was cost-effective: although the temp agency charged a 55 percent markup rate on hourly wages, it had also taken over all responsibility for employees before, during, and after the employment contract, doing all the paperwork and paying all unemployment insurance and workers' compensation costs. As a result, the firm was able to limit its expenses and avoid any legal responsibility for workers before, during, and after the employment contract.

Because the book binding company paid wages that were close to minimum wage, it had a very high turnover rate. This in turn generated additional work for the temp agency—it once called almost one hundred workers in order to hire fifteen for a two-day stint—but no extra work or cost for the firm itself. Although even the temp agency expressed frustration at the difficulty of finding so many workers for such little pay, it had not been able to convince the employer to raise wages, and in the end the agency knew it would rather keep the business than make waves. This highlights the fundamental constraint on the actions of temporary agencies in relation to disadvantaged workers: as a market-driven entity, a temp agency is governed by an incentive and interest structure in which addressing the poor quality of low-wage jobs is an option only if there is an immediate and considerable payoff to the client firm.

In some ways, temp agencies that take on the role of employer of record are simply filling the market niche created by the laissez-faire nature of U.S. employment law. Yet by filling this market niche, temp agencies are also indirectly affecting the quality of jobs. Using temporary agencies helps insulate employers from pressures on wages and working conditions, whether internal pressure from employees or external pressures from labor market conditions. One company we interviewed, for example, regularly sent off-the-street applicants to a temp agency, which then took over the hiring process. The human resource manager of this firm expressed genuine surprise when her computer records revealed the high number of temp workers she used. Sometimes the funds used to hire temporary employees are not taken from the personnel or payroll part of a firm's budget but from "materials and supplies," which typically have different processes for determining wage levels (Barley and Kunda 2004). By providing employment services, temp agencies thus indirectly change the institutional dynamics shaping employment conditions.

Temp agencies also change the structure of jobs and organizations in more direct ways. In recent years, the temp industry has undergone a marked stratification. In the lower strata remain the temp agencies of old, those that provide the requested number of people for temporary jobs. The relatively new upper tier of the temp industry, in contrast, has a more direct and deeper influence on the structure of the client company. This is seen, for example, in the growing number of temp agencies in both regions that no longer focus on temporary placements but rather primarily hire for temp-to-perm and permanent jobs. While this observed shift has been partly due to the tight labor market, it also signals a broader trend in which the agencies are becoming the key screener or interface between workers and firms.

Additionally, upper-tier temp agencies are playing an increasingly active role in firm decisions about how work is organized. The most profound manifestation of this trend is "on-premise" arrangements, whereby the temp agencies set up shop inside the client company. In Wisconsin, for example, a major temp agency created a branch of its company that specifically caters to and is physically located within a specific client company. At this firm, an on-premise manager from the temp agency has full profit-and-loss responsibility for the activities of the workers placed there by the agency. Additionally, the agency has taken over one company department entirely and others partially, controlling staffing, training, advertising, and production flow for each department. Workers under the agency's control are employees of the temp agency, not the client firm, and many become long-term employees. In one department, the agency controls over 85 percent of the workers, some of whom have been working at the firm but employed by the agency for as long as twelve years.

On-premise arrangements allow firms to functionally outsource areas of work while still keeping them physically on-site. For such arrangements, upper-tier temp agencies negotiate multi-year contracts, and they are often named the exclusive national provider for the company. As a result, they usually also become the "master vendor" and in this role subcontract with middle-tier agencies for the temporary workers they cannot provide themselves. From what we were told, temp agencies see this market-making strategy as representing a substantial future growth opportunity, and they are increasingly moving into consulting services by devising strategies for cutting costs for firms, as well as analyzing work flow, job design, and production.

Although such market-making strategies by temporary agencies often erode labor standards, this is not uniformly the case. For example, one agency we studied advised a telemarketing company suffering from high turnover to train its workers. As a result, the firm implemented a training program and increased wages, and the turnover rate decreased from 800 to 200 percent, while worker hours increased from thirty-five to forty per week. Similarly, on a more experimental level, the Working Partnerships staffing service was hopeful that by being employer of record, it could model a best-practices employment intermediary, placing workers in high-quality jobs. Similarly, subsequent to the completion of our research, the Wisconsin Regional Training Partnership launched the Professional Employer Organization; by acting as employer of record and providing long-term staff leasing services, this organization hopes to improve employment conditions in jobs for client firms. Whether these more experimental activities will have a significant impact remains to be seen, but the key point is that the power of an intermediary to affect job quality by being the legal employer is being recognized by union-linked organizations as well as by private temporary agencies.

The Labor Market Intermediary Landscape

In this chapter, we have tried to examine how a wide range of intermediaries operate in the labor market and have identified some of the forces that shape their strengths and weaknesses in providing improved employment opportunities for disadvantaged workers. In analyzing these forces, we must keep in mind that these intermediaries differ significantly in their organizational origins, functions, and activities. Temporary agencies are private-sector agencies, subject primarily to market forces. Public and nonprofit agencies are funded primarily by tax dollars and foundations and must therefore demonstrate that they are delivering a public good or social service in order to survive. Because membership agencies gain most of their revenue from their membership, they are primarily responsive to the needs of those members. Despite these differences, all these types of organizations provide intermediary services in the labor market. Since the effectiveness of these services in improving opportunities for disadvantaged workers is partly shaped by their organizational origins, we now turn to a brief discussion of the strengths and weaknesses of these organizational structures in shaping intermediary activity aimed at disadvantaged workers.

For-Profit Private-Sector Staffing Agencies

Staffing agencies are the largest type of LMI in terms of the raw number of connections they make between workers and firms, a fact confirmed by our survey. There are significant challenges, however, to improving the manner in which their activities relate to disadvantaged workers. The foremost challenge is not to motivate these LMIs to be interested in low-income workers as clients, since they already are attracted to this market. Rather, the task is to try to restructure their relationship to disadvantaged workers in a way that will prove more beneficial to improving career advancement opportunities. We saw little evidence of positive, systematic practices in this regard, and the regression results we discuss later seem to confirm this observation. Although agencies in both regional labor markets do pay some attention to workers' happiness (which makes them better able themselves to fill job orders), there was little evidence of more than idiosyncratic and highly individualized efforts to advance the careers of their temporary employees.

A private temp agency in Milwaukee was the most focused on assisting workers of all the firms we interviewed. Starting in the mid-1990s, this agency initially started working with a computer training firm, which it later bought outright and brought in-house. The training went beyond the normal self-paced computer training that most staffing services firms provide and included an individual instructor who could provide additional assistance and problem-solving to people doing the training. For a period of time, the company was even working with welfare recipients. Ultimately, however, it found that financially it could not make the training work, and it sold the training unit so that it could focus on placement work.

This story highlights the major obstacle to the possibility of staffing agencies playing a role in promoting upward mobility—the incentive structure common to all for-profit agencies. When upward mobility involves moving from a temporary to a permanent position, staffing agencies can lose their source of revenue, and thus they have little incentive to promote career mobility in this way. On the other hand, staffing agencies do have a financial incentive to place more-skilled workers, whose markup rates and pay levels are higher, and thus these agencies could benefit when the people they place move to higher positions in other firms. Indeed, one Silicon Valley agency we interviewed explicitly aimed to be a long-term employment resource for the engineers and technical personnel it placed, frequently in a series of contract positions with rising wages. This seems more possible in the limited cases where there is a substantial demand (from both workers and employers) for recurrent contract or temporary employment in skilled positions.

Alternatively, during periods of tighter labor markets, staffing agencies expand their temp-to-perm placements and direct-hire recruiting, thus diversifying their revenue sources in ways that might provide greater opportunity for some career advancement. This becomes most significant for disadvantaged workers when the placement function of the staffing agency is combined with training and support services, generally provided by a combination of public, nonprofit, and community and technical college LMIs.

Nonprofits and Publicly Funded Programs for Disadvantaged Workers and the Unemployed

Public-sector agencies are clearly the LMIs that are most focused on the lower rungs of the labor market. This focus on serving particular population groups, however, limits their effectiveness as labor market intermediaries in at least two important ways. First, their programs are limited to particular population groups (such as welfare recipients, other income-eligible people, political refugees, displaced workers, and so on). Not only are workers subject to losing access to services when their status changes slightly, but the programs themselves are frequently driven by changes in policy or funding priority, rather than directly by the needs of their constituencies. This was a common theme in many of our interviews in this category of LMI, and it was particularly evident in the transition from JTPA to WIA funding requirements. The job placement officer at a community-based organization, for instance, complained that some of his clients had been waiting months to get approval from the new workforce investment board for access to training resources.

Second, these agencies have poor outreach on the employer side of the labor market. Employment opportunities often consist of simple job listings from a range of different employers, and agencies pursue a scattershot approach that reflects little strategic planning. Many LMIs in this category work with any employer willing to provide them with listings of job openings. In this context, promoting mobility appears nearly impossible. Generally, these LMIs are working with too broad a range of employers to understand the career pathways in specific industries. Moreover, it is difficult to develop expertise in career opportunities when there are so few venues in which to interact with employers around positions other than entry-level ones.

Finally, public-sector activities are often constrained by narrow performance measures that prioritize placement measures—such as percentage placed and thirty-day retention rates—over measures related to the needs of the workers or employers. This can force agencies to "cream" on the worker side and to neglect job quality or advancement opportunities in the jobs themselves. Despite their motivating concern for worker well-being, nonprofits seem to direct their energies primarily at securing initial placements. Postplacement services are rare. Mentoring programs are present more in theory than in practice. Many clients are directed to jobs at firms that offer no opportunity for advancement, and so it is up to the workers themselves to find other opportunities for advancement. To a great extent, the contribution of these LMIs to a worker's upward mobility lies in assistance with language ability, soft skills, and work ethic improvement and achieving the first line on a future résumé. Everything else depends on the worker's own initiative.

Community and Technical Colleges

Community and technical colleges in the two regions offer some model programs, especially for worker advancement. The most successful activities are consistently marked by partnerships with industry, the community, and other LMIs. In both regions, the colleges' education and training systems reached a broad range of workers and employers, including the most disadvantaged sectors of the labor market and also higher levels. These colleges have a strong tradition of industry input into curricula, often based on industry participation on advisory boards. For more customized and employer-directed training, colleges may gain an advantage in knowing what skills are in demand and where career ladders might exist by hiring instructors who come from industry.

Our field research, however, also revealed limits to the capacities of community and technical colleges. As educational institutions, they are not always well positioned to serve in a support service capacity. Also, increasingly, they find themselves dealing with students who need more than just training. New partnerships with service providers have emerged to help deal with these issues, but there is still substantial work to be done in this regard. When they have good information on job opportunities and the technical capacity to train students to fill them, community colleges may be able to play a substantial role in advancing low-wage workers. But community and technical colleges must also move into work sites, develop relevant short-term classes, and work to remain affordable and accessible to disadvantaged communities. Community and technical colleges clearly have an essential role to play in finding systematic solutions to increasing low-wage workers' skills and advancement opportunities. But it is equally essential that their efforts in this regard include forging alliances with industry, community support providers, and other LMIs.

Unions and Membership-Based Organizations

Unions and membership-based LMIs show promise in their ability to promote job quality and advancement opportunities, though for only a limited spectrum of more advantaged workers. These organizations are often in a superior position with regard to critical industry knowledge, network building, and training delivery. They succeed by gaining intimate industry knowledge based on their long-term ties with workers who are able to share information on the industry from firsthand experience. Another part of their success in this area lies in their focus on particular industries and occupations. This industry/occupation specialization, which is rarely evidenced in other types of LMIs, seems to be critical for gaining the specific knowledge necessary for contributing to career mobility.

Membership-based LMIs are the only ones in which there is a fundamental incentive structure that supports networking efforts. For unions, it is the collective strength of their membership that ensures their bargaining power, and though their bargaining activities are not the central component of their intermediary activities, efforts to build strength through collective action also help build networks. Similarly, the members of Silicon Valley Webgrrls have an incentive to respond to other members' inquiries because they know that they may need help as well if they run across problems in the future.

The drawback here is that the membership-based LMIs we studied typically did not work extensively with the lowest levels of the labor market. The majority of the members of these LMIs were already employed workers who were skilled enough in their positions that employers were prepared to pay a union-wage premium. Similarly, for the professional association we examined, the majority of the membership already had a significant level of skill. Nonetheless, in nearly every membership-based LMI we examined, we were given examples of many people from truly disadvantaged backgrounds who had made a connection to the LMI, such as through an apprenticeship program, and then moved up in part through the successful assistance of the LMI.

Summary

Our qualitative research on the activities, structures, and motivations of intermediaries in these two labor markets was designed to understand the mechanisms and processes through which intermediaries respond to the needs of their clients, both job-seekers and employers. We were also explicitly interested in how intermediaries influence the quality of jobs. And finally, we were interested in exploring the relationship between different kinds of intermediaries and the reasons why job-seekers and employers choose to use particular types and not other types of intermediaries. From this analysis, we want to highlight four major conclusions related to economic opportunity for disadvantaged workers.

First, looking at the whole landscape of intermediary activity, we found that these organizations may have some potential for improving workers' mobility, but they seemed to have little direct impact on improving job quality in the labor market. This is not to suggest that intermediaries do not provide important services in the labor market; indeed, some of their services are likely to have a significant impact on workers' economic opportunities. Temporary intermediaries provide valuable services, networking opportunities, and political leverage. These various services, however, are limited in their ability to affect job quality. Furthermore, the short-term nature of most ties between intermediaries and their worker clients usually limits their ability to improve worker mobility.

Second, though our analysis of intermediaries here looked at different types of organizations (for-profit, nonprofit, government, membership-based, community college) within our framework of market-meeting, market-molding, and market-making, it is important to recognize that the services provided by intermediaries within any single category vary widely in quality. As we discussed in chapter 1, the organizational base of the intermediary does play an important role in shaping the organization's activity, the incentive structure to which it responds, and its priorities. But even within these constraints, there is clearly tremendous diversity of experience and quality of services. This suggests that even though using the organizational base of an intermediary is useful for analyzing intermediary impacts on the labor market—particularly given that policy debates often center on whether to regulate temporary agencies or develop better nonprofit interventions, and so on—a full analysis would require a nuanced search for other factors that shape the effectiveness of intermediaries.

This conclusion is reinforced by a third major insight that emerged from this research, namely, that many employers and workers are not able to clearly distinguish between types of intermediaries. Workers' primary goal is generally to get a job, and often they do not know whether the organization helping them is a public entity, a private firm, or a nonprofit agency. In our survey interviews, it was of course necessary to our analysis to clarify this question of which type of intermediary we were discussing, and to do so we had to both probe the interviewee and then cross-check answers against lists of intermediaries we had developed in this qualitative phase of our research. Similarly, employers' primary goal is to find people qualified to fill their positions. In most cases, they do not care whether the organization linking them with workers is a private, public, nonprofit, or membership-based organization, as long as it is effective in meeting their needs. The one exception to this is in the case of the employer-of-record service that temporary help agencies provide. There are significant administrative, legal, and time costs involved in being the employer of record, and reducing these costs was clearly one motivation for employer clients to use temporary help agencies over other kinds of intermediaries.

Finally, there is also tremendous fragmentation within the broad intermediary landscape in both regions. The negative aspects of this fragmentation include significant duplication of services, inefficiencies in government expenditures, and barriers to information sharing. On the plus side, however, different intermediaries are also able to specialize in different functions. Private temporary agencies, for example, specialize in marketing and placement services, nonprofit organizations typically specialize in support services for disadvantaged workers, and community colleges are well positioned to provide comprehensive training. Thus, in spite of the fragmentation within regional intermediary systems, there is significant potential for taking advantage of these specialties to promote effective divisions of labor within those systems. Providing services to intermediate intermediaries, so to speak, might be a productive policy intervention. We return to this issue in our concluding chapter; now we turn to a discussion of our survey findings.

Chapter Four

The Incidence and Use of
Labor Market Intermediaries

To date, there has been little comprehensive work quantifying the incidence and nature of intermediary use in the U.S. economy. There have been case studies of certain sorts of LMIs, although most of them simply highlight "best practices" and few try to profile the average experience, as we did in the previous chapter. There have also been empirical studies following certain kinds of workers using certain kinds of LMIs (see, for example, Autor and Houseman 2005b) The broadest study looking at LMI use in a full labor market context was conducted by Fredrik Andersson, Harry Holzer, and Julia Lane (2005). Their work is both pioneering and elegantly done, and we compare our results with theirs at the end of chapter 5. Nonetheless, their study is limited in certain ways. It relies on state data from unemployment insurance records, focuses only on temps (because this is the only type of LMI that can be examined in their data), has no information about individual worker characteristics (and so imputes these data), and is not able to distinguish between hours and wages.

To fill the gap in comprehensive knowledge of intermediary activity, we fielded an original survey in our two regional labor markets to assess the difference in the market experiences of those who did and did not use LMIs to find work. To our knowledge, this is the first such effort to collect a broad and representative base of quantitative information on LMI use and incidence across the whole range of types of intermediaries. The data collected allow us to comprehensively document the role and impact of LMIs and to place them in the broader context of the labor markets in which they operate. We also explore whether or not intermediaries serve as substitutes for or complements to the use of social networks for low-income workers.

An analysis of these data is presented here and in the following two chapters. In this chapter, we provide an overview of the incidence and type of intermediary use, the reasons why intermediaries are being used, and the services and satisfaction that workers get from intermediaries. We then look closely at the intermediary experiences of disadvantaged workers in the two regions, showing how their experiences differ from those of their more advantaged counterparts. We follow up in chapter 5 with an analysis of the outcomes that intermediaries appear to secure for workers, and in chapter 6 with a look at the relationship between social networks and intermediary use.

The Survey of Labor Market Intermediary Use was fielded between August 2001 and June 2002 as a random-digit-dialing phone survey in the Silicon Valley region of northern California and the Milwaukee, Wisconsin, metropolitan area. We collected responses from 1,348 individuals between the ages of twenty-five and sixty-five who had worked sometime in the past three years.[1] Survey respondents were roughly split between the two regions and between those who had and had not used an LMI to obtain a job; we used an over-sampling strategy to obtain more responses from LMI users to permit detailed analysis, then used proper weights to transform all responses back to population characteristics. We also oversampled on those living in low-income areas, using phone prefixes as a proxy, because we wished to see whether there were geographic issues with regard to social networks and LMI use, a topic taken up in chapter 6. Again, we use weights to adjust these respondent answers to their likely share in the general population (for a more detailed documentation of the survey methodology, see the appendix). In the survey, we identified and categorized the intermediaries used by workers into five groupings—private agencies, unions, nonprofit or governmental agencies, community and technical colleges or vocational schools, and professional associations.[2] Within the first category, we make some further distinctions between temporary agencies and those that function as permanent placement agencies, also known as recruiters or "headhunters."

Although intermediaries are becoming more common in our economic landscape, the concept of intermediary activity and the distinctions between organizational types are not well defined in the popular consciousness. Through repeated drafting and testing, in both focus groups and trial questionnaires, we found that individuals are most able to accurately recount their experiences with LMIs if those experiences are related to a specific job they held. Therefore, we surveyed individuals who had worked in the past three years, and as noted, we oversampled on those who had obtained through an intermediary at least one job that they held in the last three years. As such, we cannot report on the rates at which intermediaries successfully place workers in jobs, but only on the nature of the intermediary services delivered and the job placements that are actually made. The comparative success rates of intermediaries in *making* job placements and the outcomes for job-seekers who do *not* achieve a desired placement through an intermediary are fodder for future research.

An Overview of Intermediary Use, Users, Services, and Satisfaction

We look first at the overall incidence of the use of intermediaries to obtain jobs in the two regions. We have three alternative measures of the incidence of intermediary use. The structure of all three measures was dictated by the need to query people about jobs that they had held fairly recently (to minimize memory loss) and about how they had obtained those jobs. The broadest measure we constructed is the percentage of those working in the past three years who obtained a job they had held during the last three years through an intermediary. In this case, the job must have been held in the past three years, but it may have been obtained through an intermediary at any time in the past. (Later we discuss how this intermediary use is distributed over time.) Our second measure is the percentage of people working in the past three years who worked in a job obtained through an intermediary during the last three years. Our final measure is more contemporaneous and also provides us with the (conceptually) narrowest definition of intermediary use: the percentage of those currently working in a job they obtained through an LMI. This third measure provides a snapshot of how current workers got their jobs.

Results for all three measures, by region and by category of intermediary use, are presented in table 4.1. Measuring the percentage of current jobs obtained through LMIs, we estimate a rate of 20.3 percent in Milwaukee and 14.4 percent in Silicon Valley.[3] Basing the incidence measure on jobs held in the last three years, we find that in Milwaukee 29.8 percent of such jobs were

Table 4.1 Alternative Measures of the Incidence of Use of Labor Market Intermediaries for Persons Age Twenty-Five to Sixty-Five, by Type of Intermediary and Location

| | Those Working in the Last Three Years | | | | Those Currently | |
| | In a Job Obtained Through an LMI (lmi_lj) | | In a Job Obtained in the Last Three Years Through an LMI (lmi_3years) | | Working in a Job Obtained Through an LMI (lmi_cjx) | |
LMI Type	Broad Temp Measure	Narrow Temp Measure	Broad Temp Measure	Narrow Temp Measure	Broad Temp Measure	Narrow Temp Measure
Milwaukee						
Private agencies	15.1%	15.1%	8.0%	8.0%	8.7%	8.7%
Temporary agencies	12.7	8.9	6.8	5.0	6.8	3.8
Permanent placement agencies and headhunters	2.4	6.2	1.2	3.0	1.9	4.9
Union	2.7%		0.6%		2.3%	
CBOs, nonprofit and government agency	4.4		1.8		3.0	
Community college and vocational school	6.3		1.5		5.2	
Professional association	1.3		0.8		1.0	
Total	29.8		12.7		20.3[a]	
Number of cases	659					

(*continued*)

Table 4.1 Alternative Measures of the Incidence of Use of Labor Market Intermediaries for Persons Age Twenty-Five to Sixty-Five, by Type of Intermediary and Location (*Continued*)

| | Those Working in the Last Three Years | | | | | |
| | In a Job Obtained Through an LMI (lmi_lj) | | In a Job Obtained in the Last Three Years Through an LMI (lmi_3years) | | Those Currently Working in a Job Obtained Through an LMI (lmi_cjx) | |
LMI Type	Broad Temp Measure	Narrow Temp Measure	Broad Temp Measure	Narrow Temp Measure	Broad Temp Measure	Narrow Temp Measure
Silicon Valley						
Private placement agency	15.3	15.3	9.7	9.7	6.9	6.9
Temporary agencies	11.4	9.5	6.9	6.1	5.1	3.9
Permanent placement agencies and headhunters	3.9	5.8	**2.8**	3.6	1.8	3.0
Union	2.4%		1.4%		2.0%	
CBOs, nonprofit and government agency	2.7		1.8		1.7	
Community college and vocational school	4.4		1.8		**2.9**	
Professional association	1.6		1.1		0.8	
Total	26.3		15.8		14.4[a]	
Number of cases	689					

Source: Authors' compilation.

Note: **Bold** values for Silicon Valley are statistically significant from corresponding Milwaukee values at the .05 level or higher.

[a] Due to missing data, this is a lower-bound estimate. Total upper-bound estimates are 22.3 percent in Milwaukee and 15.8 percent in Silicon Valley.

obtained through an intermediary at some time in the past, and 12.7 percent were obtained through an intermediary in the past three years. The comparable figures for Silicon Valley are 26.3 percent and 15.8 percent.

As discussed in chapters 1 and 2, much has been made of the dynamic economy of Silicon Valley in the 1990s (Kenney 2000; Lee et al. 2000), leading to the expectation that the volatility of the high-tech industry in Silicon Valley in the 1990s would have fostered greater use of intermediary organizations. We find that this is not the case. Of the three measures presented, only the difference in the "current job" measure for Silicon Valley and Milwaukee is statistically significant, and here the Silicon Valley figure is nearly six points *lower* than that for Milwaukee (14.4 percent versus 20.3 percent).[4] Instead, intermediary use during this time period is as prevalent—or more so—in Milwaukee as in Silicon Valley. Finding such similar results across such disparate economies suggests that intermediary use may be just as pervasive throughout the rest of the U.S. economy. Although we do find some interesting differences in the details of intermediary use in the two regions (discussed later), the broad similarities suggest that the rise of the intermediary function is not driven by characteristics peculiar to Silicon Valley markets (for example, the rapid development of newborn industries, highly competitive market conditions, shortages of skilled labor). Instead, the rise of intermediaries must be grounded in recent developments in labor markets more broadly (see the discussion in Osterman 2004).

Looking at other job search mechanisms provides another insight into this difference in the rates of intermediary use in the two regions. Our survey asked those who had not used an intermediary how they got their current job. The single most important way in which people had found jobs in both regions was through their friends, but in Silicon Valley, 25.4 percent of all respondents had found a job this way, while in Milwaukee the figure was 19.8 percent. In addition, more Silicon Valley residents than Milwaukee residents cited the use of the Internet to get their job—4.3 percent compared to 1.6 percent. With the importance of social networks and the Internet as job search mechanisms in Silicon Valley, it seems that workers turn to intermediaries there less frequently than in Milwaukee.

Distribution of Intermediary Use Across Types

We also disaggregate the incidence of intermediary use by type of agency for each of our three incidence measures. This disaggregation is shown for both regions in table 4.1. The survey instrument included multiple questions and cues in order to generate our five-category classification of LMI use: private temporary or permanent placement agencies, recruiters, and headhunters; unions; community-based, nonprofit, and governmental organizations and agencies; public community and technical colleges and private vocational schools; and membership-based professional associations.

Note that we were careful to distinguish between general attendance at a community college and use of the community college services to obtain employment; we did this by asking certain questions in the survey and then poring over the individual answers and cross-referencing them against the knowledge of local services we acquired through the qualitative work discussed in the previous chapter.

Careful inspection of the answers was also necessary in generating a tight definition of temporary agency use. Because private agencies frequently offer multiple services that include temporary placement, permanent placement, temp-to-perm positions, and recruitment, it would have been difficult to ask survey respondents to distinguish between different types of private agencies. Instead, we included queries that would help the research team further identify the nature of the services offered by private agencies. First we obtained the name and location of the agency, and then we asked, "How many temporary/permanent/temp-to-perm jobs did you obtain through this agency?" "Who does this agency serve?" "What does this agency do?" and "Were you recruited by this agency?" We then used this information to help distinguish between "true" temporary agencies, which deal either completely or substantially in temporary placements, and permanent placement agencies, which deal primarily in permanent placements and/or recruitment (or "headhunting"). For a majority of private agency observations, the resulting classification was unambiguous. However, even with fairly rich information, in some cases the overlap in functions is such that the distinction is not clear-cut.[5] For these we applied two alternative assignment schemes, using both a broad and a narrow definition of "temporary agency" and a correspondingly narrow or broad definition of "permanent placement agency/headhunter." (The details of the construction of these definitions are offered in the appendix.) Both broad and narrow categorizations for temporary agencies and placement agencies are shown for all three incidence measures in table 4.1.

With all three incidence measures, private agencies clearly dominated the LMI landscape, accounting for roughly half of all intermediary use. About

15 percent of workers obtained a job they had held in the last three years through a private agency, and about half as many obtained their *current* job through such an agency. This category, moreover, is dominated by temp agencies, which accounted for 60 to 85 percent of private agency use, depending on whether the broad or narrow definition of "temp agency" is applied. Even applying the narrow definition of temp agency, temps accounted for 8.9 percent of the jobs held in the last three years in Milwaukee and 9.5 percent of the jobs held in Silicon Valley. Temp agencies also accounted for 3.8 and 3.9 percent of *currently held* jobs in Milwaukee and Silicon Valley, respectively. As we note later, these figures are consistent with other national and state data on temp employment as a share of nonfarm employment, a result that adds to our confidence in the representativeness of this sample.

The second most dominant LMI type is community colleges, technical colleges, and vocational schools, followed by community-based, nonprofit, or government agencies, and unions. These agency types are small in comparison, however, each operating at only 10 to 40 percent of the scale of the private agencies. Looking at all LMI use that accounted for any jobs held in the last three years, 6.3 percent of workers in Milwaukee and 4.4 percent of workers in Silicon Valley obtained their jobs through community colleges or vocational schools, while the comparable figures for community, nonprofit, or government agencies were 4.4 percent in Milwaukee and 2.7 percent in Silicon Valley. Unions accounted for less than 3 percent of jobs held, and professional associations appear to have had the smallest impact, being the source of little more than 1 percent of jobs, even using the most all-encompassing measure.

Interestingly, there are few significant differences in the distribution of LMI use among agency types between Silicon Valley and Milwaukee. Only by one measure was the use of permanent placement agencies and headhunters significantly higher in Silicon Valley than in Milwaukee (see the bolded numbers in table 4.1). Similarly, only by the "current jobs" measures was overall LMI use significantly higher in Milwaukee than in Silicon Valley, along with the use of community colleges and vocational schools. From our qualitative work, we believe that the latter may largely be a function of the relationship between the Wisconsin Works (W2) welfare-to-work system and its strong relationship to a local technical college.

Although research to date has been unable to suggest the overall scale of LMI use in the United States, our estimates are consistent with the partial estimates that do exist. Statistics collected by the U.S. Bureau of Labor Statistics (BLS) in a biennial supplement to the Current Population Survey (CPS) suggest that in 1999, 4.3 percent of the U.S. labor force was working in contingent work arrangements, defined as jobs that are short-term or temporary (Hipple 2001). Similarly, calculations from the Bureau of Labor Statistics Current Employment Statistics (CES) (shown in table 2.13) show that in the year 2000, 3.8 and 4.1 percent of workers were employed by companies in the employment services industry (NAICS 5613) in Milwaukee and Silicon Valley, respectively. As cross-sectional "snapshots," estimates from these sources are constructed in similar fashion to our "current jobs" measures, for which we obtained estimates of 3.8 and 3.9 percent for jobs obtained through temp agencies in Milwaukee and Silicon Valley, respectively.[6] Thus, CPS- and CES-based estimates of contingent and temp agency–related work are completely consistent with our "current jobs" measures of the same.

From our survey results, however, it is also clear that the scope of all LMI use in both regions is much broader than just that measured as temporary or contingent work and that it encompasses multiple types of services and relationships. Some of these aspects have been explored by other authors—for example, in the concept of "workforce intermediaries" emphasized in Giloth (2004) or in the examination of the influence of a variety of agency types (primarily welfare-to-work or temporary placement agencies) on outcomes for welfare-leavers (for example, Autor and Houseman 2005b; Heinrich, Mueser, and Troske 2005). However, no other studies to date have been able to quantify the incidence or impact of use of LMIs more generally or for most of the other agency types.

The construction of our incidence measures implies that different time frames are associated with when a reference job is actually obtained.[7] By two of the measures, a reference job that was *held* in the past three years could have been *obtained* at any time in the past. By the third measure, the reference job for LMI users must have been obtained during the previous three years. As might be expected, for LMI users, the distribution of time since beginning employment in the reference job was considerably shorter for the latter measure than for the other two. It was also influenced by the type of LMI used. For example, in Milwaukee, among those not using LMIs, 31 percent obtained their reference job in the three years preceding the interview; for those who obtained their reference job through a temp agency, this rose to 64 percent (the comparable figures for Silicon Valley are 51 and 66 percent). The mean number of years since beginning employment in the reference job is shown in

Table 4.2   Mean Years Since Reference Job Started for Alternative LMI Incidence Measures, by LMI Type and Region

| | Among Those Working in the Last Three Years | | Among Those Currently Working in a Job Obtained Through an LMI(lmi_cjx) |
	In a Job Obtained Through an LMI (lmi_lj)	In a Job Obtained in the Last Three Years Through an LMI (lmi_3years)	
Milwaukee			
No LMI	8.6	8.8	8.1
LMI	6.0[a]	1.1[a]	6.7
Temp agency (narrow)	2.4[a]	1.0[a]	2.9[a]
Placement agency	4.4[a]	1.1[a]	4.8
Nonprofit or government agency	6.3	0.9[a]	6.2
Other LMI	9.5	1.3[a]	8.9
Number of cases	659		
Silicon Valley			
No LMI	5.9[b]	6.2[b]	5.7[b]
LMI	4.1[a,b]	1.0[a]	5.6
Temp agency (narrow)	2.6[a]	1.0[a]	3.5
Placement agency	2.2[a,b]	0.9[a]	2.2[b]
Nonprofit or government agency	2.2[b]	0.9[a]	3.2
Other LMI	7.4	1.1[a]	4.9[b]
Number of cases	689		

Source: Authors' compilation.
[a]Difference from value for "no LMI" (in same region) statistically significant at the .05 level.
[b]Difference between Milwaukee and Silicon Valley statistically significant at the .05 level.

table 4.2 by type of LMI for each of our three measures and by region. Time since employment was longest for those who did not use LMIs and for those who obtained work through "other LMIs." Time since employment was generally shorter for those who used temp or placement agencies, and in Silicon

Valley compared with Milwaukee. There are particularly strong regional differences for those who used permanent placement agencies and nonprofit or government agencies.

In the analysis that follows, we apply our broadest definition of LMI use (obtained any job held in the last three years through an LMI); this measure maximizes our LMI sample and still yields fairly close correspondence in the temporal distribution of the reference job for LMI users and non-users. Thus, it should be kept in mind that the LMI experience referenced could have occurred during any time frame. When we discuss *job* characteristics in chapter 5, however, these are more compressed temporally. They refer specifically to the current (or most recent) characteristics of the LMI reference job, which has to have been held at some time in the past three years.[8]

Who Is Using Intermediaries?

From the literature documenting aspects of welfare-to-work job placements, temporary agency functions, workforce intermediaries, and unions, we know that these different organizations serve a broad array of clients with varying purposes and needs. The Survey of LMI Use allows us to begin to document these differences. In this chapter, we present estimates based on our narrow measure of temp agency use, as well as on our correspondingly "broad" measure of the use of permanent placement and recruitment agencies. Although the results using either measure are comparable, the narrow measures give the purest picture of the agencies that are most focused on temporary placements, a segment of the market that is of considerable interest in both the academic and policy literature.

An overview of the characteristics of intermediary users in both regions by type of intermediary is shown in table 4.3. Much of the picture is similar in both regions. Temp agency users are the most distinctly different from non-LMI users: they tend to be younger, are more likely to be a racial or ethnic minority and foreign-born, are more likely to live in families that have received public assistance in the past year, and have lower educational levels. Most, but not all, of these differences are statistically significant in both regions. Much of the same is true for users of nonprofit and government agencies.

There are also regional differences. The pattern of intermediary use by Hispanics varies dramatically in the two locations: the use of temp agencies by Hispanics was disproportionately high in Milwaukee and disproportionately low in Silicon Valley. And there are also some clear regional differences in the

Table 4.3 Demographic Characteristics of Workers Employed in the Past Three Years, by LMI Use (Temp Narrow)

| | Milwaukee | | | | | Silicon Valley | | | | |
| | | Private Agency | | | | | Private Agency | | | |
Characteristics	Non-LMI	Temp Agency	Permanent and Headhunter	Nonprofit and Government	Other LMI[a]	Non-LMI	Temp Agency	Permanent and Headhunter	Nonprofit and Government	Other LMI[a]
Average age (years)	44.6	38.1[b]	37.4[b]	44.4	41.0	40.8	37.5[b]	39.6	36.8	39.7
Female	56.8%	50.0%	40.0%	60.3%	53.9%	52.0%	48.8%	53.8%	68.8%	32.4%[b]
Average years of schooling	14.3	13.4	14.7	13.0	13.7	14.8	13.8	17.0[b]	13.8	16.0
Native-born	94.4%	72.1%[b]	94.3%	97.3%	94.7%	66.4%	55.4%	68.5%	70.5%	71.7%
Family received public assistance in past year	6.1%	14.4%[b]	5.3%	23.1%[b]	7.8%	5.6%	11.8%	2.5%	17.4%	2.5%
Ethnicity										
Non-Hispanic white	88.6%	39.7%[b]	84.9%	62.4%[b]	83.8%	51.8%	42.3%	68.5%	40.1%	50.3%
Hispanic	3.9	27.9[b]	1.6	5.8	3.6	28.8	12.7[b]	4.7[b]	39.5	26.7
Black	5.3	26.3[b]	5.5	24.5[b]	12.2[b]	2.6	16.8[b]	6.8	10.0	2.7
Asian or Pacific Islander	0.8	3.4	0.0	0.0	0.1	12.8	24.3[b]	9.6	1.9	13.4
Other	1.3	2.4	1.9	7.2	0.2	3.5	1.4	10.0[b]	8.5	6.5

(continued)

Table 4.3 Demographic Characteristics of Workers Employed in the Past Three Years, by LMI Use (Temp Narrow) (*Continued*)

| | Milwaukee | | | | | Silicon Valley | | | | |
| | | Private Agency | | | | | Private Agency | | | |
Characteristics	Non-LMI	Temp Agency	Permanent and Headhunter	Nonprofit and Government	Other LMI[a]	Non-LMI	Temp Agency	Permanent and Headhunter	Nonprofit and Government	Other LMI[a]
Highest level of schooling										
Less than high school	3.6%	13.3%[b]	8.5%	8.2%	2.2%	3.7%	0.9%	0.0%	6.3%	0.2%
High school or GED	38.0	41.9	28.0	69.0[b]	30.7	35.8	34.4	14.3[b]	42.3	28.1
Associate degree	14.1	9.5	7.8	7.7	32.3[b]	9.0	17.4	14.8	18.8	13.0
Bachelor's degree	26.6	32.6	39.3	7.9[b]	16.4[b]	30.8	27.1	33.0	26.1	29.0
Advanced degree	15.1	2.0[b]	12.6	6.7	4.5[b]	20.7	13.7	37.9[b]	1.0	25.4
Certificate or license	2.7	0.6	3.8	0.5	13.8[b]	0.0	6.6[b]	0.0	5.6[b]	3.2[b]
Number of cases	286	123	71	68	123	323	112	86	37	140

Source: Authors' compilation.

[a]Includes unions, professional associations, and community college and vocational school placements.

[b]Difference from the value for non-LMI value statistically significant at the .05 level or higher.

distribution of the education level of LMI users: in Milwaukee, 13.3 percent of those using temp agencies had less than a high school education and only 2 percent had an advanced degree, compared with less than 1 percent and 13.7 percent, respectively, in Silicon Valley. Similarly, the education levels of clients of permanent placement agencies vary by region. In Silicon Valley, nearly 40 percent of such clients had an advanced degree, compared to 12.6 percent in Milwaukee. It is here that the hypothesized connection between the "new economy" and the use of intermediaries may emerge. Although much of the intermediary landscape looks similar in the two regions, there may be both temporary and permanent placement agencies that cater specifically to the highly educated end of Silicon Valley's labor market that have few counterparts in Milwaukee.

Why Are People Using Intermediaries?

In the Survey of LMI Use, LMI users also reported on the circumstances under which they had sought intermediary services. A summary of this information is reported in table 4.4. In both regions, the largest group of LMI users (not surprisingly) was made up of those who went to an LMI because they were not working and they were looking for a job. They were either unemployed or (re)entering the labor market because they were leaving school or welfare, had moved into the area, or had been keeping house. In both regions, this group made up more than half of those who went to temp or nonprofit agencies but only about one-third of those who used unions, professional associations, or community college or vocational school placement services (grouped together here as "other LMIs"). Instead, users of these other LMIs were more likely to report that their primary reason for going to these organizations was related to getting a better job (seeking a better career, more pay, a second job, and so on). Here again, the use of permanent placement agencies in Silicon Valley seems to differ from such use in Milwaukee. While half of the Milwaukee clients of these agencies reported that getting a job was their primary reason, this was true for only one-third of Silicon Valley clients, who were more likely to report that they wanted a better job (30.9 percent) or that they were recruited (19.2 percent).

What Services Are People Getting from Intermediaries?

In addition to making job placements, many LMIs provide supplementary services to their clients that are aimed at meeting market needs, increasing client

Table 4.4 Reasons for Going to an LMI, by Type of LMI and Region (Temp Narrow)

	Milwaukee				Silicon Valley			
	Private Agency		Nonprofit and Government	Other LMI[a]	Private Agency		Nonprofit and Government	Other LMI[a]
Reason for Going to an LMI	Temp Agency	Permanent and Headhunter			Temp Agency	Permanent and Headhunter		
Getting a job[b]	58.3%	49.9%	61.8%	34.2%[e]	62.3%	35.3%[e]	51.9%	28.2%
Unemployed	28.5	34.7	60[e]	9[e]	47.5	19.2[e]	34	8
Moved	22.5	2.9	1[e]	2[e]	6.4	14.0	4	3
Was keeping house	4.4	0.0	0	3	2.9	0.0	4	4
Entering workforce	1.1	12.2[e]	0	19[e]	2.6	2.0	2	13
Leaving welfare	1.9	0.2	1	0	0.1	0.0	4[e]	0
Needed help finding job	0.0	0.0	0.0	0.8	2.8	0.2	4	1
Getting a better job[c]	40.2	36.8	36.6	56.3[e]	37.3	43.5	24.1	60.0
Wanted a better career	3.6	5.8	7	3	7.6	9.9	5	14
Wanted better skills	0.0	0.0	1	4[e]	0.0	0.0	0	4
Wanted better job	12.5	16.8	13	32[e]	18.8	30.9	12	38

Financial reasons (needed more money)	11.8	8.0	5	9	8.1	2.7	4	3
Needed second job	12.2	6.3	11	9	2.8	0.1	3	2
Other reasons[d]	1.5	13.2[e]	1.7	9.5[e]	0.4	21.1[e]	0.5	11.8
Other reasons	1.4	0.0	0	0	0.3	1.8	0	0
Was recruited	0.0	12.5[e]	0	2	0.0	19.2[e]	0	2
Went to school	0.0	0.7	1	2	0.0	0.0	1	6
Bored	0.1	0.0	0	0	0.1	0.1	0	0
Something else— not looking for work	0.0	0.0	0	6[e]	0.0	0.0	0	3
Number of cases	123	71	68	123	112	86	37	140

Source: Authors' compilation.

[a]Includes unions, professional associations, and community/vocational college placements.

[b]Includes unemployed, moved, was keeping house, entering workforce, leaving welfare assistance, or needed help finding a job.

[c]Includes those seeking a better job, better skills, better career, seeking more pay, or needing a second job.

[d]Includes recruited, went to school, bored, was not looking for work, or other reasons.

[e]Difference from the value for temp agency statistically significant at the .05 level or higher.

employability, improving the job-matching process, or improving the success of a placement once made. These services run the gamut from simple job-hunting advice and networking skills to training and assistance with transportation and child care. Table 4.5 shows the percentage of people who said that they received such services from the intermediary that helped them obtain their job, by region and by type of intermediary. The level and types of services provided are largely consistent with what we understand about the broad mission of the organizations in each category. Individuals generally received fewer supplementary services from temporary or permanent placement agencies than from nonprofits and other LMIs. This is the case in both regions, and the differences between temp agencies and unions and other LMIs are statistically significant for virtually every category of service. There are fewer statistically significant differences between the services offered by temporary and permanent placement agencies.

One interesting exception to the general pattern of lower levels of assistance from temp agencies is the case of transportation assistance in Milwaukee. Twenty percent of those placed by temp agencies in Milwaukee reported that they received transportation assistance from the agency that assisted them, compared with 1 percent in Silicon Valley. Only the nonprofit and government agencies in both regions provided a higher level of this service. This is consistent with observations we made during our fieldwork in Milwaukee (see chapter 3): temporary help agencies routinely got involved in solving the "spatial mismatch" problem by providing transportation (often van pools) to assist inner-city workers with commuting to suburban jobs (for documentation on spatial mismatch in cities similar to Milwaukee, see Bania, Leete, and Coulton 2001; Allard and Danziger 2003).

The service profiles of nonprofit and government agencies and of "other LMIs" in both regions are generally comparable, although there are a few differences: nonprofit and government agencies were far more likely to provide assistance with child care and transportation. This is not surprising, since this kind of assistance is often a cornerstone of welfare-to-work programs. Other LMIs are more likely to provide mentoring (often provided through professional associations) and GED/ESL classes (largely through community colleges).

Considerable note has been made in the literature on temporary help agencies that they have expanded their services to include up-to-date training, particularly in the area of computer software competency (see, for example, Freedman 1996). David Autor (2001) reports survey results suggesting that

Table 4.5 Type of Assistance Received from an LMI, by Type of LMI and Region (Temp Narrow)

	Milwaukee				Silicon Valley			
	Private Agency				Private Agency			
Type of Assistance	Temp Agency	Permanent and Headhunter	Nonprofit and Government	Other LMI[a]	Temp Agency	Permanent and Headhunter	Nonprofit and Government	Other LMI[a]
Job-finding skills								
Job-hunting advice	28%	37%	62%[b]	67%[b]	22%	46%[b]	63%[b]	69%[b]
Networking skills	20	17	36[b]	47[b]	12	29[b]	56[b]	48[b]
Help with résumé	16	11	46[b]	36[b]	11	34[b]	58[b]	40[b]
Training								
Computer training	5	2	32[b]	35[b]	10	0[b]	33[b]	38[b]
Advanced training	3	0	16[b]	36[b]	6	0	35[b]	41[b]
GED/ESL classes	0	1	7[b]	37[b]	0	0	24[b]	22[b]
Other assistance								
Mentoring	0	0	18[b]	40[b]	4	0	34[b]	41[b]
Legal help	2	0	11[b]	27[b]	3	0	35[b]	18[b]
Transportation	20	3[b]	25	8[b]	1	4	38[b]	6[b]
Child care help	0	0	12[b]	7[b]	1	2	33[b]	4
Health insurance	23	4[b]	18	28	17	3[b]	36[b]	26
Pension plan	7	1[b]	18[b]	26[b]	15	3[b]	25	27[b]
Number of cases	123	71	68	123	112	86	37	140

Source: Authors' compilation.

[a]Includes unions, professional associations, and community/vocational college placements.

[b]Difference from the value for temp agency statistically significant at the .05 level or higher.

68 percent of temporary help firms provided some form of computer training. However, our data suggest that in Milwaukee and even in computer-laden Silicon Valley the share of temp agency *clients* receiving computer training from temp agencies is relatively low (5 and 10 percent, respectively). The discrepancy here could lie in the unit of measurement: it may be that a large percentage of firms provide training to only a small share of their clients. Or it may be that the survey respondents were not reporting as training the availability of the self-paced computer training that we observed in our qualitative work (see chapter 3). In any case, the source of this discrepancy bears further investigation.

Satisfaction with Intermediary Assistance

Different intermediaries are likely to vary in the nature and quality of the jobs to which they provide access. We inquired as to whether LMI users felt that their agency had assisted them in obtaining a job that they enjoyed more, that was more stable, that had better working conditions, that offered better career opportunities, and so on. Their answers are reported in table 4.6. In most categories, something less than a majority of LMI users reported that the assistance they received from the LMI helped them get a better job or an improved employment situation. There is, however, variation across regions and types of LMIs. In both regions and in all categories, those who used LMIs *other than* temp agencies were more likely to report that their agency had helped them get a better work situation than were their counterparts who had used temp agencies (and most of these differences are statistically significant). Nonetheless, between one-quarter and one-third of temp agency users in each region said that their agency had helped them get a job that they enjoyed more or that offered higher wages, better career opportunities, better working conditions, or more stability. For those who used nonprofit agencies, roughly half or more in both regions felt that the LMI had helped them get a job with better career opportunities, a more stable job, or a job that they enjoyed more. In most categories, however, it was users of other LMIs (unions, community colleges, and professional associations) who were most likely to report that they were satisfied with the jobs they obtained.

Labor Market Intermediaries and Disadvantaged Workers

Labor market developments in the United States in recent decades have sometimes resulted in problematic outcomes for workers with low levels of education

Table 4.6 Satisfaction with the Assistance Provided by LMIs, by Type of LMI and Region (Temp Narrow)

| | Milwaukee | | | | Silicon Valley | | | |
| | Private Agency | | | | Private Agency | | | |
Agreed with Statement That Assistance from LMI Helped Them Get . . .	Temp Agency	Permanent and Headhunter	Nonprofit and Government	Other LMI[a]	Temp Agency	Permanent Pand Headhunter	Nonprofit and Government	Other LMI[a]
Job they enjoyed more	36%	57%[b]	53%[b]	67%[b]	36%	74%[b]	59%[b]	70%[b]
Job that was more stable	34	47	75[b]	59[b]	31	33	54[b]	54[b]
Job with better working conditions	26	44[b]	46[b]	60[b]	32	32	50	47[b]
Job with better career opportunities	26	43[b]	49[b]	64[b]	36	51[b]	44	62[b]
Job with higher wages	32	29	31	48[b]	36	51[b]	49	48
Job with better schedule	31	19	35	39	23	19	56[b]	31
Job with better medical coverage	18	33[b]	47[b]	47[b]	15	27	33[b]	38[b]
Job with better pension	10	41	54[b]	46[b]	19	17	34	41[b]
Better commute	13	22	23	17	9	15	46[b]	23[b]
Better child care	2	7	12[b]	11[b]	2	0	50[b]	10[b]
Something else	8	5	9	23[b]	8	14	23[b]	25[b]
Number of cases	169	25	68	123	151	47	37	140

Source: Authors' compilation.

[a]Includes unions, professional associations, and community/vocational college placements.

[b]Difference from the value for temp agency statistically significant at the .05 level or higher.

and skills. Wage and hours distributions have become polarized, and involuntary unemployment and underemployment has risen (Bluestone and Harrison 1988; Leete-Guy and Schor 1994), and advancement out of low-wage work has become more difficult (Bernhardt et al. 2001; Harrison and Weiss 1998; Melendez and Falcón 1999). In this section, we look at the relationship of disadvantaged workers to the full range of labor market intermediaries. We cast a broad net in defining disadvantage and examine outcomes for workers in three groups: those living in households with low incomes (in the bottom one-third of the regional distribution of household income),[9] those with low education levels (a high school diploma or less), and members of nonwhite racial or ethnic minorities.

That the pattern of intermediary usage varies for those who do and do not have some level of disadvantage is shown in table 4.7. In both regions, those with low incomes were more likely to use temp or nonprofit and government agencies. However, in Silicon Valley those with low income or low education were significantly less likely to use permanent placement agencies than their higher-income and more-educated counterparts, while there were no significant differences in this regard in Milwaukee.

Turning to race and ethnicity, we divide the population into four groups: black, Hispanic (of any race), and non-Hispanic black, white, and Asian and other races; for ease, we drop the "non-Hispanic preface" and just use black, white, and Asian and other. The use of intermediaries across different races was largely similar in both regions: temp agency and nonprofit and government agency usage was generally higher for nonwhites than for whites. In Milwaukee, 41.7 percent of Hispanics and 27 percent of blacks reported having obtained a job they held in the last three years through a temp agency, as compared with only 4.4 percent of whites. Similarly, in Silicon Valley, 37.3 percent of blacks and 13 percent of Asians (and those of other races) used temp agencies, compared with only 8.1 percent of whites. There is one striking exception to this pattern, however: Hispanics in Silicon Valley used all intermediaries at a far lower rate than any other racial-ethnic group, and at a rate lower than whites in either Milwaukee or Silicon Valley. Furthermore, whereas blacks and Asians (and other nonwhites) reported having obtained jobs through temp agencies at high rates, only 4.7 percent of Hispanics in Silicon Valley reported using this kind of agency.

Differences in choice of LMIs undoubtedly reflect differences in the underlying reason for going to an LMI. In table 4.8, we show the reasons individuals

Table 4.7 Use of LMIs to Obtain a Job Held in the Past Three Years, by Income, Education, Race, and Region (Temp Narrow)

Type of LMI Used	All	Household Income		Education Level		Race			
		Bottom 33 Percent	Top 67 Percent	High School Graduate or Less	Some College or More	Black	Hispanic	Asian and Other	White
Milwaukee	29.9%	33.8%	26.7%[a]	32.4%	27.8%	57.9%[a]	54.1%[a]	32.6%	24.9%
Temp agency	8.9	13.0	5.6[a]	11.2	7.1	27.0[a]	41.7[a]	12.0	4.4
Permanent and headhunter	6.2	6.6	5.9	5.3	6.9	4.0	1.6	10.8	6.5
Community college	6.3	5.1	7.2	4.4	7.7	9.5	2.1	0.5	6.6
Nonprofit, government	4.5	6.4	2.9[a]	8.0	1.8[a]	12.6[a]	4.4	7.5	3.4
Union	2.7	1.8	3.4	2.6	2.8	1.3	3.4	1.9	2.8
Professional association	1.3	1.0	1.6	0.9	1.6	3.5	0.9	0.0	1.2
Number of cases	659	379	280	345	311	172	62	39	386
Silicon Valley	26.3	26.4	26.2	21.5	29.3[a]	57.7[a]	18.8[a]	29.2	26.3
Temp agency	9.5	12.0	7.5[a]	9.2	9.7	37.3[a]	4.7	13.0	8.1
Permanent and headhunter	5.8	3.3	7.8[a]	2.3	7.8[a]	8.7	1.0[a]	6.9	7.5
Community college	4.4	2.8	5.6	3.0	5.1	2.4	3.8	6.2	4.1
Nonprofit, government	2.7	4.6	1.2[a]	3.6	2.3	6.4	4.2	1.4	2.2
Union	2.4	3.5	1.4	3.5	1.6	3.0	3.5	0.1[a]	2.7
Professional association	1.6	0.1	2.7[a]	0.0	2.5[a]	0.0	1.5	1.7	1.7
Number of cases	659	379	280	345	311	172	62	39	386
Number of cases	689	328	361	264	417	32	177	135	345

Source: Authors' compilation.

[a]Difference between categories (high versus low education or income, other races versus white) is statistically significant at the .05 level or higher.

Table 4.8   Reason for Using an LMI to Obtain a Job Held
in the Past Three Years, by Education Level and Region

| | Milwaukee | | Silicon Valley | |
| | Low | High | Low | High |
Reason for Using an LMI	Education	Education	Education	Education
To get a job	53%	45%	47%	43%
Unemployed	35	21[a]	30	26
Moved	10	6	5	8
Was keeping house	1	3	5	1[a]
Entering workforce	5	14[a]	2	7
Leaving welfare	2	0	2	0[a]
Needed help finding a job	0	1	3	1
To get a better job	43	46	47	44
Wanted a better job	14	26[a]	26	27
Wanted better skills	3	0[a]	1	1
Wanted a better career	5	3	12	9
Financial reasons				
(needed more money)	12	6[a]	8	4
Needed a second job	9	10	1	2
Other reasons	4	9	6	13[a]
Recruited	1	5[a]	3	9[a]
Other reasons	0	0	2	0[a]
Went to school	1	1	1	3
Bored	0	0	0	0
For something else;				
not looking for work	3	2	0	2
Number of cases	264	417	345	311

Source: Authors' compilation.
[a]Differences between education groups are statistically significant at the .05 level.

reported for going to the LMI, separately by education level and for each region. As we did with table 4.7, we group the reasons for going to an LMI into three categories: those that related to a job search for the unemployed, those that related to obtaining either a better (or better-paying) job or a second job, and other reasons. Differences between those with higher and lower levels of education are not as apparent in the broad groupings as they are in the under-lying detail. For instance, those with lower education levels were far more likely to be unemployed, leaving welfare, seeking a better career, or citing financial need. Those with higher levels of education were more likely to be just enter-ing the workforce, seeking a better job, or reporting that they had been recruited. Finally, some interesting differences are clearly regional, independent of education level. For instance, those with both low and high levels of educa-tion in Silicon Valley were more likely to be seeking a better career than their counterparts in Milwaukee, while seeking a second job or citing financial need was far more common in Milwaukee.

If those likely to be disadvantaged have different reasons for seeking assis-tance from an LMI and use different types of LMIs, then a remaining question is whether they also receive different kinds of services or have a different inten-sity of contact with LMIs. However, we found few significant differences accord-ing to income, education, or race in the range of services that people received from particular types of intermediaries (along the lines of the measures shown in table 4.5). Measures of intensity of contact with an LMI include the length of time individuals had ongoing contact with the organization; the amount of time spent in GED, computer, or advanced training classes; and whether train-ing led to some kind of certificate or diploma or was helpful in finding a job. Reported levels of such measures were minimal for those who used temp agen-cies but relatively high for those who obtained their jobs through any other type of intermediaries. The latter are shown in table 4.9 according to region, income, education, and race. These measures suggest that client-agency contact is rela-tively deep in these "other intermediaries"—duration of agency contact averaged close to a year, and average training enrollments often ranged from a month to two months. However, these levels are also consistent across income, education, and racial groups, with few statistically significant differences between them. This tends to suggest that the services that were available and their use were more a function of the intermediary than of the client.

Summary

Fielding a unique survey, we find a high level and wide range of LMI involve-ment in our two labor markets. This activity was not only a characteristic of the churning and volatility thought to be characteristic of Silicon Valley's boom-ing high-tech economy in the 1990s but was equally pervasive in the more tra-ditional economy of Milwaukee, Wisconsin. This suggests that intermediaries

Table 4.9 Intensity of Intermediary Contact, by Income, Education, Race, and Region, for Users of Agencies Other Than Temp Agencies (Temp Narrow)

Length of Contact with LMI/Outcome	All	Household Income		Education Level		Race	
		Bottom 33 Percent	Top 67 Percent	High School Graduate or Less	Some College or More	White	Nonwhite
Milwaukee							
Length of contact (days)	297	236	342[a]	244	335	328	166
Days spent in GED classes with LMI	44	43	44	43	44	45	39
Days spent in computer classes with LMI	28	40	19	17	37	27	32
Days spent in advanced training with LMI	46	15	71[a]	50	42	51	26
Percentage for whom . . .							
LMI training led to a diploma	22	20	23	16	26	20	28
LMI training helped find a job	26	29	24	28	25	25	34
Number of cases	262	138	124	131	131	165	94

Silicon Valley

Length of contact (days)	268	286	259	219	285	282	264
Days spent in GED classes with LMI	30	25	33	18	35	28	34
Days spent in computer classes with LMI	38	30	43	32	41	42	32
Days spent in advanced training with LMI	57	70	50	19	73[a]	66	49
Percentage for whom . . .							
LMI training led to a diploma	20	25	17	24	19	17	25
LMI training helped find a job	26	32	22	31	23	21	31
Number of cases	263	112	151	93	170	132	127

Source: Authors' compilation.

[a]Differences between groups (low- versus high-income, high school graduate versus higher education, white versus nonwhite) are statistically significant at the .05 level.

are likely to be just as important throughout U.S. regional labor markets and that they are rooted in market transitions that transcend regional developments, particular technologies, or volatility per se. This is consistent with findings by other researchers that LMIs are developing in similar fashion in other nations as well (see, for example, Peck, Theodore, and Ward 2005).

Until this chapter's report of our survey results, neither the magnitude of LMI activity nor its diversity had been definitively illustrated. Previous researchers have focused on particular types of intermediaries, but it is clear here that many kinds of organizations—ranging from temp agencies to welfare-to-work agencies to unions—are playing a wide range of roles for a diverse group of people. In the regions studied here, private for-profit placement agencies, both temporary and permanent, are a particularly important element of the inter-mediary picture; they account for about half of all intermediary use—far more than any other single type of agency. But temp agencies in particular are also the least likely to provide supportive services to workers, and temp agency clients are the least likely to report that their agency helped them get a better work situation.

Disadvantaged workers—those who are low-income, low-education, or a racial or ethnic minority—make disproportionate use of intermediary agencies and tend to use temp agencies and nonprofit or government agencies more than members of more-advantaged groups. They are most likely to be seeking work after being unemployed or upon entering the labor market. In contrast, more-advantaged populations use intermediaries when they are seeking some improve-ment in their career and are more likely to do so through organizations such as unions, community colleges, vocational schools, and professional associations.

That said, there are some important differences between the two regions that run somewhat counter to these generalities. First, Hispanics in Silicon Valley use all intermediaries, and particularly temp and permanent placement agencies, at considerably lower rates than any other racial-ethnic groups. Second, permanent placement agencies play somewhat different roles in the two regions. In Silicon Valley, higher-income and more highly educated work-ers are more likely to obtain work through permanent placement agencies—a phenomenon not observed as distinctly in Milwaukee. The role of this type of intermediary seems to have diverged in the two locations. We investigate this split further as we examine the relationship between intermediaries and job outcomes in the next chapter.

Chapter Five

The Impact of Intermediaries on Job Outcomes

In the previous chapter, we reviewed data from the Survey of Labor Market Intermediary Use to examine the nature of LMI use by workers in two regions, and we considered the differential experience of workers who are disadvantaged by education, income, or race. Here we give further consideration to the impact of intermediaries. We look at job outcomes—occupation, industry, wages, hours, and benefits—with an eye to whether workers obtained their job through an intermediary agency, the kind of agency used, and their level of disadvantage.

Job outcomes, of course, are jointly determined by complex factors on both the supply and demand sides of the market. Raw outcomes may reflect not only the efficacy of the agency making the job placement but also differences in the mix of workers who do or do not use each type of agency. Thus, although a simple comparison of wages and other outcomes across intermediary types is an important descriptive exercise, these comparisons cannot be taken as indicative of causality. In the analysis that follows, we first evaluate raw outcomes across LMI users and non-users, disadvantaged and otherwise. We then turn to a multivariate analysis of outcomes, measuring the impact of intermediary use in the presence of other controls for worker and job characteristics. Even though this latter analysis still cannot definitively identify causality, it is more suggestive of potential causal factors.

In particular, we find a strong negative relationship between temporary agency use and wage and benefits outcomes. We compare these findings with those of other authors, reconciling differences in datasets and reproducing a variety of specifications. We pay particular attention to a study by Fredrik Andersson and his colleagues (2005), who found a positive association between previous temp use and earnings for low-income workers; we rework our data to mimic their results and illustrate how the positive impact is likely to be due to longer hours rather than higher wages, with the net welfare benefits up for evaluation by observers and policymakers. In general, we find that the negative relationship between temporary agency use and hourly wages is robust and holds up in any comparison of jobs obtained through temp agencies and jobs obtained without LMI intervention.

Occupations and Industries

The nature of a job can in part be inferred from its occupational and industrial location. In figures 5.1 to 5.4, we show the distribution of jobs according to industry and occupation and according to whether the job was obtained through a temp agency (narrowly defined), some other type of LMI, or no LMI. It is clear (if not surprising) that both the occupational and industrial distribution of jobs vary according to how the jobs were obtained. In both regions, temp users were largely found in administrative support occupations, machine operator and assembler occupations, and transportation and material moving occupations. They were also more likely to be located in the manufacturing sector than were other workers, perhaps belying a common notion that temp workers are mostly found in office occupations.[1] Differences between those who used other LMIs and those who used no LMI were much less stark.

A separate question is whether job placements made by LMIs are more highly concentrated in a narrower slice of the economy. We measure this by calculating the cumulative percentage employed in occupation or industry categories, sorted by concentration of employment. We conduct this analysis separately by region and for temp agency users, other LMI users, and non-LMI users. We also repeat the analysis separately for those with low education levels only. We find that *across all education levels,* LMI users are *not* more or less concentrated than non-users in their industry or occupation locations. However, among those with low levels of education (high school diploma or less), the industry/occupation locations of those who obtained jobs through LMIs were

(*text continues on page 131*)

Figure 5.1   Distribution of Employment by Occupation and
LMI Status, Milwaukee

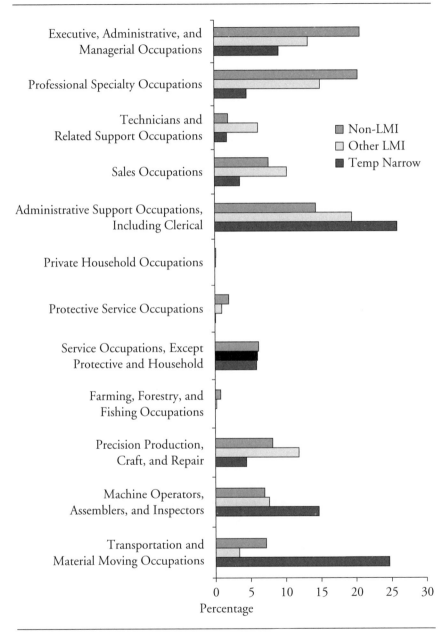

Source: Authors' compilation.

Figure 5.2   Distribution of Employment by Industry and LMI Status, Milwaukee

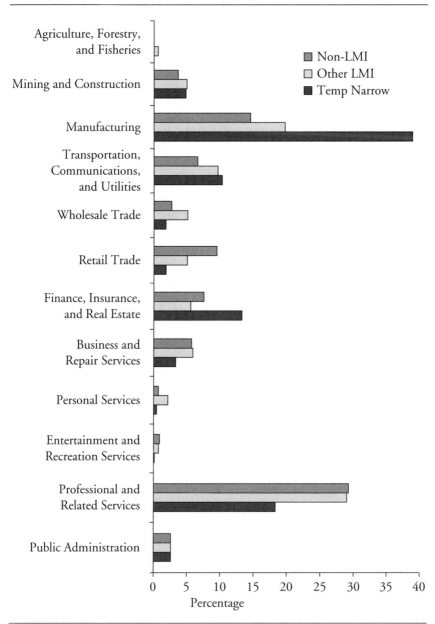

Figure 5.3   Distribution of Employment by Occupation and
LMI Status, Silicon Valley

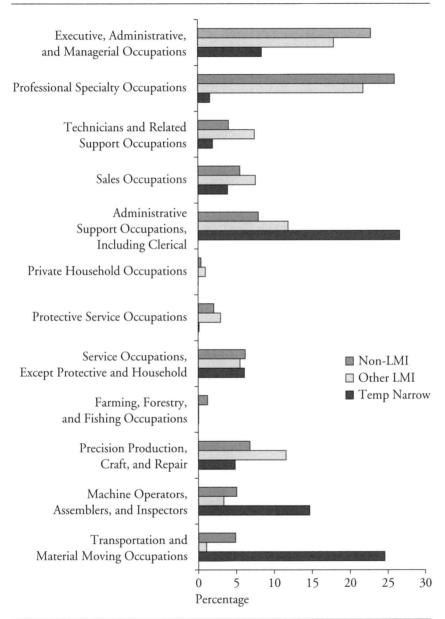

Source: Authors' compilation.

Figure 5.4   Distribution of Employment by Industry and
LMI Status, Silicon Valley

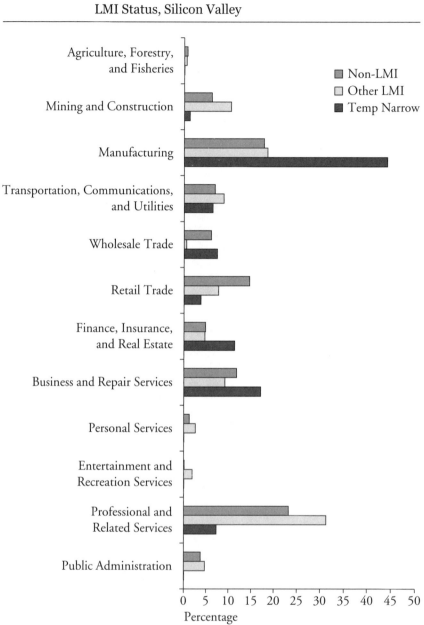

Source: Authors' compilation.

more concentrated than for those who obtained their jobs through other means. In Milwaukee, temp agency users with low levels of education were more concentrated by both occupation and industry than either users of other LMIs or non-LMI users. The results by occupation are illustrated in figure 5.5. Seventy-five percent of temp agency users can be found in the top three occupational categories for this group, as compared with only 64 percent of other LMI users and 47 percent of non-LMI users. In Silicon Valley, the same pattern holds by industry, but when we look at concentrations by occupation, we see that it is the users of other LMIs who appear to be more highly concentrated than the others (with more than 80 percent found in administrative support occupations, technicians and related support occupations, and professional specialty occupations).

Wages, Hours, and Benefits

Outcomes such as wages, hours, and benefits vary somewhat according to what type of agency was used to obtain a job. Table 5.1 (see p. 134) displays the mean levels of the real hourly wage, usual hours worked per week, part-time status (less than twenty hours per week), and the receipt of training, health insurance, or pension benefits from the employer in each region according to type of LMI used. The most distinct differences (and statistically significant ones) are between those who used temp agencies and those who did not use LMIs. In both regions, the mean wage for temp agency users was well below that of the non-LMI sample, as was their rate of receiving health insurance or pension benefits.[2]

Although there are uniformly lower wages for temp users in both regions, a distinction emerges between temp agency users in Milwaukee and those in Silicon Valley with regard to lower hours and training levels: temp users had significantly lower hours and less training than their non-LMI counterparts in Milwaukee, but not in Silicon Valley. This is consistent with the view that temp agencies were responding to the superheated labor market in Silicon Valley in the late 1990s (when unemployment rates were as low as 3.2 percent) by moving into market segments with both more investment in and return to workers. The outcomes for private permanent placement agencies ("headhunters") in Silicon Valley may also reflect this phenomenon: those LMI users also reported significantly higher wages, hours, and benefits. Outcomes for other LMIs are less distinctive: wages for users of nonprofit and government agencies were also significantly lower in both regions, but little else varied by type of LMI.

Figure 5.5   Concentration of Occupational Employment for
Workers with Low Education, by LMI Status, Milwaukee

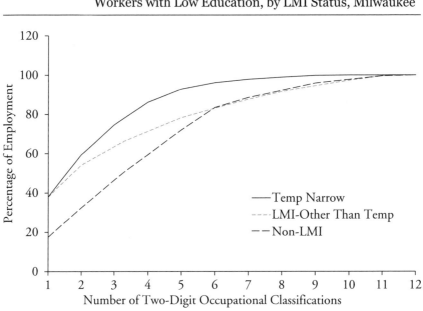

Source: Authors' compilation.

We are also interested in outcomes that correspond to the LMI use of more-
or less-disadvantaged workers. In figures 5.6 and 5.7 (see pp. 136–37), we
show median real hourly wages for those who did not obtain their job through
an intermediary, for those who used a temporary agency, and for those who
used all other intermediaries. In each case, we distinguish between those from
low-income households and others, those with lower and higher levels of education, and members of white and nonwhite racial-ethnic groups. The results
are quite striking and indicate, among other things, either considerable sorting of workers into temp agencies, differential impact in temp agencies, or
both. In Milwaukee, wages for temp agency workers were lower among both
advantaged and disadvantaged workers, while differences between "other
LMI" users and "non-LMI" users were less distinct. In Silicon Valley, the same
pattern holds for more advantaged workers. However, among Silicon Valley's
disadvantaged workers, those with temp agency placements were faring about
as well as those who had found jobs through non-LMI avenues. This again

may reflect the movement of temp agencies into higher market segments in Silicon Valley and the effects of very strong employment demand.

In figures 5.8 through 5.13 (see pp. 138–43), we display differences in obtaining employer-provided health insurance, pension plans, and job training. The results are quite similar, with outcomes for disadvantaged workers in Silicon Valley falling in line with the others. In all cases, those who obtained work through temp agencies received fewer benefits than others, with minimal differentials between outcomes for non-LMI users and other LMI users. These results hold for both the relatively disadvantaged and advantaged, and in both locations. The same pattern holds for employer-provided training in Milwaukee. The exceptions to the pattern are again in Silicon Valley. The provision of employer-provided training there (shown in figure 5.13) was lower than in Milwaukee among non-LMI and other LMI placements, and higher among temp agency placements. The result is that the training levels in Silicon Valley were much closer to being comparable across LMI type regardless of level of advantage or disadvantage. The higher level among temp agencies, again, may have reflected their presence in more segments of the market.

Of course, the distribution of job outcomes among workers depends on both supply- and demand-side characteristics of the worker and the job. Clearly, different kinds of workers are hired for different kinds of jobs, and as we showed in chapter 4 and explore in more depth in chapter 6, they also use different kinds of intermediaries. As a result of both of these influences, they also experience different job outcomes. To identify these various factors separately, we turn to a multivariate analysis of wage and benefit outcomes.

Intermediaries and Job Outcomes: A Multivariate Analysis

Data from the Survey of LMI Use allow for an initial investigation into critical questions about the performance of labor market intermediaries. Do intermediaries secure better outcomes for those who use them? Does the answer depend on the type of intermediary and the type of outcome being considered? Do intermediaries function in different ways for those who have attended college than for those who have not? And in particular, are disadvantaged workers better off or worse off using temp agencies? Answering these questions is not simply an academic exercise. These questions are at the very core of debates about public investment in workforce development capacity, the

Table 5.1   Labor Market Outcomes for Workers Employed in
Past Three Years, by LMI Use (Temp Narrow)

| | Milwaukee | | | | |
| | Non-LMI | Private Agency | | Nonprofit or Government | Other LMI[a] |
Outcomes		Temp Agency	Permanent or Headhunter		
Hourly wage (in 2002 dollars)	$ 19.01	$ 10.69[b]	$ 23.35	$ 13.46[b]	$ 18.95
Hours per week	40.8	37.0[b]	43.3	38.6	42.4
Part-time work (less than 20 per week)	9%	12	12%	11%	3%
Training from employer	54	20[b]	56	61	65
Health insurance from employer	79	40[b]	87	65	75
Health premiums paid in full by employer	13	4	16	11	16
Pension benefits from employer	68	17[b]	83	68	72
Number of cases	274	123	71	68	123

Source: Authors' compilation.
[a]Includes unions, professional associations, and community college and vocational school placements.
[b]Difference from the value for non-LMI value statistically significant at the .05 level or higher.

ability of the public sector to meet the employment needs of low-wage workers, and the extent to which successful intermediaries might serve as models for others. These are key policy questions, and yet relatively few data have been brought to bear on them.

We offer several caveats to our analysis. First, the LMI users we interviewed were limited to those who had successfully obtained work through an LMI. Thus, our data cannot speak to the important question of whether intermediaries are effective in *finding* jobs for workers. This, of course, is one of the central outcomes of interest in the current discourse on labor market inter-

| | Silicon Valley | | | |
| | Private Agency | | | |
Non-LMI	Temp Agency	Permanent or Headhunter	Nonprofit or Government	Other LMI[a]
$ 25.81	$ 17.49[b]	$ 34.65[b]	$ 11.92[b]	$ 24.95
41.8	41.6	50.0[b]	34.9[b]	42.7
10%	3%	0%	21%	6%
52	44	37	44	47
72	46[b]	93[b]	68	80
27	8[b]	40	21	31
64	32[b]	77	50	72
311	112	86	37	140

mediaries. Second, the data analyzed here offer a snapshot of only two regional economies during relatively good economic times; they are not necessarily indicative of what might be found in other regions or at other points in the business cycle. Finally, our data are neither experimental nor explicitly longitudinal—they do not allow a fully controlled cause-and-effect isolation of intermediary effects.

On the other hand, the nature of our data collection introduces a longitudinal component to our outcomes data. Although reported LMI usage may have occurred at any point in the past, job outcomes are measured contemporaneously

Figure 5.6   Real Median Hourly Wage, by Type of LMI Used, Income, Education, and Race, Milwaukee

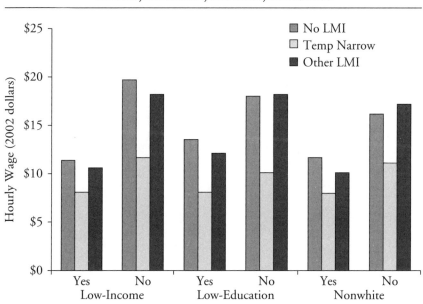

Source: Authors' compilation.

with the survey. Thus, our wage and outcome models are suggestive of longer-term effects of LMI usage. Moreover, we have a rich set of cross-sectional controls here for individual worker characteristics that are much more detailed than those that have been available to most other researchers asking related questions. The inclusion of these controls tempers many of the results, suggesting both that selection is at work and that we have captured at least some of its effects. Thus, we suggest that these results may cautiously be interpreted as indicative of possible causal patterns, but we cannot conclusively ascribe causality, for instance, from LMI use to outcome, nor can we infer general patterns that go too far beyond these labor markets and this time period. Nonetheless, we believe that there may be useful lessons here for researchers and policymakers.

In what follows, we estimate several multivariate models explaining wages and benefits for workers in each region. The dependent variable in the wage models is the log of the real hourly wage (set to 2002 prices). In the benefits equations, the dependent variables are dummy variables indicating variously

Figure 5.7   Real Median Hourly Wage, by Type of LMI Used,
Income, Education, and Race, Silicon Valley

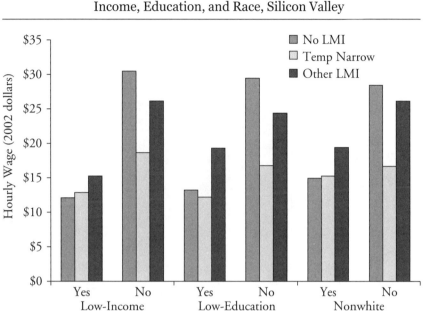

Source: Authors' compilation.

the availability of an employer-provided pension plan, the availability of an employer-provided health insurance plan, or an employer who provides full payment of the health insurance premium. In all cases, the models estimate the relationship between type of LMI used (if any) and the outcome in question, controlling for various personal and job characteristics.[3]

Hourly Wages

Five separate models explaining real wages are estimated, progressively adding and testing a range of explanatory variables. The means and standard errors of all model variables are shown in table 5.2 (see pp. 144–45). Model 1 shows the LMI wage differentials estimated without the inclusion of other controls, and model 2 adds worker characteristics, including controls for the highest level of education completed, the receipt of training, gender, race (black, Hispanic, and Asian and other), foreign-born status, level of English fluency, potential work experience (and potential work experience squared), and tenure on the reference

Figure 5.8   Availability of Employer-Provided Health Insurance
by Type of LMI Used, Income, Education, and
Race, Milwaukee

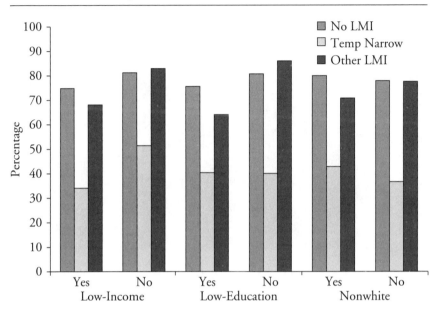

Source: Authors' compilation.

job.[4] Model 3 adds job characteristics—controls for one-digit industry and for
union contract coverage and an indicator for part-time work (less than twenty
hours per week)—and in model 4 a control for temporary jobs is tested. In
Model 5, separate LMI effects for those who have not attended college are added.

The models explaining the hourly wage generate interesting and provocative
results (see table 5.3 on pp. 146–49). In both regions, a strong negative wage
effect is estimated for individuals who obtained jobs through a temporary agency
as compared with individuals who did not use an LMI to find work; strong positive effects are found for individuals who obtained work through private placement agencies. In Silicon Valley only, a negative effect is also estimated for the
use of nonprofit and government agencies. Estimated effects decrease considerably with the inclusion of controls for individual characteristics in model 2, suggesting that a significant portion of the effects estimated in model 1 are the result
of individuals with different characteristics (which have differential returns in the

Figure 5.9   Availability of Employer-Provided Health Insurance,
by Type of LMI Used, Income, Education, and
Race, Silicon Valley

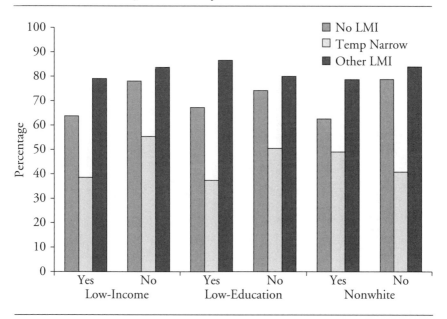

Source: Authors' compilation.

market) using different methods to obtain jobs. The estimated effects do not
change much, however, with the further inclusion of job characteristics in
model 3. The resultant effect of temp agency placement is 21 percent lower wages
in Milwaukee and 28 percent lower wages in Silicon Valley; the nonprofit wage
reduction in Silicon Valley is 34 percent. In contrast, private placement agencies
confer a wage advantage of 21 and 25 percent in Milwaukee and Silicon Valley,
respectively. It should be noted that these estimates could reflect either the real
effects associated with obtaining work through different types of agencies or differential sorting of workers (with different unobservable and wage-related characteristics) into different types of LMIs. However, as noted earlier, a wide range
of worker and job characteristics are already included, and they should account
for much of the differential sorting of workers into different LMIs.[5]

In model 4, we test the inclusion of a variable indicating whether a job is a
temporary placement, regardless of how that job was obtained. In both regions,

Figure 5.10   Availability of Employer-Provided Pension Plan, by Type of LMI Used, Income, Education, and Race, Milwaukee

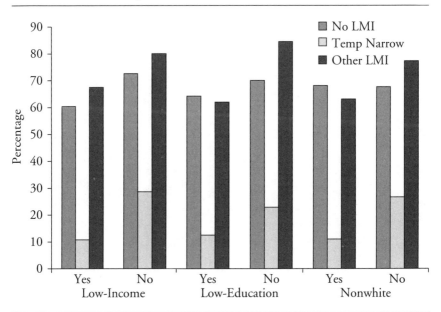

Source: Authors' compilation.

controlling for temporary placements causes the *temp agency* effect to drop—in Milwaukee by 42 percent, and in Silicon Valley by 25 percent. This suggests that the remaining temp agency effect (12 percent in Milwaukee and 21 percent in Silicon Valley) is over and above any effect associated with temporary placements per se and is associated specifically with the use of the temporary agency.

We also test for differences in LMI effects among those with and without any college education. These are shown in model 5, where we include a separate LMI term for those without a college education. In both regions, the results suggest that the strong positive effect of private placement agencies is experienced only by those with at least some college education.

Benefits
Pension Plans   We follow a similar strategy in testing for LMI effects on the receipt of benefits such as an employer-provided pension or health insurance

Figure 5.11   Availability of Employer-Provided Pension Plan, by Type of LMI Used, Income, Education, and Race, Silicon Valley

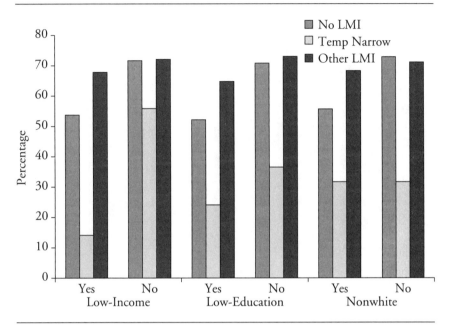

Source: Authors' compilation.

plan. The results closely parallel those found for wages. In table 5.4 (see pp. 150–51), we present coefficient estimates and the corresponding odds ratio effects from logistic regressions modeling the odds of having access to an employer-provided pension plan; estimates corresponding to models 3 and 4 are shown. Model 3 includes the full range of controls for worker and job characteristics, except the control for temporary placements. Model 4 adds that control.[6] In both regions, individuals who obtained work through temporary agencies were considerably less likely to receive pension benefits than others; in Milwaukee the odds ratio effect is 0.15 and in Silicon Valley it is 0.18. Adding the control for temporary placements about doubles the odds ratio in both regions, but the effect is still large and statistically significant. This suggests that workers who obtained temporary placements through temp agencies were still far less likely to receive pension benefits than otherwise comparable workers who made temporary placements by other means. In Milwaukee, we also estimate a positive and significant

Figure 5.12   Availability of Employer-Provided Training, by Type of
LMI Used, Income, Education, and Race, Milwaukee

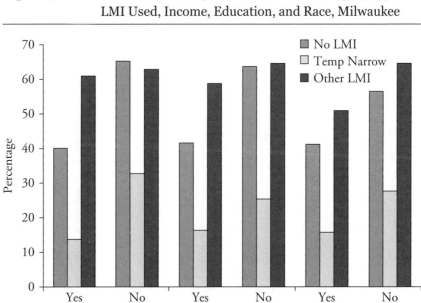

Source: Authors' compilation.

effect of permanent placement agencies on the odds of receiving pension benefits. However, all other LMI effects are statistically insignificant. We found no
statistically significant separate LMI effects for those without college.

Health Insurance   We extend our estimation strategy further to look at the
determinants of the availability of health insurance through employers; model
estimates are shown in table 5.5 (see pp. 152–53). The results for the effect of
temp agency placements on the availability of employer-provided health insurance closely parallel those found for pensions, both in direction and size: temp
agency users in both regions were less likely than others to have health insurance available through their employer. The odds ratio for those using temp
agencies is only a fraction of the odds ratio for non-LMI users (0.14 in
Milwaukee and 0.13 in Silicon Valley). However, these effects lose their size
and significance when we separately control for temporary placements regardless of their source in model 4.

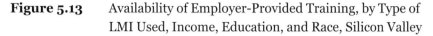

Figure 5.13   Availability of Employer-Provided Training, by Type of LMI Used, Income, Education, and Race, Silicon Valley

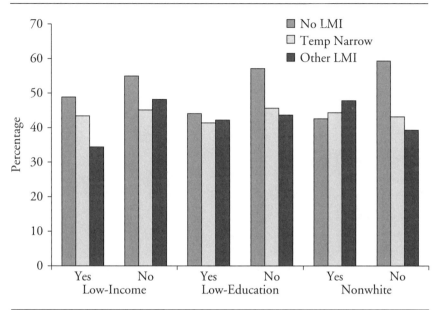

Source: Authors' compilation.

We also investigate health insurance in more detail, modeling the extent to which employers paid health insurance premiums, either in part or in full. When the dependent variable is whether the employer paid *any* of the health insurance premium, the results (not surprisingly) are virtually identical to those in table 5.5 that model whether employer-provided health insurance was available at all through the employer. The findings diverge somewhat, however, when we model whether the health insurance premiums were paid *in full* by the employer. In this case (shown in table 5.6 on pp. 154–57), we find that full premiums are strongly tied to education levels, part-time status, union status, and industry of employment. In Milwaukee the outcome is largely unrelated to LMI status. In Silicon Valley, however, this is not the case: we find a strong negative effect associated with both temporary jobs and with the use of temporary agencies. The magnitude of this effect is comparable to those found in the preceding benefits models. When we estimate model 5 in either location, we find little in the way of differential impact of LMIs for those without a college education.

Table 5.2   Summary Statistics for Model Variables

	Milwaukee		Silicon Valley	
	Mean	Standard Error	Mean	Standard Error
Log real hourly wage	2.73	0.039	3.03	0.041
Health insurance from employer	0.75	0.025	0.71	0.028
Pension benefits from employer	0.65	0.028	0.62	0.030
Health premiums paid in full by employer	0.13	0.019	0.27	0.027
Percentage Using LMI				
Temp agency	0.09	0.012	0.10	0.014
Private placement agency and headhunter	0.06	0.011	0.06	0.009
Union	0.03	0.007	0.02	0.006
Nonprofit, CBO, government	0.04	0.008	0.03	0.007
Community and technical college	0.06	0.011	0.04	0.008
Professional association	0.01	0.006	0.02	0.005
Individual characteristics				
Potential experience (years)	23.09	0.746	19.14	0.660
Job tenure (months)	99.93	6.486	69.57	5.677
Percentage with other training	0.66	0.028	0.62	0.029
Percentage with LMI training	0.09	0.014	0.07	0.011
English limited	0.21	0.024	0.28	0.028
Foreign-born	0.07	0.015	0.34	0.029
Female	0.55	0.030	0.51	0.030
White	0.82	0.019	0.51	0.031
Hispanic	0.06	0.011	0.26	0.030
Black	0.09	0.013	0.04	0.012
Asian or other race	0.03	0.008	0.18	0.022
Educational attainment				
High school dropout	0.05	0.011	0.03	0.010
High school graduate	0.38	0.029	0.33	0.029
Associate's degree	0.15	0.022	0.11	0.018
Four-year college graduate	0.38	0.029	0.52	0.030

Table 5.2   Summary Statistics for Model Variables (*Continued*)

	Milwaukee		Silicon Valley	
	Mean	Standard Error	Mean	Standard Error
Job characteristics				
Union	0.22	0.024	0.18	0.023
Temporary job	0.09	0.013	0.12	0.016
Part-time job	0.09	0.017	0.08	0.017
(less than 20 hours per week)				
Industry of employment				
Manufacturing	0.20	0.023	0.21	0.024
Construction	0.05	0.013	0.06	0.012
Retail	0.11	0.020	0.12	0.022
Services	0.08	0.015	0.13	0.019
FIRE	0.40	0.030	0.27	0.026
Agriculture and mining	0.00	0.001	0.01	0.005
Public administration	0.03	0.010	0.03	0.010
Public transportation	0.08	0.016	0.07	0.016
Wholesale	0.03	0.010	0.05	0.015

Source: Authors' compilation.

Comparison with Other Studies

Our most consistent findings across both regions are statistically significant and strongly negative relationships between temporary agency use and several labor market outcomes—namely, hourly wages, the availability of pension and health insurance benefits, and the payment of health insurance premiums by employers. Several other recent studies have also looked specifically at the relationship between temporary agency use and earnings, particularly among low-income workers (for example, Andersson et al. 2005; Autor and Houseman 2005a; Ferber and Waldfogel 1998; Heinrich, Mueser, and Troske 2005; Lane et al. 2003). Some authors have reached conclusions parallel to those here, but others have had quite opposite findings. Of course, each of these studies incorporates different data, populations, and research methodologies, making direct comparisons something of an "apples and oranges" exercise. In

(*text continues on page 158*)

Table 5.3   Wage Outcomes and LMIs, Milwaukee and Silicon Valley, OLS Regressions (Dependent Variable: Log Real Hourly Wage)

	Milwaukee				
	Model 1 Coefficient	Model 2 Coefficient	Model 3 Coefficient	Model 4 Coefficient	Model 5 Coefficient
Intercept	2.79***	2.57***	2.60***	2.60***	2.62***
LMI use (most recent LMI job)					
Professional association	−0.08	−0.07	−0.06	−0.05	−0.06
Community and vocational college	−0.11	−0.08	−0.08	−0.08	−0.09
Nonprofit, government and CBO	−0.27***	−0.11	−0.08	−0.07	−0.06
Private placement agency	0.11	0.18*	0.21*	0.20*	0.35***
Temp agency	−0.52***	−0.20***	−0.21***	−0.12	−0.23**
Union	0.31***	0.07	−0.08	−0.08	−0.08
Education level					
Less than high school		−0.25***	−0.23***	−0.23***	−0.19**
Associate's degree		0.12*	0.10	0.09	0.09
College graduate		0.36***	0.35***	0.35***	0.32***
Race					
Asian or other		−0.12	−0.09	−0.09	−0.07
Black		−0.15**	−0.17***	−0.15**	−0.19***
Hispanic		−0.09	−0.16	−0.14	−0.16
Female		−0.31***	−0.30***	−0.29***	−0.29***
English Limited		−0.03	−0.02	−0.02	−0.03
Foreign-born		−0.11	−0.08	−0.07	−0.08
Training from LMI		0.04	0.02	0.02	0.02
Job tenure		0.002***	0.002***	0.002***	0.002***
Training		0.11*	0.09	0.10	0.09
Work experience		0.006	0.00	0.00	0.00
Work experience-squared		−0.0002	0.00	0.00	0.00

	Silicon Valley			
Model 1 Coefficient	Model 2 Coefficient	Model 3 Coefficient	Model 4 Coefficient	Model 5 Coefficient
	3.10***	3.17***	3.17***	3.17***
0.10	−0.11	−0.05	0.02	−0.07
0.05	−0.13	0.03	0.05	0.01
−0.63***	−0.41***	−0.34**	−0.34**	−0.42*
0.39***	0.25***	0.25***	0.25***	0.29***
−0.29***	−0.25***	−0.28***	−0.21*	−0.28***
0.08	−0.01	0.01	0.05	−0.10
	−0.37***	−0.36***	−0.36***	−0.36***
	0.06	0.11	0.11	0.11
	0.32***	0.33***	0.33***	0.33***
	0.03	0.01	0.02	0.01
	−0.21**	−0.20*	−0.20*	−0.19*
	−0.29***	−0.26**	−0.26**	−0.27**
	−0.19***	−0.18**	−0.18**	−0.17**
	−0.17*	−0.18*	−0.16*	−0.18*
	−0.08	−0.08	−0.08	−0.08
	0.01	−0.12	−0.13	−0.08
	0.001***	0.001***	0.001***	0.001***
	0.03	0.05	0.05	0.05
		0.00	0.00	0.00
		0.00	0.00	0.00

(*continued*)

Table 5.3   Wage Outcomes and LMIs, Milwaukee and Silicon Valley, OLS Regressions (Dependent Variable: Log Real Hourly Wage) (*Continued*)

| | Milwaukee | | | | |
	Model 1 Coefficient	Model 2 Coefficient	Model 3 Coefficient	Model 4 Coefficient	Model 5 Coefficient
Part-time			−0.17*	−0.17*	−0.17*
Union			0.03	0.02	0.02
Industry					
Agriculture, mining			−0.08	−0.08	−0.18
Construction			0.25**	0.26**	0.27**
FIRE			0.01	0.01	0.03
Public administration			−0.21**	−0.21*	−0.15
Public transit			−0.06	−0.05	−0.02
Retail			−0.07	−0.08	−0.07
Services			−0.09	−0.09	−0.06
Wholesale			0.03	0.06	−0.01
Temporary job				−0.17**	
LMI effects for noncollege sample					
Community and vocational college					0.19
Nonprofit and government CBO					−0.05
Private placement agency					−0.05***
Temp agency					0.03
Union					0.07
R-squared	0.1058	0.4332	0.4621	0.4669	0.4738
Number of cases	528	498	494	494	494

Source: Authors' compilation.
*significant at the .10 level
**significant at the .05 level
***significant at the .01 level

		Silicon Valley		
Model 1 Coefficient	Model 2 Coefficient	Model 3 Coefficient	Model 4 Coefficient	Model 5 Coefficient
		0.03	0.04	0.03
		−0.02	−0.02	−0.02
		−0.12	−0.13	−0.11
		0.02	0.02	0.02
		−0.12	−0.12	−0.13
		−0.11	−0.11	−0.11
		−0.22	−0.21	−0.23
		−0.13	−0.13	−0.13
		−0.13	−0.13	−0.13
		−0.02	−0.02	−0.02
			−0.11	
				−0.10
				0.21
				−0.41**
				0.00
				0.34*
0.0816	0.4084	0.4312	0.4337	0.436
574	518	513	513	513

Table 5-4 Benefits and LMIs, Milwaukee and Silicon Valley, Logistic Regressions (Dependent Variable: Employer-Provided Pension Plan)

	Milwaukee				Silicon Valley			
	Model 3		Model 4		Model 3		Model 4	
	Coefficient Estimate	Odds Ratio	Coefficient Estimate	Odds Ratio	Coefficient Estimate	Odds Ratio	Coefficient Estimate	Odds Ratio
Intercept	−0.64	0.00	−0.39	0.00	0.53	0.00	0.61	0.00
LMI use (most recent LMI job)								
Professional association	−1.56	0.21	−1.64	0.19	−1.04	0.35	−0.26	0.77
Community or vocational college	−0.61	0.54	−0.72	0.48	0.16	1.18	0.53	1.71
Nonprofit, government and CBO	−0.11	0.90	−0.13	0.88	−0.30	0.74	−0.14	0.87
Private placement agency	1.23**	3.42	1.07*	2.92	0.62	1.86	0.59	1.80
Temp agency	−1.89***	0.15	−1.16**	0.31	−1.74***	0.18	−0.97*	0.38
Union	−0.44	0.64	−0.54	0.58	1.26	3.51	2.04	7.70
Education level								
Less than high school	−0.25	0.78	−0.24	0.78	−0.44	0.64	−0.49	0.61
Associate's degree	0.37	1.45	0.28	1.32	1.01*	2.74	1.03*	2.79
College graduate	0.66	1.93	0.66	1.94	0.08	1.09	0.04	1.04
Race								
Asian or other	2.25***	9.48	2.22***	9.24	−0.13	0.88	−0.09	0.91
Black	−0.99**	0.37	−0.93**	0.39	1.05	2.85	1.09	2.99
Hispanic	0.25	1.29	0.49	1.64	−0.60	0.55	−0.62	0.54
Female	0.01	1.01	0.06	1.06	−0.19	0.83	−0.20	0.82
English limited	0.70	2.01	0.74	2.09	−0.99**	0.37	−0.84*	0.43

Foreign-born	−1.73**	0.18	−1.63**	0.20	0.36	1.44	0.32	1.37
Training from LMI	0.83	2.28	0.92*	2.52	−0.49	0.61	−0.82	0.44
Job tenure	0.005**	1.005	0.005***	1.005	0.015***	1.015	0.014***	1.014
Training	1.04***	2.84	1.08***	2.94	0.59*	1.81	0.60*	1.83
Work experience	0.07	1.07	0.05	1.05	−0.04	0.96	−0.04	0.96
Work experience-squared	0.00*	1.00	0.00	1.00	0.00	1.00	0.00	1.00
Part-time	−2.33***	0.10	−2.29***	0.10	−1.91***	0.15	−1.81***	0.16
Union	1.68***	5.35	1.68***	5.37	0.00	0.00	−1.30**	0.27
Temporary job			−2.00***	0.14	0.00	0.00	−1.30**	0.27
Industry								
Agriculture, mining	1.67	5.31	1.45	4.26	1.18**	3.25	1.14**	3.14
Construction	−2.04**	0.13	−2.08**	0.13	0.73	2.08	0.78	2.18
FIRE	−0.35	0.70	−0.41	0.66	−0.95	0.39	−0.96	0.38
Public administration	0.47	1.61	0.85	2.33	0.34	1.41	0.41	1.51
Public transit	−0.49	0.61	−0.46	0.63	0.18	1.20	0.29	1.33
Retail	−0.40	0.67	−0.48	0.62	−0.39	0.68	−0.40	0.67
Services	−1.17**	0.31	−1.22**	0.29	0.42	1.53	0.40	1.50
Wholesale	1.06	2.89	1.85	6.35	−0.07	0.93	−0.03	0.97
Likelihood ratio	256.9		271.8		196.3		205.4	
c-statistic	0.838		0.851		0.757		0.771	
Number of cases	659		659		686		686	

Source: Authors' compilation.
*significant at the .10 level
**significant at the .05 level
***significant at the .01 level

Table 5.5 Benefits and LMIs, Milwaukee and Silicon Valley, Logistic Regressions (Dependent Variable: Health Insurance Available Through Employer)

	Milwaukee				Silicon Valley			
	Model 3		Model 4		Model 3		Model 4	
	Coefficient Estimate	Odds Ratio	Coefficient Estimate	Odds Ratio	Coefficient Estimate	Odds Ratio	Coefficient Estimate	Odds Ratio
Intercept	2.74***	0.00	3.62***	0.00	3.08***	0.00	3.15***	0.00
LMI use (most recent LMI job)								
Professional association	-3.49***	0.03	-3.89***	0.02	-0.56	0.57	0.77	2.15
Community and vocational college	-0.92	0.40	-1.13	0.32	-0.17	0.85	0.26	1.30
Nonprofit, government and CBO	-0.63	0.53	-0.67	0.51	1.10	3.00	1.67*	5.33
Private placement agency	1.54**	4.66	1.39*	4.02	0.95	2.59	0.87	2.40
Temp agency	-1.98***	0.14	-0.80	0.45	-2.02***	0.13	-0.25	0.78
Union	0.82	2.27	0.94	2.56	1.19	3.30	2.54*	12.65
Education level								
Less than high school	-1.47**	0.23	-1.91***	0.15	0.79	2.20	0.80	2.23
Associate's degree	-0.18	0.83	-0.35	0.71	0.13	1.14	0.13	1.14
College graduate	0.16	1.17	0.09	1.09	-0.02	0.98	-0.08	0.92
Race								
Asian or other	-1.53**	0.22	-1.92**	0.15	0.10	1.11	0.12	1.13
Black	-0.32	0.73	0.05	0.96	1.00	2.72	1.26	3.53
Hispanic	-0.40	0.67	-0.08	0.92	-1.08	0.34	-1.14	0.32
Female	0.03	1.03	0.20	1.22	-0.54	0.58	-0.51	0.60
English limited	0.11	1.11	0.15	1.17	-1.12**	0.33	-1.06*	0.35

	Model 1		Model 2		Model 3		Model 4	
Foreign-born	1.40*	4.07	1.95**	7.05	−0.61	0.54	−0.55	0.58
Training from LMI	0.50	1.65	0.60	1.83	0.64	1.90	0.37	1.44
Job tenure	0.006**	1.006	0.006**	1.006	0.004	1.004	0.002	1.002
Training	0.38	1.46	0.33	1.40	0.59	1.81	0.68	1.98
Work experience	−0.05	0.95	−0.09*	0.91	−0.05	0.95	−0.05	0.95
Work experience-squared	0.00	1.00	0.00	1.00	0.00	1.00	0.00	1.00
Part-time	−4.98***	0.01	−5.05***	0.01	−6.87***	0.00	−6.77***	0.00
Union	0.00	0.00	−2.96***	0.05	0.00	0.00	−2.78***	0.06
Temporary job			0.88	2.40	0.00	0.00	2.18***	8.85
Industry								
Agriculture, mining	1.63	5.1	1.48	4.4	1.93	6.90	2.14	8.53
Construction	−2.16**	0.12	−2.29**	0.10	−1.00	0.37	−0.85	0.43
FIRE	−0.72	0.49	−0.92	0.40	−0.87	0.42	−0.84	0.43
Public administration	−0.29	0.75	−0.03	0.97	0.10	1.11	0.73	2.07
Public transit	0.34	1.40	0.50	1.64	−1.11*	0.33	−1.10	0.33
Retail	−0.63	0.53	−0.95	0.39	0.39	1.47	0.32	1.38
Services	−0.59	0.55	−0.70	0.50	−0.72	0.49	−0.56	0.57
Wholesale	2.12**	8.32	3.35***	28.56	−0.50	0.61	−0.30	0.74
Likelihood ratio	250.16		273.07		221.97		256.04	
c-statistic	0.850		0.857		0.809		0.842	
Number of cases	659		659		686		686	

Source: Authors' compilation.
*significant at the .10 level
**significant at the .05 level
***significant at the .01 level

Table 5.6 Benefits and LMIs, Milwaukee and Silicon Valley, Logistic Regressions (Dependent Variable: Health Insurance Premium Paid Fully by Employer)

| | Milwaukee | | | | | |
| | Model 3 | | Model 4 | | Model 5 | |
	Coefficient Estimate	Odds Ratio	Coefficient Estimate	Odds Ratio	Coefficient Estimate	Odds Ratio
Intercept	−2.99**		−3.01**		−2.90**	
LMI use (most recent LMI job)						
Professional association	−0.52	0.59	−0.52	0.60	−0.49	0.62
Community and vocational college	−1.12	0.32	−1.12	0.33	−1.09	0.34
Nonprofit, government and CBO	−1.06	0.34	−1.08	0.34	−0.98	0.37
Private placement agency	0.51	1.66	0.51	1.66	0.63	1.88
Temp agency	−1.02	0.36	−1.14	0.32	−0.91	0.40
Union	0.59	1.81	0.60	1.81	0.60	1.82
Education level						
Associate's degree	−0.22	0.81	−0.21	0.81	−0.25	0.78
College graduate	1.08*	2.96	1.09*	2.97	1.03*	2.80
Less than high school	−2.89**	0.06	−2.88**	0.06	−2.14*	0.12
Race						
Asian or other	2.26***	9.58	2.27***	9.71	2.27***	9.72
Black	0.79	2.21	0.79	2.20	0.77	2.17
Hispanic	1.08	2.93	1.08	2.93	1.09	2.96
Female	−0.63	0.53	−0.63	0.53	−0.63	0.53
English limited	0.09	1.09	0.09	1.10	0.09	1.09
Foreign-born	−1.45**	0.23	−1.46**	0.23	−1.47*	0.23
Training from LMI	0.93	2.54	0.93	2.52	0.90	2.47
Job tenure	0.003	1.003	0.003	1.003	0.003	1.003
Training	−0.57	0.57	−0.57	0.57	−0.58	0.56

| | Silicon Valley | | | | |
| Model 3 | | Model 4 | | Model 5 | |
Coefficient Estimate	Odds Ratio	Coefficient Estimate	Odds Ratio	Coefficient Estimate	Odds Ratio
0.68		0.82	0.00	0.66	
0.57	1.78	1.26	3.54	0.49	1.63
−0.59	0.55	−0.53	0.59	−0.75	0.47
−1.40	0.25	−1.48	0.23	−1.85*	0.16
0.11	1.12	0.08	1.08	0.08	1.08
−2.18***	0.11	−1.42*	0.24	−2.21***	0.11
0.19	1.21	0.59	1.80	−0.24	0.79
0.88	2.41	0.86	2.35	0.93	2.52
−0.56	0.57	−0.62	0.54	−0.53	0.59
−0.69	0.50	−0.74	0.48	−0.72	0.49
0.05	1.05	0.07	1.07	0.04	1.04
0.95	2.59	1.02	2.76	1.01	2.75
0.02	1.02	−0.01	0.99	−0.0001	1.00
0.03	1.03	0.05	1.05	0.02	1.02
−0.69	0.50	−0.56	0.57	−0.69	0.50
0.10	1.11	0.08	1.08	0.09	1.09
−0.44	0.65	−0.52	0.59	−0.24	0.78
−0.003*	0.997	−0.004**	0.996	−0.004*	0.996
0.14	1.15	0.12	1.13	0.15	1.17

(*continued*)

Table 5.6   Benefits and LMIs, Milwaukee and Silicon Valley, Logistic Regressions (Dependent Variable: Health Insurance Premium Paid Fully by Employer) (*Continued*)

| | Milwaukee | | | | | |
| | Model 3 | | Model 4 | | Model 5 | |
	Coefficient Estimate	Odds Ratio	Coefficient Estimate	Odds Ratio	Coefficient Estimate	Odds Ratio
Work experience	0.01	1.01	0.01	1.01	0.01	1.01
Work experience-squared	−0.001	1.00	−0.001	1.00	−0.001	1.00
Part-time	−16.13***	0.00	−16.13***	0.00	−16.09***	0.00
Union	1.12**	3.05	1.12**	3.07	1.10**	3.01
Industry						
Agriculture, mining	−13.61***	0.00	−13.61***	0.00	−13.66***	0.00
Construction	−0.01	0.99	−0.01	0.99	0.03	1.03
FIRE	1.12*	3.08	1.12*	3.07	1.13*	3.08
Public administration	−1.15	0.32	−1.16	0.31	−1.09	0.34
Public transit	1.72**	5.59	1.71**	5.54	1.74**	5.72
Retail	0.86	2.36	0.86	2.36	0.83	2.30
Services	1.54*	4.67	1.54*	4.67	1.51*	4.51
Wholesale	0.51	1.66	0.51	1.66	0.42	1.53
Temporary job			0.19	1.21		
LMI effects for noncollege sample						
Private placement agency					−2.67*	0.070
Temp agency					−0.48	0.618
Other LMI[a]					−0.20	0.820
Likelihood ratio	256.9		271.8		261.4	
c-statistic	0.838		0.851		0.761	
Number of cases	596		596		596	

Source: Authors' compilation.

[a]Other LMI includes unions, community/vocational colleges, nonprofit, government, and community-based organizations and professional associations.

*significant at the .10 level

**significant at the .05 level

***significant at the .01 level

| | Silicon Valley | | | | | |
| Model 3 | | Model 4 | | Model 5 | | |
Coefficient Estimate	Odds Ratio	Coefficient Estimate	Odds Ratio	Coefficient Estimate	Odds Ratio
−0.10	0.90	−0.11	0.90	−0.10	0.90
0.002	1.00	0.002	1.00	0.002	1.00
−4.84***	0.01	−4.76***	0.01	−4.85***	0.01
0.80	2.21	0.81	2.26	0.78	2.19
4.31**	74.70	4.30**	73.71	4.37**	79.16
0.34	1.41	0.29	1.33	0.39	1.47
0.04	1.05	−0.01	0.99	0.07	1.07
−0.08	0.92	−0.06	0.94	−0.07	0.93
0.23	1.26	0.18	1.19	0.24	1.28
−1.08*	0.34	−1.16*	0.31	−1.06	0.35
0.16	1.17	0.18	1.20	0.18	1.20
−0.88	0.41	−0.94	0.39	−0.84	0.43
		−1.34**	0.26		
				0.13	1.14
				−0.26	0.77
				1.20	3.31
196.3		205.4		197.6	
0.757		0.771		0.683	
585		585		585	

this section, we explore some of the similarities and differences between our study and others, looking particularly at one study that finds similar results (Autor and Houseman 2005b) and one that does not (Andersson et al. 2005). We find that differences between the studies can be reconciled when we take into account the different populations and locations sampled and the different outcome and control measures used.

Studying welfare recipients transitioning to work in Michigan, Autor and Houseman (2005b) find that temporary agency placements result in lower earnings (in both the first quarter and subsequent quarters) than direct-hire placements. Although Autor and Houseman pursue numerous econometric strategies, their results are consistent: those who initially take temp agency placements earn substantially less per year over the subsequent two years than those who are placed in direct-hire positions. Those results are parallel to ours, and their study has the distinct advantage over numerous others in drawing on a near random assignment of workers to temp agency placements, thus helping limit concerns about the relationship between worker characteristics, self-selection into temp agency employment, and job outcomes.

Autor and Houseman's findings of negative impacts of temp agency use on earnings may seem surprising in light of recent work by Andersson, Holzer, and Lane (2005, 161), who report that, even though they find negative impacts from the contemporaneous employment of workers by temp agencies, they also find that use of a temporary help agency during either the first three years or the middle three years of the sample period had a *positive* and often significant effect on an individual's earnings during the last three years of the sample period. We consider this variation in results—both within the findings of Andersson and his colleagues and across different studies—to be an anomaly worth exploring.

Even though the empirical strategies used in both studies are significantly different from ours, we set out to replicate both specifications as closely as possible and to reconcile any differences between their results and ours. Here we first consider each specification in turn and then discuss how the results differ and why. Both studies draw on longitudinal quarterly earnings data drawn from the unemployment insurance system. Autor and Houseman focus on welfare recipients who were provided assistance in seeking employment from program service providers in one city in Michigan, measuring how those who were sent to temp agencies fared compared with others. Independent variables in their specification include controls for race, gender, age (and age-squared), education, earnings, and work experience in the previous four quarters. Autor and

Houseman's data are drawn from program participation spells that began between 1999 and 2003, a period that partially matches our survey's time frame.

To make the closest comparison we could with Autor and Houseman's sample, we restricted our analysis to Milwaukee, which is a closer match to Michigan's economy than Silicon Valley. To match Autor and Houseman's sample of welfare recipients, we tried two sample restrictions. First, we used only those Milwaukee respondents who reported that their household received public assistance in the past year. This gave us the closest match to Autor and Houseman's population but restricted the sample size. Second, we took advantage of the low-income phone prefix oversample strategy that had been developed for testing geographic effects and limited the sample to be tested to those with such prefixes in Milwaukee. To further control for differences in our samples, we included our full range of LMI controls (temp agencies, permanent placement agencies, unions, and so on) to account for the fact that those in our sample were pursuing multiple kinds of job placement strategies. Lacking the work history controls available in the UI data, we included our job tenure variable and used potential work experience in place of age.

Autor and Houseman's data measure actual earnings as reported to the UI system, while our measure of annual earnings is an estimate based on a point-in-time reporting of earnings on the LMI survey. To more closely match their specification, we generated an annual earnings measure from survey information. Respondents were asked for an earnings figure from their current or most recent job, and then a follow-up question regarding the basis of those earnings, with possible responses including hourly, weekly, biweekly, monthly, or annual. We inferred annual earnings from this information.

Our inferred annual earnings are, however, only an estimate. We needed a measure that could help us project whether the reported income in our snapshot was likely to persist for a full year. To create such a dummy variable, we made use of an interesting pattern in our data. As it turns out, those who reported their earnings on a biweekly, monthly, or annual basis seemed to have much more stable employment than those who reported their earnings on an hourly or weekly basis. Specifically, nearly one-quarter of those in low-income prefixes that reported income on an hourly or weekly basis were not employed at the time of the survey (and were reporting income on their last job). Given the usual relationships between current unemployment and the probability of unemployment,[7] this suggests that nearly half of this portion of the sample might experience unemployment in the coming year.[8] By contrast, nearly all of those who reported income on a biweekly or monthly basis were currently employed; those who reported on an annual basis had a current unemployment rate close to that of those in the hourly and weekly group, but they also had average job tenures for the previous job of almost seven years, and it was that job whose earnings they were reporting. (Recall that we can pick up currently unemployed individuals in our sample since they may be non-LMI users and the only requirement to be in the LMI sample was that one had obtained a job in the last three years through an LMI, not that one currently had it.) Thus, we proxy stable employment with a dummy variable ("Stable") that equals one if the respondent reported being paid on a biweekly, monthly, or annual basis.[9]

The results of the OLS estimations that apply these modifications are shown in columns 1 and 2 of table 5.7. The results are strikingly similar to Autor and Houseman's.[10] We estimate that compared with direct-hire placements, temporary job placements resulted in earnings that were lower by $3,026 annually for the Milwaukee public assistance households and by $3,885 for those in the Milwaukee low-income prefix sample. In comparison, Autor and Houseman (2005b, table 7, column 8) estimate a $3,566 annual pay difference in their two-stage least squares specification with fixed effects. For comparison with other results reported in this chapter, we also replicated the Autor and Houseman specification for log annual earnings using the Milwaukee low-income prefix sample (see column 3 of table 5.7) and then for the combined low-income prefix samples of both Milwaukee and Silicon Valley (column 4). The resulting percentage differentials are 11.6 percent and 4.7 percent, respectively. (The former is the percentage equivalent of the $3,885 estimated for Milwaukee in absolute terms.)

We now shift to constructing an earnings regression that is close in spirit to the work of Andersson, Holzer, and Lane (2005). To do so, several additional data considerations are needed: Andersson and his colleagues draw on panel data from the UI data system for individuals residing in five states over the nine-year period from 1993 to 2001, and their sample is restricted to persons with initially low earnings (less than $12,000 per year for each of the first three years of the nine-year period). The goal of their effort is to track these workers over time to gain insight into the evolution of earnings. They regress the natural log of quarterly earnings for the final three years of the sample period (1999 to 2001) on individual fixed effects, potential work experience and its square, job tenure and its square, firm fixed effects for an earlier period, interactions between tenure/squared tenure and those firm fixed effects, a dummy

Table 5.7   Autor and Houseman (2005b) Specification: Earnings and Temp Agency Use

	Milwaukee Only		Milwaukee and Silicon Valley
	Public Assistance Families	Low-Income Prefixes	
	Annual Earnings		Log Annual Earnings
	(1)	(2)	(3)	(4)
---	---	---	---	---
Intercept	37843.5***	37036.4***	10.310***	10.624***
LMI use (most recent LMI job)				
Temp agency	−3026.1	−3884.5*	−0.116	−0.047
Private placement agency	117.0	791.0	0.033	0.122
Union	6005.7	8849.0	0.265	0.164
Nonprofit, government and CBO	−4147.2	−2540.1	−0.173	−0.633*
Community and vocational college	5298.4	4196.8	0.077	0.171
Professional association	−42572.6***	−31330.8***	−2.005***	−0.222
Education level				
Less than high school	−5474.3	−3199.0	−0.019	0.185*
High school dropout	−1552.6	−789.0	0.088	0.042
College or more	−511.2	1499.2	0.074	−0.067
Race				
Black	−3712.0	−5648.8*	−0.192*	−0.287*
Hispanic	−5900.2	−4983.7	−0.127	−0.346**
Asian or other	−5561.9	−12751.6***	−0.602***	−0.129
Work experience	−977.7	−317.0	−0.006	−0.038**
Work experience-squared	22.9	3.7	−0.00001	0.001**

(continued)

Table 5.7   Autor and Houseman (2005b) Specification:
Earnings and Temp Agency Use (*Continued*)

	Milwaukee Only		Milwaukee and Silicon Valley
	Public Assistance Families	Low-Income Prefixes	
	Annual Earnings		Log Annual Earnings	
	(1)	(2)	(3)	(4)
Job tenure	117.5*	14.5	0.001**	0.002***
Stable	3788.8	6636.0***	0.219*	0.399***
English limited	2056.2	−3757.3	−0.156	−0.343***
Foreign-born	−3502.9	−3807.5	−0.220	−0.001
Female	−13602.6***	−7532.1***	−0.271***	−0.238***
Silicon Valley sample			0.360***	0.354***
R-squared	0.536	0.389	0.313	0.490
Number of cases	76	211	211	492

Source: Authors' compilation.
*significant at the .10 level
**significant at the .05 level
***significant at the .01 level

variable for having been employed for the full quarter, and, finally, a dummy variable indicating whether the individual used a temp agency during either the first three years or the middle three years of the period.

Andersson and his colleagues collected a limited set of variables on the same individuals over a nine-year time span; indeed, their individual (and firm) fixed effects were derived through panel regression techniques and are meant to stand in for the human capital variables they lacked. We, on the other hand, had cross-sectional data that were far richer in terms of variables that captured individual labor market and human capital characteristics, but we did not have data over time. Most critically, in the LMI survey we did not know who was low-income some years before—we only had their income now. To use current income as a way to restrict the sample would bias the results by eliminating all those who moved up in earnings. To proxy past low-income status, we restricted the regression again to individuals living in low-income telephone prefixes. Our logic was that those who had seen their economic prospects improve might wait some time before moving from a low-income area and so such a geographically constrained sample would be close to one that captures individuals with initial low incomes. Given our data, this seemed like the best way to construct a parallel sample.

As for our key explanatory variable—temp agency use—our earlier regressions had generally relied on a dummy variable that indicated whether a temp agency was used to obtain the *most recent* LMI job held during the three years prior to the survey. A more appropriate parallel to Andersson et al. (2005) is whether a temp agency was used to obtain *any job* that was held during the three years prior to the survey—very similar to their middle-three-years dummy variable—and so we utilized that construction instead. We applied the broad rather than the narrow definition of temp agency when classifying LMI use for the last job. We did this to set the highest bar for hypothesis-testing, given our hypothesis that temp agencies are associated with lower wages and the finding we were trying to replicate from Andersson et al. (2005) that temp agencies are associated in a positive way with earnings. Of course, a bias working in the other direction was the fact that while our specification allowed for the use of a temp agency sometime prior to the reported earnings, the temp agency use could be contemporaneous. Therefore, we could not capture the lagged effect of temp agencies as well as Andersson and his colleagues did, but this was as close as we would get with this dataset. By using a broad definition of temp agency, we hoped to be stacking the cards against ourselves in the hypothesis testing.

In addition to temp agency use, we included several other explanatory variables that control for the respondent-specific human capital and labor market characteristics picked up by the individual fixed effects used by Andersson and his colleagues. These include geographic region, gender, potential work experience and its square, dummy variables for significant breaks in education status (high school and above, BA degree and better), job tenure and its square, ethnicity, limited English-language ability, and nativity; some of these variables, particularly the quadratic specification for job tenure, are slightly different than what we used in our own preferred wage regressions earlier, but are closer to the variables deployed in Andersson et al. (2005, 94–101). In some runs we also added controls for industry to proxy the firm-specific effects utilized by

Andersson and his colleagues. Finally, Andersson and his colleagues included a dummy variable for whether the individual was engaged in a full quarter's worth of work, on the logical grounds that spells of unemployment lower earnings. To proxy this, we included our employment stability measure discussed earlier.[11]

With this regression specification in place, we first calculated the effects on the log of annual earnings. (Because of the construction of our earnings variable, the results for quarterly and annual earnings will be identical.) The regression results on log earnings turn out to be remarkably similar to those obtained by Andersson and his colleagues: for the use of a temp agency, we obtain a coefficient of 0.106 (column 2, table 5.8; marginally significant at $p = 0.25$) that matches the Andersson et al. (2005, 101) estimate of 0.103 almost exactly. The addition of industry controls (column 3, table 5.8) reduces both our coefficient and the t-statistic by about one-half, similar to the results obtained when Andersson et al. (2005) enter firm effects.[12]

What explains the difference between these findings and those that mirror the Autor and Houseman (2005b) specification? One critical difference in the specifications is the use of the alternative measure of temp agency usage and the elimination of controls for other kinds of LMI use. This suggests that how we specify temp agency use and which other alternative job-finding mechanisms are controlled are critical in measuring the impact of temp agency use. In particular, both our original specification and Autor and Houseman's make an explicit comparison between temp agency placements and direct-hire placements. The Andersson et al. (2005) specification, in contrast, implicitly compares outcomes for former temp agency users to all other outcomes. In addition, the use of the quadratic form for job tenure increases the estimated return to job tenure considerably. Since temp agency users are likely to have low levels of job tenure, this reallocation leads to an assignment of higher relative return to temp agency use.

But the most important difference we wish to probe is the difference between these positive results of temp use on earnings—which we were able to reproduce with our dataset—and the negative results highlighted in our earlier analysis. In our view, one critical factor is the focus on earnings and not wages: lack of information on usual hours worked per week is one drawback of the UI data utilized by these other authors. When we reproduced the specification of Andersson and his colleagues using our log hourly wages as the dependent variable, the coefficient on temp agency use once again turned negative (a coeffi-

Table 5.8 Andersson et al. (2005) Specification: Log Annual Earnings and Temp Agency Use, Low-Income Telephone Prefixes in Milwaukee and Silicon Valley

Model	(1)	(2)	(3)
Intercept	10.523***	10.395***	10.081***
Temp agency use (any job, broad definition)	0.060	0.106	0.053
Education level			
High school and above (no BA)	0.014	0.026	0.049
College and more	−0.026	0.001	0.135
Race			
Black	−0.327**	−0.279**	−0.292**
Hispanic	−0.334**	−0.294**	−0.333***
Asian or other	−0.093	−0.069	−0.073
Work experience	−0.038**	−0.041**	−0.032*
Work experience-squared	0.001	0.001*	0.001
Job tenure	0.002***	0.006***	0.006***
Job tenure-squared		−0.00002***	−0.00002***
Stable	0.395***	0.382***	0.354***
English limited	−0.281***	−0.262***	−0.259***
Foreign-born	0.027	0.003	−0.076
Female	−0.266***	−0.258***	−0.196**
Industry			
Agriculture, mining			0.726***
Construction			0.399***
FIRE			0.491***
Public administration			0.127
Public transit			0.292**
Retail			0.320***
Wholesale			−0.088
Armed forces			0.000***
Manufacturing			0.337***
Unemployed, not classified			0.339*

(continued)

Table 5.8   Andersson et al. (2005) Specification: Log Annual
Earnings and Temp Agency Use, Low-Income Telephone
Prefixes in Milwaukee and Silicon Valley (*Continued*)

Model	(1)	(2)	(3)
Silicon Valley sample	0.365***	0.372***	0.464***
R-squared	0.439	0.458	0.502
Number of cases	492	492	492

Source: Authors' compilation.
*significant at the .10 level
**significant at the .05 level
***significant at the .01 level

cient of −0.039; see column 1, table 5.9). When industry controls were entered (a coefficient of −0.077; see column 2, table 5.9), the result became significant at the 0.20 level, with a t-statistic well above one (a usual marker of interest in such a small sample). When we reverted to using the whole sample from both regions and to our preferred measure of temp agency use (whether the respondent's last job was obtained though a temp agency, not whether he or she used a temp agency at some point in the past) and entered controls for the other possible intermediary types as well as for industries, we found a negative impact of 14.6 percent on wages that is statistically significant at the .05 level (column 3, table 5.9). Remaining differences between these results and those we reported in table 5.3 are accounted for by other changes in the specification: the inclusion of job tenure-squared, the variable for stability of schedule, and other controls for human capital and job training available in our dataset.

What explains the range of results that we find here for workers in low-income areas? There are three relevant factors. First, the results for hourly wages are consistently negative regardless of specification: those working in temp agency placements earned lower hourly wages than comparable workers who obtained work through other means. Second, the inclusion of other controls for factors such as industry, job characteristics, and measures of human capital (including training) matters for both the magnitude and significance of the estimated effect, with additional controls generally increasing both. Finally, the estimated relationship between temp agency use and total earnings depends on how we control for other LMI usage.

Table 5.9   Alternative Specifications: Log Hourly Wages and Temp Agency Use, Low-Income Telephone Prefixes in Milwaukee and Silicon Valley

	Low-Income Prefixes		Whole Sample
	(1)	(2)	(3)
Intercept	2.827***	2.637***	2.454***
Temp agency use (any job, broad definition)	−0.039	−0.077	
LMI use (most recent LMI job)			
Temp agency			−0.146**
Private placement agency			0.205***
Union			0.085
Nonprofit, government and CBO			−0.167**
Community and vocational college			−0.034
Professional association			−0.076
Race			
Black	−0.303***	−0.297***	−0.199***
Hispanic	−0.307***	−0.335***	−0.217***
Asian or other	−0.025	−0.022	0.033
Education level			
High school dropout			−0.224***
Associate's degree			0.096
High school and above (no BA)	0.123*	0.125*	
College and more	0.164	0.239**	0.324***
Work experience	−0.034**	−0.027**	−0.0012
Work experience-squared	0.001**	0.001**	0.00002
Job tenure	0.004***	0.004**	0.002***
Job tenure-squared	−0.00001**	−0.00001**	
Stable	0.190***	0.166**	0.233***
English limited	−0.288***	−0.284***	−0.085
Foreign-born	0.031	−0.014	−0.106
Female	−0.110*	−0.087	−0.216***

(continued)

Table 5.9   Alternative Specifications: Log Hourly Wages and Temp Agency Use, Low-Income Telephone Prefixes in Milwaukee and Silicon Valley (*Continued*)

	Low-Income Prefixes		Whole Sample
	(1)	(2)	(3)
Industry			
Agriculture, mining		0.920***	−0.121
Construction		0.266**	0.231**
FIRE		0.360***	0.344***
Public administration		0.027	−0.023
Public transit		0.087	0.027
Retail		0.165	0.023
Wholesale		0.185	0.167
Armed forces		0.000***	0.000***
Manufacturing		0.207**	0.151***
Unemployed, not classified		0.130	0.111
Silicon Valley sample	0.418***	0.404***	0.365***
R-squared	0.527	0.561	0.499
Number of cases	495	495	1017

Source: Authors' compilation.
*significant at the .10 level
**significant at the .05 level
***significant at the .01 level

With regard to the last point, when we control for other LMI usage along with temp usage and the relevant comparison is between jobs obtained through temp agencies and jobs obtained by direct hire, we find a negative earnings impact for temp agency use. This is the format we use in table 5.3 and when replicating Autor and Houseman's work. When we mirror Andersson and his colleagues' specification, however, we eliminate controls for other LMIs and use the broadest possible measure of previous temp agency use. In this case, the implicit comparison is between temp agency use and all other labor market outcomes, and we estimate a positive impact of temp agencies on earnings. Given that the same specification yields a negative impact of temp agency use on hourly wages, this can only suggest that those who have used temp agencies increase their earnings relative to the mix of *all* other labor market participants through increases in their hours of work or the stability of their work schedule. The same is not true, however, when we compare temp agency users with direct-hire placements; comparing these two groups directly makes clear that the earnings (as well as the hourly wages) of temp agency users still fall short.

But the distinction between earnings and wages is also quite critical. It may be useful to qualify the finding of Andersson and his colleagues (2005, 100) that temp agencies "help initial low earners by improving their access to better jobs" by clarifying that "better" may refer only to *more* work, while the hourly return to that work is still lower. Furthermore, this statement may hold only for temp users relative to other LMI users and not relative to direct-hire placements, another alternative for LMI use. Combined with our earlier findings regarding the lower availability of benefits such as employer-provided health insurance or pensions for temp agency users, these qualifications cast doubt on the efficacy of temp agency use for low-wage workers as a means to better outcomes.

Summary

We find interesting and provocative correlations between intermediary use, type of intermediary used, and the nature of job outcomes for workers in Silicon Valley and Milwaukee. In both regions, temporary agency use is consistently and strongly associated with lower hourly wages and lesser availability of employer-provided pensions and health insurance. This holds true even after controlling for detailed worker and job characteristics and after separating the effect of temp agencies from temporary job placements per se. We also frequently find correspondingly positive effects associated with the use of private placement agencies and headhunters, although these effects are sometimes limited to those with a college education.

Significantly, we find few other clear relationships in either region between outcomes and the use of other types of labor market intermediaries—professional associations, community and vocational colleges, unions, and nonprofit or government agencies. This lack of apparent relationship may be due to too few observations in these groups or to inadequate precision in defining these categories. By necessity, we grouped together very different kinds of agencies—for instance, including neighborhood churches, federally funded job centers, and welfare-to-work programs under the rubric of nonprofit and government agencies. Further, we know that even within homogenous groups of intermediaries, individuals receive very different services. If, as many have argued, only a few very well structured programs are able to make a difference for disadvantaged workers, our analysis certainly cannot pinpoint those programs. We observed in chapter 4 that nontemp intermediaries often bring considerably more resources to the support of their clients. Yet in the analysis here, there is no evidence that these agencies as a group have any strong positive effects on worker outcomes. If true, this might suggest that the policy focus needs to turn to the general determinants of job quality rather than the structure and services of intermediary organizations.

Finally, we have reconciled our findings with two other studies that highlight the impact of temp agency use on earnings for low-income workers. Our results suggest that differences across specifications largely depend on how the relevant comparison groups are specified and on whether we model annual earnings or hourly wages. Hourly wage and annual earnings outcomes are clearly negative for temp agency users from low-income areas when they are compared with direct-hire placements. The same lower-income temp agency users may have an annual earnings advantage over other labor market participants generally, but the root of this advantage seems to lie in the greater number of hours they work, not in a higher hourly wage. Furthermore, our work here stresses a broader focus on job quality, one that emphasizes not only wage and earnings levels but also access to health insurance and pension plans. It is for policymakers and others to decide which of these foci are more important at any given time and for any given population.

Chapter Six

The Role of Social Capital in Choosing
Labor Market Intermediaries

Many workers solve the dual problem of job-seeking—that is, how to collect information about jobs and how to signal their reliability to employers through referrals—without using formal intermediaries. One could, for example, seek employment possibilities via newspaper classified ads, the Internet, and other outlets, and then use an elegantly written résumé to seize an employer's attention. Many job-seekers also use social networks (Fernandez and Weinberg 1997; Granovetter 1995). As noted in chapter 4, around 23 percent of our survey respondents used friends to secure employment, while 8 percent were in a family business or self-employed.[1]

Not all labor market participants, however, find that their networks of friends and family are broad enough or effective enough to help them find employment. For those living in conditions of concentrated poverty and already facing problems of spatial mismatch, inadequate transportation, and other challenges (Jargowsky 1997; Pastor and Adams 1996; Wilson 1996), networks that lead to better opportunity seem especially important. However, recent studies suggest that the limited connections of friends and family for job-seekers living in such situations may steer them toward lower-wage opportunities (Johnson et al. 1999; Pastor and Marcelli 2000). Indeed, one of the reasons for the growing policy interest in the potential of LMIs by those concerned about low-income individuals, especially those who live in poorer neighbor-hoods, is to help connect job-seekers who have weaker or less efficacious social networks with better employment opportunities (Harrison and Weiss 1998; Massey and Shibuya 1995).

What is the relationship between "social capital" (or networks) and the use of intermediaries? In this chapter, we look at which survey respondents used or did not use an LMI to secure employment. In a multivariate logit analysis, we control for various characteristics that might be associated with LMI use (for example, whether the individual tends to enter the labor market frequently and so might be more likely to use many means of job search) and test for the effect of social capital. The central finding of this exercise—and one that supports the theories of the importance of social networks in shaping labor-market outcomes—is that those labor market participants with higher levels of social capital or more social connections are less likely to select into the group of LMI users.

Of course, even within this group, there is some variation in the level of social capital, and we make use of this variation to try to see whether social capital makes a difference in terms of which sort of LMI is utilized by job-seekers. The notion here is that better social connections may help one choose or find a higher-quality LMI, perhaps because of the additional information afforded by those in one's social circle. We first test this notion on the entire sample. We find that while social capital has a significant negative effect on the probability of using either private-sector temporary or permanent placement agencies over no LMI, its effect on the probability of using any of the other LMI types is not sta-tistically significant.[2] We also estimate these relationships for subgroups of the population (by location, ethnicity, and gender). Across cases, we consistently find that those with higher levels of social capital or social connection are more likely to avoid temp agencies as well as permanent placement agencies.

Finally, we consider the intersection of social capital and geography. Social capital, after all, is at least partly about overcoming geographic divides: farther-reaching network connections help one go past local horizons to secure employ-ment. However, those living in poor communities may also find that their own social capital, however rich in friends, is less useful at this task: since many net-works are neighborhood-based (Sampson and Groves 1989) and their own neighborhoods are poor, their social connections may not necessarily facilitate job-finding. Thus, we also examine the relative impacts of social capital on LMI choices for those living in lower-income areas. We find results that are different from those for the overall sample: in lower-income areas, social capital turns out to have a negligible effect in reducing LMI use in general, but it has some influence on the type of LMI used. One interesting difference is that in the low-income prefixes social capital also has the effect of guiding people toward nonprofit and government LMI types. This may indicate a positive effect of social capital given the low overall performance of temp agencies with regard to labor market outcomes, but given the mixed performance of nonprofits, any conclusions in this regard would require more careful case study research and analysis of specific LMIs.

We begin the next section by defining our key measure of social connectedness, or social capital, and offering some simple comparative statistics. We then develop and test a model of the likelihood of using an LMI and add the social capital variable to it. We go on to explore whether social connectedness plays any role in the sorting into different types of LMIs. We also investigate whether the impact of social capital differs if we limit the geographical boundaries of our analysis to lower-income areas. We conclude with a brief discussion of the implications of this social capital analysis for research and policy.

Measuring Social Capital

Although recent analysis suggests that social capital can play an important role in individuals' labor market experiences (Lichter and Oliver 2000; Pastor and Marcelli 2000), measuring social capital presents a challenge. After all, we could easily ask about a respondent's level of schooling and thus arrive at a rough measure of human capital. Asking a respondent about his or her level of social capital, however, is likely to draw a blank stare.

Previous work has tried to approximate social capital either with neighborhood quality measures (based on the notion that networks are often geographic; see O'Regan 1993; Pastor and Adams 1996) or with more direct questions about the particular people in a respondent's social circle, how close the respondent is to the identified persons (by, say, degree of a favor that might be asked of each person), and the relative position of each identified person in the labor market and social hierarchy (Johnson, Oliver, and Bobo 1994). In designing our own survey measure for a respondent's interactions with others, we built from questions on previous survey instruments provided to us by colleagues (for descriptions of these instruments, see Briggs 1998; Johnson et al. 1994; Marcelli and Heer 1997). We were able to ask questions of all respondents in three social interaction areas that squared well with previous work on social capital: the number and type of meetings the respondent attends; the tendency to communicate regularly with friends and/or relatives; and the respondent's subjective feeling about how many friends or relatives he or she might be able to ask for help in finding a job.[3] Because of the era in which the survey was conducted—as well as the location, particularly Silicon Valley—we also looked at a measure of connectedness not usually used in social capital studies: the use of the Internet as a communication device.

We combined these four dimensions of interaction into a single measure of social connectedness that took a value of one if the respondent (1) had attended at least three different types of meetings in the past year, (2) talked to close friends or relatives at least once a week, (3) had at least one to two friends or relatives whom they would feel comfortable asking for help finding a job, and (4) had access to the Internet. We tested this variable, which could be constructed for nearly the whole sample, against the answers for a smaller group of respondents who were asked far more detailed questions about their social networks. These were respondents who had not used LMIs, and so there was time in the interview frame to go into detail on either their actual or potential use of friends to find employment; the downside was that since none of these respondents had used LMIs, none of those measures could be used directly in the tests considered in this chapter. However, as we note in the appendix, the very high and statistically significant correlation between our crude but broad measure for nearly all respondents and these more complex measures that were limited to a subsample of non-LMI users give us confidence in the more limited measure used here.

Although we find the combination of meetings, communication, willingness to use friendship networks for employment, and use of the Internet for communication to be a theoretically satisfying construction of social capital, there may be some concerns. For example, is the use of friends, like the use of an LMI, just one means of job search, and so a negative relationship simply reflects the straightforward outcome of addition and subtraction? Recall, however, that we are not contrasting the actual use of friends to obtain employment with the use of LMIs; we are contrasting respondents' ability to identify a hypothetical employment network with their use of LMIs. These strategies are not necessarily related in theory or even in these data—a person who has not utilized his social network to find employment may still have a network that *would* be useful should the occasion arise. In any case, we estimated a series of models in which we dropped this component, and the pattern of results was very similar to our preferred measure.

We discuss Internet access and other methodological issues in more detail in the appendix, but the broadest concern about Internet access as a variable is that it is itself a method of job search, not just a signal of social capital, and hence there could be an issue of identification, as with friends. We should stress, however, that having Internet access for communication is not the same thing as using it for job search. We are not simply labeling everyone with Internet access "socially connected," but instead using Internet access to differentiate between those who have already passed, say, the attendance at meetings restriction. In fact, there is some evidence that the group that is socially connected as measured by our other measures tends to use the Internet more for communication than for job search, further alleviating identification concerns and actually imposing a much stricter test on our composite measure.[4] Moreover, there is now a growing literature about the relationship between Internet access and social capital. For example, one study at the neighborhood level indicates that having Internet access in one's community is positively correlated with other community characteristics that can be taken to indicate a "socially connected" community, such as participation in community organizations that address local problems, sports leagues, youth groups, religious organizations, and community charities (Dutta-Bergman 2005). In another study at the individual level, Dhavan V. Shah, Nojin Kwak, and Lance Holbert (2001) find that the use of the Internet as a medium of informational exchange was significantly related to increased engagement in community activities. A final issue regarding the Internet access variable may be that the use of the Internet is often related to income; since many LMI users tend to have lower incomes, perhaps causality is running in the other direction. For this reason, we ran a series of regressions that either dropped Internet access alone or dropped both the number of friends who could help with job search (discussed previously) and the Internet; the pattern of results was nevertheless the same.

Although these results help to assuage concerns over the inclusion of Internet access as a component in our social capital measure, it may still be the case that the Internet itself is an important explanatory variable in predicting LMI use, outside of its role of filtering out the "socially connected" from those passing the other three criteria in our composite measure. This could justify its inclusion as a separate independent variable in our models. Recall that our reason for including Internet access in our composite measure is that it is increasingly being used as a communication device and therefore a facilitator of social capital. However, based on two other aspects—its use as an alternative job search mechanism and its positive correlation with income—we would expect it to have a negative effect on LMI use. To determine whether Internet access itself is an important explanatory variable in predicting LMI use, we also ran the regressions discussed later in this chapter with Internet access included as a separate independent variable, along with the version of our social capital measure that excludes Internet access, and found its coefficient to be positive but highly insignificant—the opposite of what we would expect if we had the concerns just discussed. For all these theoretical and empirical reasons, we feel confident about including Internet access in our social capital measure.

Finally, for good measure, we dropped the indicator of how often the respondent communicated with close friends or relatives, leaving us with a measure of social connectedness based solely on meetings. While communicating with friends and relatives is a reasonable measure of social capital or connectedness, it can also simply indicate a closer family rather than the "strength of weak ties" that is so essential to employment and is perhaps better captured by simply the willingness to go to meetings. Once again, paring back a component of the measure does not change the basic pattern of results; indeed, any component of the measure (save the base measure of meetings attended) can be dropped and the pattern of results is the same. We therefore stick with the four-dimensional measure—which eventually identified about one-fourth of the sample as socially connected—both because we find it to be more theoretically appealing and because our preferred measure is the most robust of all the variations considered across the many subgroups that we included.

Who Chooses to Use an LMI?

As can be seen from figure 6.1, there is a dramatic difference in the likelihood of using an LMI when we consider the sample split by our measure of social capital or connectedness. Considering both regions, those who were "socially connected" had an incidence of LMI use of 20 percent; for those who were not socially connected, the incidence rate was 31 percent. The gaps are quite similar if we break the sample down by region (also depicted in figure 6.1).

Do the gaps revealed in this simple comparison hold up once we control for the other variables that might predict the likelihood of LMI use? To conduct this multivariate analysis of who uses an LMI, we developed a logistic model in which the dependent or "response" variable was a dummy for having held a job during the three years prior to the survey that was obtained through an LMI. We then regressed this against a series of human capital variables similar to

Figure 6.1   LMI Users by Social Connectedness

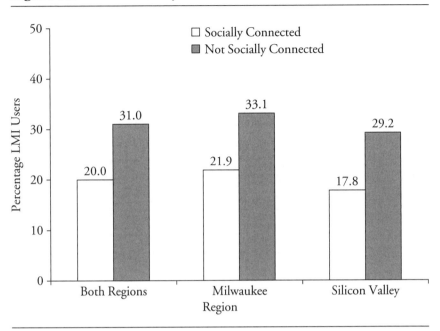

Source: Authors' compilation.

those used in models to predict employment versus unemployment, with a few modifications to reflect the specificities of analyzing LMI use and this sample.

On the right-hand side of our regression, we entered the usual demographic and locational variables (gender, race, and marital status, as well as residence in Silicon Valley or Milwaukee when we pooled the two regional samples). We also used age and its squared value, with the notion that it might be the very young and those in the last years of their work life who are more likely to turn to help in navigating the labor market; there was little difference in the basic regression if we instead used a potential work experience measure.[5] As controls for education, we used dummy variables for two educational levels that we would expect to have an impact on the use of LMIs: having some level of education higher than a high school diploma but not a bachelor's degree (measured by the variable "above high school education [no BA])", and having earned a bachelor's degree or higher (measured by the variable "college and more").[6] Our view was that both of these gradients of educational attainment might correlate with additional knowledge of the labor market and job search institutions, but that the way in which they affect LMI use could differ.

In addition to these measures of education level, we also included a temporal measure for education, that is, of when training was completed or a degree was earned. This measure takes the form of another dummy variable labeled "received degree in last three years" and takes a value of one for all respondents who completed their highest degree, at whatever level, during the three years prior to the survey and a value of zero otherwise.[7] It was included to control for the high likelihood that those who had experienced a recent increase in educational level would be actively searching for a job and perhaps have a higher proclivity to try out the many existing avenues of job search, including LMIs.

Respondents also reported on the number of different jobs they had held in the past three years; from this, we created a dummy called "frequent job changer" that equaled one for those who had held three or more jobs in that time period. This variable is meant to pick up volatility, voluntary or otherwise, that might lead to LMI use.[8]

We also used a variable, "English limited," that was set equal to one if the respondent reported that he or she could not speak English "very well." This specification of limited English-language ability is common in the literature on labor market outcomes (see, for example, Reimers 1985; Trejo 1997); our thought in this case was that such individuals might face particular challenges in employment but that they would also face challenges in reaching out to LMIs, many of which do not offer multilingual services. Finally, we included a dummy variable for having someone living in the respondent's household who is on welfare ("household member on welfare"), hoping to pick up any effects that being low-income might have on a person's social network or lack thereof—without necessarily being synonymous with his or her wage outcome—and therefore on their need to use an LMI.

We first ran the regression using all the base variables, that is, without including our key measure of social connectedness.[9] All the binomial logit regressions discussed here and the multinomial logits to follow were run using survey regression techniques to account for the complex sampling and weighting involved in the survey.[10] We report the results in the first column of table 6.1; in that table and the ones that follow, rather than including the parameter estimates on each of the explanatory variables from the regression (which are not so easily interpreted), we simply report an estimate of the marginal effect that variable has on the dependent. This effect approximates the average increase or decrease in the

Table 6.1 Logit Model on the Probability of Using an LMI, Both Regions

Explanatory Variables	All, Not Controlling for Social Capital		All, Controlling for Social Capital		Males		Females	
	Marginal Effect	Significance	Marginal Effect	Significance	Marginal Effect	Significance	Marginal Effect	Significance
Silicon Valley sample	-4.1%		-5.0%	#	-9.8%	*	-3.0%	
Female	-4.6		-3.8		—		—	
Age	1.1		1.7	#	1.8		1.8	
Age-squared	-0.0		-0.0	*	-0.0		-0.0	#
Above high school education (no BA)	10.4	#	11.1	*	3.8		20.6	**
College or more	-2.1		0.4		4.7		-3.2	
Received degree in last three years	-1.6		-1.2		8.4		-9.3	#
Hispanic	-5.4		-5.0		-3.4		-4.9	
Black	23.0	**	24.0	***	20.2		28.2	***
Asian or other	3.8		3.9		-0.4		11.9	
Married	-2.3		-0.6		-1.0		0.4	
English limited	4.1		3.5		4.0		2.3	

(continued)

Table 6.1 Logit Model on the Probability of Using an LMI, Both Regions (*Continued*)

Explanatory Variables	All, Not Controlling for Social Capital		All, Controlling for Social Capital		Males		Females	
	Marginal Effect	Significance	Marginal Effect	Significance	Marginal Effect	Significance	Marginal Effect	Significance
Frequent job changer	23.3	***	23.6	***	21.6	***	29.9	***
Household member on welfare	2.6		0.9		−14.9	*	7.3	
Socially connected	—		−13.3	***	−13.3	**	−14.7	***
Number of cases	1,241		1,241		596		645	
F-statistic	2.81		4.17		1.84		4.87	
Probability > F	0.0004		0.0000		0.0286		0.0000	
Pseudo R-squared	0.0674		0.0724		0.0684		0.0846	
Percent predicted correctly	0.7331		0.7359		0.7008		0.7722	

Source: Authors' compilation.
Note: Response variable: dummy variable that is equal to one if respondent used an LMI during the three years prior to the survey.
*significant at .10 level
**significant at .05 level
***significant at .01 level
#significant at .20 level

probability of using an LMI for changes in that variable, with interpretation easiest for the dummy variables that can move only from zero to one. The statistical significance is based on the calculated probability levels from the marginal effects and parallels those for the actual regression coefficients.[11]

Before we describe the results, a few words of caution are in order. First, as with studies of the location of environmental hazards in minority communities (see, for example, Sadd et al. 1999), this is less a causal model of LMI use than a multivariate map of the factors associated with those who use and do not use LMIs. Second, we do not have the whole world of those who sort into LMIs; because of the nature of our survey sampling strategy, we have only those who actually found jobs through LMIs, and so we have no specific information on individuals who tried to use an LMI but found employment through other search mechanisms (although such individuals may be in our non-LMI group), perhaps because the LMI served them poorly or perhaps because other methods yielded payoffs more quickly.

As can be seen in the first regression without social capital, there is a negative but insignificant effect for living in Silicon Valley, as there is for being female. Age is positively correlated with LMI use up to a certain point, but the negative coefficient on the age-squared variable indicates that, as we might expect, the effect diminishes in later years—it is likely that more experience allows one to use other means of job search. The education dummies show that having more than a high school diploma but less than a BA makes an individual about 10 percent more likely to use an LMI than someone with a high school diploma or less (the effect is significant at the .20 level). There is no significant effect on LMI use, however, for having either a BA or higher, or for having completed one's education recently. When we estimate this regression for Silicon Valley and Milwaukee separately (not shown in the table because the results are mostly similar for each region), we find that the positive coefficient on having more than a high school diploma but less than a BA is largely a Silicon Valley effect. This squares with both our qualitative results in chapter 3 and our descriptive findings in chapter 4 that suggest that there are many more intermediaries serving people with associate's degrees or higher in Silicon Valley.

The dummy variable for being black is one of the two highly significant variables in the regression: it increases the probability of LMI use by about 23 percent. The high job turnover variable, "frequent job changer," is significant at the .01 level, showing an increased probability of LMI use of just over 23 percent for respondents of this type. Having someone in the house on welfare has the expected positive effect, although it is quite insignificant. To gauge the overall "goodness of fit," we calculated a pseudo R-squared in addition to the reported F-statistic; it suggests that we can explain about 7 percent of the variation in LMI use. Although this seems to be a relatively low level of explanatory power, this is quite typical of the figures for pseudo R-squareds in logit estimations.

When we add our measure of social capital to the model, the pseudo R-squared value increases, and the coefficient on the social capital variable itself, "socially connected," is also negative and significant at better than the .01 level (see column 2 of table 6.1). The marginal effect calculation indicates that those who were socially connected were about 13 percent *less* likely to use an LMI, or more precisely, to have held a job in the past three years that was obtained through an LMI. Interestingly, the estimated marginal effects are quite stable for the other significant variables, indicating that we are not simply "stealing" significance from another important but collinear variable. When we run the regression for Silicon Valley and Milwaukee separately, we also find that the negative effect of being socially connected on the probability of being in the LMI user group is very stable in both locations, with nearly identical statistical significance and a marginal effect that differs only by about 2.5 percent (see column 1 of tables 6.2 and 6.3).[12]

Although the effect that social capital has on LMI use does not differ much overall by region, there is considerable difference if we split the sample by race or gender. Simple comparisons show a gap in the percentage of LMI users of nearly 12 percent between females who were socially connected and those who were not; by contrast, the gap for men is less than 10 percent (see figure 6.2). There are also fairly clear differences by race within the sample. Figure 6.3 shows that virtually all groups show an increase in LMI use for those who were less socially connected; however, the difference is especially striking for African Americans. One interesting exception to the general pattern is that of Hispanics: those who were socially connected (as we have defined it) and those who were not had roughly equivalent levels of LMI use.

How do these differences manifest themselves in the regression analysis? The last two columns of table 6.1 show the results when the sample is split between males and females. The "socially connected" variable is significant for both groups, but it has both a larger marginal effect and a higher level of significance for female respondents. The number of recent employers is significant for both

(*text continues on page 188*)

Table 6.2 Logit Model on the Probability of Using an LMI, Silicon Valley

Explanatory Variables	Silicon Valley Sample		Whites in Silicon Valley		Nonwhites in Silicon Valley		Hispanics in Silicon Valley		Non-Hispanics in Silicon Valley	
	Marginal Effect	Significance	Marginal Effect	Significance	Marginal Effect	Significance	Marginal Effect	Significance	Marginal Effect	Significance
Female	-2.2%		-1.2%		-2.2%		-0.2%		-0.9%	
Age	0.1		-0.8		2.1		3.3	#	-1.5	
Age-squared	-0.0		0.0		-0.0		-0.0	#	0.0	
Above high school education (no BA)	21.9	**	14.8		26.7	*	7.7		22.7	**
College or more	7.0		6.5		3.0		16.2		3.3	
Received degree in last three years	-2.0		-12.3	#	7.9		66.4	***	-12.0	*

(continued)

Table 6.2 Logit Model on the Probability of Using an LMI, Silicon Valley (*Continued*)

Explanatory Variables	Silicon Valley Sample		Whites in Silicon Valley		Nonwhites in Silicon Valley		Hispanics in Silicon Valley		Non-Hispanics in Silicon Valley	
	Marginal Effect	Significance	Marginal Effect	Significance	Marginal Effect	Significance	Marginal Effect	Significance	Marginal Effect	Significance
Hispanic	−12.1	**	—		−10.1		—		—	
Black	26.1	#	—		30.2	*	—		25.4	#
Asian or other	−2.3		—		—		—		−1.1	
Married	−4.3		−1.1		−4.5		2.2		−5.9	
English limited	6.3		17.6	*	−0.4		−2.4		12.0	#
Frequent job changer	24.0	***	33.2	***	14.5	#	14.4		28.8	***
Household member on welfare	14.0		2.9		14.3		31.9	*	4.3	

Socially connected	-12.8 ***	-11.9 *	-13.9 *	-12.8 ***	-14.2 **
Number of cases	627	323	304	164	463
F-statistic	2.89	2.14	2.27	2.07	2.93
Probability > F	0.0003	0.0154	0.006	0.0195	0.0003
Pseudo R-squared	0.0753	0.1021	0.0757	0.0641	0.0988
Percent predicted correctly	0.7613	0.7169	0.7638	0.8539	0.7198

Source: Authors' compilation.

Note: Response variable: dummy variable that is equal to one if the respondent used an LMI during the three years prior to the survey.

*significant at .10 level
**significant at .05 level
***significant at .01 level
#significant at .20 level

Table 6.3 Logit Model on the Probability of Using an LMI, Milwaukee

Explanatory Variables	Milwaukee Sample		Whites in Milwaukee		Nonwhites in Milwaukee	
	Marginal Effect	Significance	Marginal Effect	Significance	Marginal Effect	Significance
Female	−5.3%		−5.8%		5.3%	
Age	2.9	#	2.9	#	0.7	
Age-squared	−0.0	*	−0.0	*	−0.0	
Above high school education (no BA)	3.9		9.9		−15.0	
College or more	−7.1		−3.3		−24.9	#
Received degree in last three years	0.6		−8.1		16.8	
Hispanic	19.0	#	—		0.7	
Black	26.4	**	—		−1.9	
Asian or other	18.4	#	—		—	

Married	3.8	0.5	14.8
English limited	1.0	9.8 #	-19.9 *
Frequent job changer	20.9 **	19.6 **	33.1 ***
Household member on welfare	-7.2	-6.3	-16.8
Socially connected	-15.4 ***	-11.9 **	-27.9 **
Number of cases	614	369	245
F-statistic	3.42	2.09	2.18
Probability > F	0.0000	0.0185	0.0086
Pseudo R-squared	0.0878	0.0861	0.1064
Percent predicted correctly	0.7278	0.7436	0.6624

Source: Authors' compilation.

Note: Response variable: dummy variable that is equal to one if the respondent used an LMI during the three years prior to the survey.

*significant at .10 level
**significant at .05 level
***significant at .01 level
#significant at .20 level

Figure 6.2   LMI Use by Social Connectedness and Gender

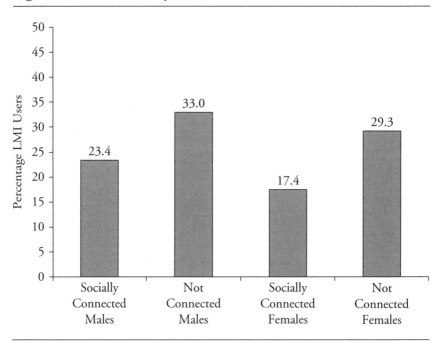

Source: Authors' compilation.

sexes but has a higher marginal effect for females; being black is highly significant for females, a pattern in line with information gleaned from more detailed
case studies and individual accounts, particularly in Wisconsin.

As for the racial pattern, when we use the logit regression to compare the
experience of non-Hispanic whites and all others in a sample that includes both
Silicon Valley and Milwaukee, we find that whites who were "connected" were
about 11 percent less likely to use an LMI, while "connected" nonwhites were
a full 23 percent less likely to use an LMI. In the second and third columns of
tables 6.2 and 6.3, we show the results when these regressions are restricted to
Milwaukee and Silicon Valley separately. As can be seen, being socially connected has a much larger negative correlation with LMI use for nonwhites overall and is especially significant in Milwaukee.

What about the Hispanic anomaly noted earlier? The final two columns of
table 6.2 show the logit regressions for Hispanics and non-Hispanics separately

Figure 6.3   LMI Use by Social Connectedness and Race

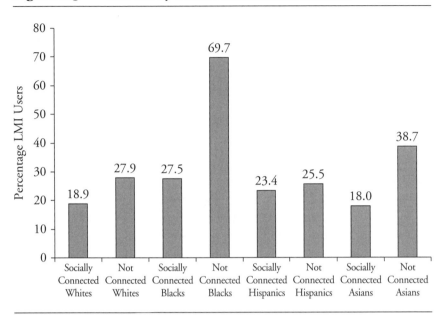

Source: Authors' compilation.

in Silicon Valley. (We concentrate on Silicon Valley because the percentage of Hispanics is so much lower in Milwaukee.) The significant variables in the regression restricted to Hispanics are age and its square, having obtained a degree in the last three years (which dominates the positive and near-significant coefficient on the education dummy variable for having a BA or better), and having a person in the house on welfare. This suggests that it is older, more-experienced, and more-educated workers, those who completed their education recently, and those who were able to gain access to the welfare system who made use of LMIs. Individuals who were younger, less educated, and/or less recently educated apparently had to make use of informal job search mechanisms rather than turn to an LMI. This pattern squares with findings by both Luis Falcón (1995) and Manuel Pastor and Enrico Marcelli (2000) that Hispanics rely more on informal social networks than do non-Hispanics. In any case, the key finding here is that our social capital measure does matter for Hispanics (despite the simple comparison in figure 6.3) once we account for other sorting variables. Social capital significantly decreases the probability of LMI use for Hispanics in Silicon

Valley by about the same percentage as it does for the rest of the Silicon Valley population.

To Temp or Not to Temp?

This analysis suggests that social capital or connectedness does indeed play a role in determining whether an individual will tend to use an LMI: those with lower levels of social connectedness may find that their networks are inadequate and hence may turn to a formal institution as a substitute. Does social capital also play a role in their selection of a particular type of LMI? Both general theory and our qualitative interviews suggest that social connectedness has an impact on the choice of an LMI, partly because friends and family can provide steering information similar to the typical job search help provided through social networks. We might also expect that social capital could help find a more effective LMI.

In testing the impact of social networks, particularly on the choice of an "effective" LMI, it would be preferable to have quality ratings for the various individual agencies in the sample: not all temp agency, nonprofit, or union intermediaries are created equal. However, we have only broad categorizations of LMI type, with temp agencies being by far the most used: about one-third of all LMI users in the sample went to a temp agency.[13] As it turns out, temps are also the LMI type for which both our qualitative work and regression analysis consistently suggest the lowest level of services and the lowest likelihood of yielding positive outcomes for workers. Thus, per the general classifications, we would expect that being socially connected, aside from making people less likely to have experienced the world of LMIs as a whole, should have the effect of guiding those looking for work away from temps and perhaps toward more effective nontemp LMIs.

On the surface at least, temp avoidance appears to be the case. In figure 6.4, we have taken the sample of LMI users from the survey (those respondents who held a job during the three years prior to the survey that was obtained through an LMI) and charted the types of LMIs used by those whom we have defined as "socially connected" or "not connected" under our measure. As can be seen, there are some large and apparently significant differences in the types of LMIs used. We find that among socially connected LMI users, about 17 percent used temps, 19 percent used placement agencies or headhunters, 15 percent used unions, 12 percent used nonprofits or government organizations, 26 percent used community colleges, and 10 percent used business or professional organizations. Of those defined as not connected, more than one-third used temps (36 percent),

Figure 6.4   Sorting into LMIs: Social Connectedness by Type of LMI
Used to Get Last LMI Job

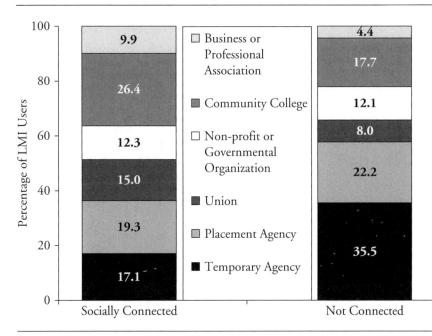

Source: Authors' compilation.

22 percent used placement agencies or headhunters, 8 percent used unions,
12 percent used nonprofits or government organizations, 18 percent used
community colleges, and 4 percent used business or professional organizations. It seems that social capital generally leads those who use LMIs away from
temps—and to some degree away from placement agencies—and that there
might be a slight steering effect toward unions and perhaps toward community colleges and associations.

To decipher the effect of social capital on individuals' choice of LMI type, we
estimated a multinomial logit model of the decisionmaking process, one that
simultaneously modeled the probability of choosing. In this case, we set "no
LMI" as the base category and modeled the probability of selecting into each of
the six LMI types over not using an LMI.[14] Independent variables were the same
set of explanatory variables that were used in the earlier logistical regression modeling the probability of LMI use. As before, we first ran the regression omitting
our measure of social capital to get a sense of the multivariate relationships that
set the stage for our variable of interest, and then we included the social capital

measure to estimate its effect on the relative probability of sorting into each type of LMI over no LMI. The response variable used in the regression is polychotomous, taking discrete values depending on the respondent's LMI experience as described earlier. As with the previously reported logistic regressions, we calculated marginal effects and report them along with their associated levels of statistical significance.

As can be seen in table 6.4, the fit of this model is actually better than the model for use versus non-use of LMIs when judging by the pseudo R-squared value, but not quite as good when judging by the percentage predicted correctly, which is not surprising given the much greater range of possible outcomes we are trying to predict.[15] The statistically significant variables of note are "frequent job changer," "English limited," "college or more," and, to some degree, "household member on welfare." The results for the high job-turnover variable square with our notion that people who are more actively searching for employment may be more anxious to find work and thus hastily match up with a temp agency. These results indicate that those taking a value of one for this variable were 16 percent more likely to use a temp agency than no LMI, a result that is significant at the .01 level, while they were less than 2 percent more likely to use a union or business or professional association over no LMI, with the effect significant at the .20 level.

Limited English communication skills have a less dramatic but significant impact, slightly decreasing the probability of choosing a business or professional association or permanent placement agency and slightly increasing the probability of choosing a union LMI. This makes sense given that members of associations and those who use placement agencies tend to be better educated (as indicated by the small positive and significant effect on "college or more" for choosing either an association or placement agency over no LMI) and that union LMIs may be more attractive or more accessible to those who do not have excellent English language skills. Holding a BA degree or higher, as compared to a high school diploma, makes one a bit more likely to use an association-type LMI and significantly less likely to use a nonprofit or governmental LMI (although this latter marginal effect is also small). Having more than a high school degree but no BA also steers one away from nonprofit and governmental LMIs and is significantly (and perhaps naturally) associated with the use of a community college as a job search mechanism.

The variable for having a household member on welfare also has small but significant effects; the largest of these is a 6 percent increase in the use of nonprofit or governmental LMIs. This result is not surprising, since welfare use may also provide household members with more information about state agencies and nonprofits. On the other hand, having someone in the house on welfare is negatively associated with choosing a union LMI.

To test the effect of social capital on the choice between multiple types of LMIs and no LMI, we added our "socially connected" variable to the above regression. As can be seen in table 6.5, the explanatory power (as indicated by the pseudo R-squared) rises slightly with the inclusion of this variable. Our social capital dummy variable is associated with a 7 percent decrease in the probability of using a temp LMI over no LMI that is significant at the .01 level. Permanent placement agencies have an effect of similar significance but only about half the magnitude. The latter effect suggests that even among better-educated populations and those better endowed with other measures of human capital, a strong social network can mean the difference between obtaining the next job upgrade through a personal contact or through a placement agency.

When looking at the effect of social capital on sorting into the other LMI types over no LMI, the results are as expected: social capital steers individuals away from most LMIs but has a positive effect on utilizing a union LMI; these effects, however, are always insignificant. Our previous binomial logits suggested that social capital generally steers people *away* from LMIs. Multinomial logit results, however, indicate that while this is the case for temp agencies and placement agencies, social capital does not seem to have significant bearing on the decision to use other types of LMIs. This finding may simply be due to small subsample size, but it also suggests that we may be able to collapse all non-temp and nonplacement LMIs into a single group, an approach taken later in this chapter.

Finally, note that the other marginal effects are generally the same after the social capital measure is introduced, suggesting a robust specification. However, it is worth noting that when we include social capital in this regression, both the positive effect of age and the negative effect of age-squared on the probability of using a temp agency become more significant. In particular, the latter becomes significant at the .05 level (see column 1 of table 6.5), indicating that, especially with regard to temp agencies, increasing years and presumably labor market experience eventually lead people away from temps. Note, by contrast, that the effect of increasing age on using any of the other LMI types over no LMI is insignificant without exception.

(*text continues on page 202*)

Table 6.4   Multinomial Logit Model on the Probability of Using Various Types of LMIs over No LMI, Both Regions, Not Controlling for Social Capital

Explanatory Variables	Temp Agency Marginal Effect	Significance	Permanent Placement Agency Marginal Effect	Significance	Union Marginal Effect	Significance
Silicon Valley sample	−0.6%		−0.5%		−0.1%	
Female	−0.6		−1.4		−2.4	***
Age	0.8	#	−0.5		0.2	
Age-squared	0.0	#	0.0		−0.0	
Above high school education (no BA)	−0.1		1.2		0.1	
College or more	−1.8		2.7	#	−0.7	#
Received degree in last three years	0.1		−3.2	**	0.2	
Hispanic	3.5		−5.3	***	−0.6	#
Black	18.0	**	−0.4		−0.6	
Asian or other	5.5		−0.1		−1.6	***
Married	0.7		−1.7		−0.3	
English limited	3.0		−2.6	*	1.5	*
Frequent job changer	16.0	***	2.2		1.5	#

Nonprofit and Government Organization		Community College		Business and Professional Association	
Marginal Effect	Significance	Marginal Effect	Significance	Marginal Effect	Significance
−1.2%		−1.3%		0.1%	
0.5		−0.4		0.5	
−0.0		0.4		0.1	
0.0		−0.0		−0.0	
−1.8	**	10.8	**	1.3	
−2.4	**	−0.5		1.4	*
−2.2	**	2.2		0.9	
−0.3		−2.6	#	1.4	
4.2	#	1.3		0.6	
1.5		0.9		−0.0	
−0.8		−0.7		0.3	
−0.6		2.1		−1.0	*
0.4		−0.7		1.7	#

(continued)

Table 6.4   Multinomial Logit Model on the Probability of Using Various Types of LMIs over No LMI, Both Regions, Not Controlling for Social Capital (*Continued*)

Explanatory Variables	Temp Agency		Permanent Placement Agency		Union	
	Marginal Effect	Significance	Marginal Effect	Significance	Marginal Effect	Significance
Household member on welfare	1.1		−2.6	*	−1.1	***
Socially connected	—		—		—	
Number of cases						1,235
F-statistic						3.67
Probability > F						0.0000
Pseudo R-squared						0.1063
Percent predicted correctly						0.7110

Source: Authors' compilation.
Note: Response variable: polychotomous variable that takes one of seven possible unique values for each respondent that indicates whether he or she was not an LMI user (the base alternative) or, if an LMI user, that indicates the type of LMI that was used to obtain the most recently held LMI job during the three years prior to the survey, with possible LMI types including temp agencies, permanent placement agencies/headhunters, unions, nonprofit/government organizations, community colleges, and business/professional associations.

Nonprofit and Government Organization		Community College		Business and Professional Association	
Marginal Effect	Significance	Marginal Effect	Significance	Marginal Effect	Significance
6.5	*	−0.3		−0.8	*
—		—		—	

*significant at .10 level
**significant at .05 level
***significant at .01 level
#significant at .20 level

Table 6.5   Multinomial Logit Model on the Probability of Using Various Types of LMIs over No LMI, Both Regions, Controlling for Social Capital

Explanatory Variables	Temp Agency		Permanent Placement Agency		Union	
	Marginal Effect	Significance	Marginal Effect	Significance	Marginal Effect	Significance
Silicon Valley sample	−1.1%		−0.9%		0.0%	
Female	0.0		−1.3		−2.4	***
Age	1.0	*	−0.3		0.2	
Age-squared	−0.0	**	0.0		−0.0	
Above high school education (no BA)	0.4		1.3		0.0	
College or more	−0.4		3.3	*	−0.8	#
Received degree in last three years	0.6		−3.1	**	0.1	
Hispanic	3.2		−4.9	***	−0.6	#
Black	18.5	**	−0.1		−0.7	#
Asian or other	5.0		0.1		−1.6	***
Married	1.1		−1.1		−0.4	
English limited	2.7		−2.7	**	1.4	*
Frequent job changer	15.6	***	2.3		1.5	#

Nonprofit and Government Organization		Community College		Business and Professional Association	
Marginal Effect	Significance	Marginal Effect	Significance	Marginal Effect	Significance
−1.3%		−1.3%		0.0%	
0.5		−0.3		0.5	
0.0		0.4		0.1	
0.0		−0.0		−0.0	
−1.8	*	10.9	**	1.3	
−2.3	**	−0.4		1.5	*
−2.2	**	2.2		0.9	
−0.3		−2.5	#	1.5	
4.5	#	1.2		0.6	
1.6		1.0		−0.0	
−0.7		−0.5		0.3	
−0.7		2.0		−1.1	#
0.4		−0.7		1.8	

(continued)

Table 6.5   Multinomial Logit Model on the Probability of Using Various Types of LMIs over No LMI, Both Regions, Controlling for Social Capital (*Continued*)

Explanatory Variables	Temp Agency		Permanent Placement Agency		Union	
	Marginal Effect	Significance	Marginal Effect	Significance	Marginal Effect	Significance
Household member on welfare	−0.2		−2.8	*	−1.0	***
Socially connected	−6.9	***	−3.7	***	0.3	
Number of cases						1,235
F-statistic						4.11
Probability > F						0.0000
Pseudo R-squared						0.1125
Percent predicted correctly						0.7158

Source: Authors' compilation.

Note: Response variable: polychotomous variable that takes one of seven possible unique values for each respondent that indicates whether he or she was not an LMI user (the base alternative) or, if an LMI user, that indicates the type of LMI that was used to obtain the most recently held LMI job during the three years prior to the survey, with possible LMI types including temp agencies, permanent placement agencies/headhunters, unions, nonprofit/government organizations, community colleges, and business/professional associations.

Nonprofit and Government Organization		Community College		Business and Professional Association	
Marginal Effect	Significance	Marginal Effect	Significance	Marginal Effect	Significance
6.3	*	−0.3		−0.8	#
−0.7		−0.8		−0.2	

*significant at .10 level
**significant at .05 level
***significant at .01 level
#significant at .20 level

What happens when we examine the impacts by demographic subgroup? To do this, we collapsed all LMI types other than temps and permanent placement agencies into one category, resulting in a response variable with only four outcomes. (This was necessary given the small samples for each of the six LMI types once the sample was divided into demographic subgroups, and it was reasonable given the finding of few significant effects for the other LMIs.) The "no LMI" group was kept as the base alternative, with the remaining alternatives being "temp LMI," "placement LMI," and "nontemp, nonplacement LMI." After we revised the multinomial logit specification in this way, the results for various subgroups were as follows.

For gender, we found that the socially connected variable has a larger effect for males than for females in reducing temp agency use, but both effects have similar significance levels (see table 6.6). The pattern is reversed in the case of social capital and permanent placement agency use: the effect of social capital in reducing placement agency use is larger and quite a bit more significant for females than males. The larger (and more statistically significant) positive effect of the variable "frequent job changer" for women suggests that labor market volatility has a greater impact on steering women toward temps than men. As for race, we found that social connections seem to be slightly more likely to reduce temp agency use for nonwhites than for whites in Silicon Valley. By contrast, in Milwaukee the marginal effect of social capital in reducing temp agency use is nearly five times as large for nonwhites as it is for whites (see tables 6.7 and 6.8). Similarly, the effect of social capital in placement agency use is more important for nonwhites than for whites in Milwaukee, but much more important for whites than for nonwhites in Silicon Valley. Thus, the pattern across a range of subpopulations suggests that social connectedness is indeed a factor in explaining the differential use of temp agencies, placement agencies, and other LMIs.

Does the Effect of Being Socially Connected Differ in Low-Income Areas?

Previous research has suggested that for individuals in lower-income areas, with their tight, geographically determined social boundaries, the extensive social networks of the sort we measure—meetings attended, relatives and friends in the communication loop, and friends who can be asked for employment assistance—do not necessarily lead to positive labor market outcomes.[16] Thus, we would expect networks in these areas to be less important in steering individuals away from LMI use or toward better LMIs.

Note that the argument has less to do with whether the household is low-income than with whether the household is in a low-income area. To proxy this, we make use of the fact that our survey was designed to oversample in low-income areas, with the area-level income ascertained at the level of telephone prefix. We construct our low-income area sample from the low-income telephone prefix oversample and from other individuals whose telephone prefix might have fallen in that range but who were randomly called in the process of constructing the larger sample. We can then look specifically at those who may be confined to neighborhoods where making good contacts is more difficult, or where even being socially connected does not take one very far into the labor market.

We begin by checking on the probability of using an LMI for those living in low-income prefixes. Recall that "socially connected" had a significant negative effect on the probability of using an LMI over the whole sample, as well as in all of the subsamples examined. However, as shown in the first column of table 6.9, in lower-income areas we get an insignificant coefficient on our measure of social capital, with the result holding if we conduct the regressions separately for Silicon Valley and Milwaukee (not shown in the table). This finding supports the idea that social connections in low-income areas are not as likely to assist in job search (as they often do in higher-income areas). As a result, higher levels of social connectedness do not necessarily substitute for the use of LMIs in low-income areas.

Although social networks of people in lower-income areas do not reduce intermediary use, a remaining question is whether they influence the type of intermediary used. To test this, we ran the same seven-outcome multinomial logit model that we used previously, restricted in this case to low-income prefixes. The results are reported in the last six columns of table 6.9. Here the effect of social capital becomes significant. In these low-income areas, social capital is negatively related to temp agency use (decreasing the probability of using a temp over no LMI by just over 4 percent; significant at the .20 level), and it is positively associated with the use of nonprofit and government LMIs (increasing the probability by 9 percent; significant at the .20 level). We also find a highly significant negative effect of social capital on the use of permanent placement agencies (reducing use by 3 percent, significant at the .01 level).[17]

Thus, while social capital apparently reduces the use of temp agencies in lower-income areas (just as in other geographic areas and across other subsamples),

(*text continues on page 220*)

Table 6.6   Multinomial Logit Model on the Probability of Using Various Types of LMIs over No LMI, Both Regions

	Males					
	Temp Agency		Permanent Placement Agency		Other LMI	
Explanatory Variables	Marginal Effect	Significance	Marginal Effect	Significance	Marginal Effect	Significance
Silicon Valley sample	−4.3%	#	−3.7%	*	0.1%	
Age	0.5		−0.4		1.6	
Age-squared	−0.0		0.0		−0.0	
Above high school education (no BA)	−2.2		−1.2		8.0	
College or more	−0.2		6.5	**	−3.3	
Received degree in last three years	8.6		−2.5	#	2.3	
Hispanic	9.9	#	−4.9	***	−6.8	#
Black	25.2	*	−1.9		−0.4	
Asian or other	11.3	#	−2.5	#	−5.8	
Married	0.7		0.4		−2.5	
English limited	−1.1		−1.3		7.1	#
Frequent job changer	10.8	**	1.2		6.8	
Household member on welfare	−3.3	#	−2.0		−8.9	**
Socially connected	−7.0	***	−2.4	#	−1.9	

| Females | | | | | |
| Temp Agency | | Permanent Placement Agency | | Other LMI | |
Marginal Effect	Significance	Marginal Effect	Significance	Marginal Effect	Significance
0.9%		1.3%		−6.2%	*
1.1	*	−0.3		1.0	
−0.0	**	0.0		−0.0	
4.3		4.1	#	9.5	
−0.5		0.3		−3.1	
−3.0	*	−3.4	***	1.1	
−1.5		−3.4	***	2.7	
11.9	**	1.1		11.6	#
0.0		5.7	#	4.5	
1.2		−1.4		−0.6	
7.8	**	−3.5	***	−3.0	
21.1	***	2.7		5.5	
1.4		−2.6	**	11.2	
−5.7	***	−4.4	***	−1.8	

(continued)

Table 6.6   Multinomial Logit Model on the Probability of Using Various Types of LMIs over No LMI, Both Regions (*Continued*)

	Males					
	Temp Agency		Permanent Placement Agency		Other LMI	
Explanatory Variables	Marginal Effect	Significance	Marginal Effect	Significance	Marginal Effect	Significance
Number of cases			595			
F-statistic			2.85			
Probability > F			0.0000			
Pseudo R-squared			0.0932			
Percent predicted correctly			0.6842			

Source: Authors' compilation.
Note: Response variable: polychotomous variable that takes one of four possible unique values for each respondent that indicates whether he or she was not an LMI user (the base alternative) or, if an LMI user, that indicates whether he or she used a temp agency, a permanent placement agency/headhunter, or some other type of LMI to obtain the most recently held LMI job during the three years prior to the survey.

		Females			
Temp Agency		Permanent Placement Agency		Other LMI	
Marginal Effect	Significance	Marginal Effect	Significance	Marginal Effect	Significance
		640			
		3.54			
		0.0000			
		0.0985			
		0.7626			

*significant at .10 level
**significant at .05 level
***significant at .01 level
#significant at .20 level

Table 6.7   Multinomial Logit Model on the Probability of Using Various
Types of LMIs over No LMI, Silicon Valley

	Whites in Silicon Valley					
	Temp Agency		Permanent Placement Agency		Other LMI	
Explanatory Variables	Marginal Effect	Significance	Marginal Effect	Significance	Marginal Effect	Significance
Female	2.1%		0.2%		−3.9%	
Age	−0.7		−0.1		0.0	
Age-squared	0.0		0.0		−0.0	
Above high school education (no BA)	3.2		8.4	#	3.5	
College or more	−4.5	#	7.7	***	2.6	
Received degree in last three years	−1.0		−7.2	***	−1.4	
Hispanic	—		—		—	
Black	—		—		—	
Married	1.1		−0.1		−2.2	
English limited	1.7		6.9	**	7.9	
Frequent job changer	8.5	*	4.5	**	18.8	**
Household member on welfare	7.5		−4.4	#	−4.4	
Socially connected	−6.5	**	−4.3	*	0.0	

| Nonwhites in Silicon Valley | | | | | |
| Temp Agency | | Permanent Placement Agency | | Other LMI | |
Marginal Effect	Significance	Marginal Effect	Significance	Marginal Effect	Significance
−1.1%		1.3%	*	−5.8%	#
0.5		−0.2		2.4	#
0.0		0.0		−0.0	#
13.2		0.8		12.4	
2.8		0.3		0.5	
−3.8		0.0		13.0	
−7.3		−1.8	*	2.7	
14.9		0.2		10.8	
−0.4		−0.5		−5.9	
3.9		−1.6	*	−0.9	
18.1	**	−0.4		−0.3	
9.8		−0.8	*	6.9	
−7.3	**	−0.9	*	0.7	

(continued)

Table 6.7   Multinomial Logit Model on the Probability of Using Various Types of LMIs over No LMI, Silicon Valley (*Continued*)

Explanatory Variables	Whites in Silicon Valley					
	Temp Agency		Permanent Placement Agency		Other LMI	
	Marginal Effect	Significance	Marginal Effect	Significance	Marginal Effect	Significance
Number of cases			323			
F-statistic			1.84			
Probability > F			0.0029			
Pseudo R-squared			0.0857			
Percent predicted correctly			0.7460			

Source: Authors' compilation.
Note: Response variable: polychotomous variable that takes one of four possible unique values for each respondent that indicates whether he or she was not an LMI user (the base alternative) or, if an LMI user, that indicates whether he or she used a temp agency, a permanent placement agency/headhunter, or some other type of LMI to obtain the most recently held LMI job during the three years prior to the survey.

	Nonwhites in Silicon Valley				
Temp Agency		Permanent Placement Agency		Other LMI	
Marginal Effect	Significance	Marginal Effect	Significance	Marginal Effect	Significance
		302			
		2.45			
		0.0000			
		0.1110			
		0.7731			

*significant at .10 level
**significant at .05 level
***significant at .01 level
#significant at .20 level

Table 6.8   Multinomial Logit Model on the Probability of Using Various Types of LMIs over No LMI, Milwaukee

| | Whites in Milwaukee | | | | | |
| | Temp Agency | | Permanent Placement Agency | | Other LMI | |
Explanatory Variables	Marginal Effect	Significance	Marginal Effect	Significance	Marginal Effect	Significance
Female	0.0%		−5.1%	*	−0.1%	
Age	0.7	#	0.0		2.1	#
Age-squared	0.0	#	0.0		−0.0	#
Above high school education (no BA)	−2.5	**	−2.2		11.8	*
College or more	2.2	#	1.7		−10.1	**
Received degree in last three years	0.9		−2.7		−5.6	
Hispanic	—		—		—	
Black	—		—		—	
Married	0.1		−0.2		0.6	
English limited	0.6		−3.8	**	11.9	*
Frequent job changer	7.5	#	1.8		6.2	
Household member on welfare	0.5		−3.0	*	−0.7	
Socially connected	−3.6	***	−3.1	*	−2.2	

| | Nonwhites in Milwaukee | | | | |
| Temp Agency | | Permanent Placement Agency | | Other LMI | |
Marginal Effect	Significance	Marginal Effect	Significance	Marginal Effect	Significance
5.3%		0.0%		6.4%	
13.6	***	0.0		−7.0	**
−0.2	***	0.0		−0.1	**
−16.3	**	0.0		−0.2	
−18.7	**	0.0		−2.2	
16.2		0.0	#	4.9	
27.6	#	0.0	**	−9.6	
21.4	#	0.0	**	−1.4	
12.6		0.0	#	2.1	
4.5		0.0		−21.5	**
35.3	***	0.0		−0.5	
−13.6	*	0.0		0.1	
−17.5	**	−4.8	**	−2.9	

(continued)

Table 6.8   Multinomial Logit Model on the Probability of Using Various Types of LMIs over No LMI, Milwaukee (*Continued*)

	Whites in Milwaukee					
	Temp Agency		Permanent Placement Agency		Other LMI	
Explanatory Variables	Marginal Effect	Significance	Marginal Effect	Significance	Marginal Effect	Significance
Number of cases			368			
F-statistic			2.88			
Probability > F			0.0000			
Pseudo R-squared			0.1064			
Percent predicted correctly			0.7613			

Source: Authors' compilation.

Note: Response variable: polychotomous variable that takes one of four possible unique values for each respondent that indicates whether he or she was not an LMI user (the base alternative) or, if an LMI user, that indicates whether he or she used a temp agency, a permanent placement agency/headhunter, or some other type of LMI to obtain the most recently held LMI job during the three years prior to the survey.

			Nonwhites in Milwaukee			
Temp Agency			Permanent Placement Agency		Other LMI	
Marginal Effect	Significance		Marginal Effect	Significance	Marginal Effect	Significance
		242				
		210.37				
		0.0000				
		0.1472				
		0.5927				

*significant at .10 level
**significant at .05 level
***significant at .01 level
#significant at .20 level

Table 6.9   Models for Low-Income Prefixes Only

	Logit Model on the Probability of Using an LMI[a]					
	All, Controlling for Social Capital		Temp Agency		Permanent Placement Agency	
Explanatory Variables	Marginal Effect	Significance	Marginal Effect	Significance	Marginal Effect	Significance
Silicon Valley sample	−27.1%	***	−19.7%	***	−3.9%	**
Female	−0.2		−0.6		0.9	
Age	4.3	*	1.8	#	−0.5	*
Age-squared	−0.0	*	−0.0	#	0.0	#
Above high school education (no BA)	27.3	***	5.4		1.0	
College or more	10.1		−2.9		3.1	#
Received degree in last three years	4.0		14.5	*	−2.4	***
Hispanic	3.3		4.2		−2.0	#
Black	−4.7		3.9		−2.4	**
Asian or other	−5.3		−6.0	**	9.1	#
Married	5.3		1.8		0.2	
English limited	4.0		3.8		−1.7	#
Frequent job changer	26.2	***	19.7	***	−0.4	
Household member on welfare	12.1		−5.3	*	−0.3	
Socially connected	1.2		−4.2	#	−3.1	***

Multinomial Logit Model on the Probability of
Using Various Types of LMIs Over No LMI[b]

	Union		Nonprofit and Government Organization		Community College		Business and Professional Association	
	Marginal Effect	Significance	Marginal Effect	Significance	Marginal Effect	Significance	Marginal Effect	Significance
	0.9%	*	0.5%		−1.0%		−0.0%	
	−1.2	#	1.8		−0.4		−0.0	
	0.3	#	1.3		0.7	*	0.0	#
	−0.0		−0.0		−0.0	*	−0.0	
	1.5		−2.3		17.8	***	0.0	
	2.3		0.3		2.1		0.0	
	−0.9	#	−1.7		0.0		0.0	
	1.8	#	1.5		−3.0	**	0.0	
	−0.7		−0.4		−1.7	**	−0.2	
	−1.1	**	−8.6	***	−0.9		−0.0	
	−0.4		1.9		−0.3		−0.0	
	0.5		−3.4		5.0	**	−0.0	
	2.4	**	3.1		−0.8		0.0	
	−1.1	**	19.5	**	2.1		0.0	
	−0.4		9.0	#	−0.4		0.0	

(*continued*)

Table 6.9   Models for Low-Income Prefixes Only (*Continued*)

	Logit Model on the Probability of Using an LMI[a]					
	All, Controlling for Social Capital		Temp Agency		Permanent Placement Agency	
Explanatory Variables	Marginal Effect	Significance	Marginal Effect	Significance	Marginal Effect	Significance
Number of cases	571					
F-statistic	2.38					
Probability > F	0.0021					
Pseudo R-squared	0.0790					
Percent predicted correctly	0.7090					

Source: Authors' compilation.

[a]Response variable: dummy variable that is equal to one if the respondent used an LMI during the three years prior to the survey.

[b]Response variable: polychotomous variable that takes one of six possible unique values for each respondent that indicates whether he or she was not an LMI user (the base alternative) or, if an LMI user, that indicates the type of LMI that was used to obtain the most recently held LMI job during the three years prior to the survey, with possible LMI types including temp agencies, unions, nonprofit/government organizations, colleges, business/professional associations, and permanent placement agencies/headhunters.

Multinomial Logit Model on the Probability of
Using Various Types of LMIs Over No LMI[b]

	Union		Nonprofit and Government Organization		Community College		Business and Professional Association	
Marginal Effect	Significance	Marginal Effect	Significance	Marginal Effect	Significance	Marginal Effect	Significance
567							
128.01							
0.0000							
0.1409							
0.6794							

*significant at .10 level
**significant at .05 level
***significant at .01 level
#significant at .20 level

being socially connected in lower-income areas is associated with an *increase* in the use of nonprofit and government LMIs. Such organizations may be the best resort for people in lower-income areas in need of employment and employment support services, but there are mixed qualitative and quantitative results concerning the wage and other outcomes associated with utilizing nonprofit and government LMIs (see chapters 3, 4, and 5).

To see whether social connectedness might be steering users to the more effective of these agencies, we estimated wage equations restricted to the low-income prefixes. The natural log of respondents' wages was modeled as a function of geographic location (Milwaukee or Silicon Valley); gender; age and its square; education; job tenure; limited English-language ability; foreign-born; Hispanic, black, Asian, or other race; and dummy variables for each of the six broad LMI types. Use of a nonprofit or government LMI was modeled separately for those who were or were not defined as socially connected.[18] We estimate a negative relationship between wages and both variables indicating nonprofit or government LMI use, but only the effect for "not socially connected" nonprofit or government LMI use is statistically significant. This suggests that while the wages of the not socially connected users of nonprofit or government–type LMIs were significantly lower than those of the average person in a low-income area, those of the socially connected nonprofit or /government LMI users were not. These results should not be given a great amount of weight, owing to the small sample size, but they may indicate that social connections in poorer neighborhoods help guide job-seekers to the more effective of the nonprofit and government LMIs.

More generally, we should stress one further limitation to this work: our measure of social connectedness does not distinguish between "bonding" and "bridging" social capital (Briggs 1998). Bridging social capital is associated with connections to those who might have more resources to help with job search, while bonding social capital, which involves connections to individuals more of one's social class and milieu, may be less effective at securing employment or finding better LMIs. This finding is consistent with the notion that geography affects network quality, leading to more bonding and less bridging. This distinction may be important to the interpretation of these results: on the one hand, social connections appear to reduce usage of temporary agencies, but they may increase usage of nonprofit and government organizations that does not necessarily lead to positive outcomes. On the other hand, there is some tentative evidence that social connectedness improves the choice of which nonprofit or government LMIs to use.

Given this pattern of results, it may be useful to improve information about LMI quality in geographic areas of concentrated poverty so that residents could make more effective choices. It may also be useful to persuade higher-quality LMIs to target workers living in such areas. Finally, there may be some benefit in thinking more systematically about LMI activities and how they lead to the construction of new social networks and thus influence social connectedness.

Summary

This chapter has explored the dynamics of choice with regard to LMIs, focusing specifically on the role that social capital plays in LMI choice. We expected that those with higher levels of social capital or connectedness would be less likely to use the services of an LMI; this notion is supported by both general comparisons and multivariate regression analysis. We then explored whether social connectedness might play a role in *which* type of LMI is selected: in fact, those with higher levels of social capital do tend to select away from temporary agencies, and they are also less likely to use permanent placement agencies. Finally, we explored the effect of social capital within low-income areas: the results suggest that social capital has less effect on LMI choice in general because of the bounded nature of the social contacts included in our measure. On the other hand, social connectedness does seem to have some impact on steering those in low-income communities to what might be higher-quality LMIs—that is, ones with more services and better outcomes.

These results raise the intriguing notion that improving social connectedness for low-income individuals could improve LMI choice. Indeed, LMIs themselves could help if they were to conceive as one of their tasks the development of new bridging social networks for those least connected to labor markets and social resources. Like some of the union-based intermediaries we explore in our qualitative work, LMIs might be more conscious about building what Chris Benner (2003c) calls an "occupational community." This might include LMIs developing ongoing training programs, focus groups, monthly meetings, consistent postplacement follow-up of other LMI users, and additional ways to both maintain ties over time and pursue career development. One nonprofit LMI in Silicon Valley, Springboard Forward, has taken on exactly this issue with a newly created network training program and a specific effort to network its low-income clients with well-placed members of its advisory board and business allies.

Whether more LMIs will in fact take up this central task for improving worker welfare depends in part on whether they see themselves as "marketmeeters" or "market-molders," as well as on how they see themselves striking a balance between the interests of employers and employees. In our qualitative work, we saw a higher attention to the deliberate creation of community among unions, nonprofits, community colleges, and associations than among temp agencies. Nonetheless, organizations other than temp agencies are hardly uniform in their provision of services and outcomes. We take up both the broader policy implications of this and our earlier qualitative and quantitative findings in the final chapter of this book.

Chapter Seven

Conclusions and Implications for Future Research and Policy

When the planning for this research project began in the late 1990s, the term "labor market intermediary" was nearly unknown. Indeed, a full-text search of nearly four thousand scholarly journals indexed by ProQuest reveals only ten articles from 1987 to 1996 that mention the term. Though still hardly a household term, in recent years scholarly interest in labor market intermediaries has increased significantly. In 2004 and 2005, more than ten articles each year were published that mention the term—a tenfold increase. A search for terms related to particular types of intermediaries, including temporary help agencies and new forms of workforce intermediaries, would undoubtedly show a significantly greater number of articles. This reflects a clear growth of new interest in institutions that engage in job matching and new inquiries into the broader effects of these institutions on labor market flows and outcomes for both workers and employers.

Despite this growth in research, our knowledge of the activities and impacts of labor market intermediaries remains partial and incomplete. Rather than focusing on particular types of intermediaries, as much of the previous research in the field has done, this book has tried to fill in some of the gaps in this knowledge by taking a comprehensive approach to understanding all intermediaries within just two regional labor markets. Our goal was to provide a baseline measurement for the incidence of intermediary use and to provide insights into why people use particular types of intermediaries, how different types of intermediaries relate to their clients and to each other, and how intermediaries affect labor market outcomes, particularly for different types of workers.

In this concluding chapter, we begin by pulling together what we see as the most significant conclusions we have drawn from the results of our research. Then we discuss what we see as the most important and promising avenues for future research on labor market intermediaries that could build from this work. Finally, since our research is motivated at least in part by a normative concern about reaching better outcomes for workers by improving labor market intermediaries, we conclude with some thoughts on the implications of our research findings for public policy.

The Prevalence of Labor Market Intermediaries

The most basic conclusion that emerges from this research is that intermediaries of various types are widely used in the labor market. This is particularly evident in our broadest incidence measure, which shows that more than one-quarter of the labor force in each region *held a job* in the previous three years that they got through an intermediary. More than 15 percent of labor force participants in Silicon Valley and nearly 13 percent in Milwaukee *obtained* a job in the last three years through an intermediary. Furthermore over 20 percent of people currently working in Milwaukee, and 14.4 percent in Silicon Valley, *were currently in a job* obtained through an LMI. Although, as we might expect, intermediary use was most prevalent among disadvantaged workers, it is significant that intermediary use was also widespread among more-advantaged workers. It is also significant that at least half of all users of LMIs were using intermediaries not simply because they were unemployed or entering the labor market, but because they wanted to get a better job or for some other reason related to career advancement. We believe that these numbers are large enough to warrant more research and policy attention. Any set of institutions that helps one out of every five to seven people get their current job (and helps one out of every four people get a job they held in the last three years), and can at least potentially play a role in building cross-firm career ladders, is worth understanding better.

Our interest in intermediaries was driven in part by the hypothesis that increasing volatility in the labor market leads to increasing use of intermediaries as more people are looking for jobs and more new hires are being made. However, in comparing intermediary use in each region, it is clear that there is no simple linear relationship between volatility and intermediary use. By nearly all measures, volatility in Silicon Valley is higher than in Milwaukee, yet intermediary use is no higher in Silicon Valley than in Milwaukee, and by some measurements it is even lower. LMIs are clearly only one option that job-seekers have for finding work; most people continue to get jobs through friends or by responding directly to advertisements. The lower level of intermediary use in Silicon Valley, despite higher levels of volatility, appears to be the result of people there more often using friends (25.4 percent in Silicon Valley versus 19.8 percent in Milwaukee in our survey) and the Internet (4.3 percent versus 1.6 percent) to find work. The nature and character of social networks clearly play an important role in shaping intermediary use and moderating any relationship between intermediary use and labor market volatility, and the greater use of social networks to find work in Silicon Valley helps explain the different patterns of LMI use in each region.

Though we have emphasized the widespread prevalence of intermediaries in both regions as a sign of their potential importance in multiple economic contexts, it is also worthwhile to highlight some of the differences between the two regions. The most significant difference is the presence in Silicon Valley of various LMIs that either specialize in or have some significant concentration in supporting more highly skilled workers, particularly those information technology professionals who work in the often project-based and rapidly changing production systems in the region's information technology industries. The importance in Silicon Valley of these professional associations and private agencies, including both permanent and temporary placement agencies, was apparent in our qualitative data. It also appeared in the survey data in various ways, including a higher incidence of use of permanent placement agencies and professional associations and the patterns of LMI use among more highly educated and higher-income households. Although there is some LMI use among more-advantaged workers in the Milwaukee labor market as well, it is less than in Silicon Valley.

The other major difference between the two regions emerged in the racial patterns of intermediary use. The lower level of intermediary use in the Hispanic population of Silicon Valley is entirely accounted for by the striking differences in use of temporary agencies by Hispanics in the two regions: levels of temp agency use are very low in Silicon Valley and disproportionately high in Milwaukee. There are also racial differences in the use of other types of intermediaries in each region; community colleges in Milwaukee, for example, disproportionately serve blacks, those in Silicon Valley disproportionately serve Asians and Hispanics, and nonprofit and government agencies in Silicon Valley apparently disproportionately underserve the Asian population. Whether these differences are related to characteristics of the various racial groups in each city or to differences in the intermediaries in each region is unclear from our data.[1] But it is clear that there is some variation across our two regions in the relationship between race and intermediary use, particularly among temporary agencies.

The Impact of Labor Market Intermediaries

As discussed in chapter 5, the most consistent and significant relationships we found between intermediary use and outcomes for workers in the labor market were negative correlations between temporary agency use and both hourly wages and access to employer-provided benefits. Reconfiguring our data to mirror the data used in the study by Andersson, Holzer, and Lane (2005), we did find some evidence of increased *earnings* among temp agency users, but this result is driven by longer hours of employment, not higher wages. We did find a positive relationship between the use of permanent placement agencies or headhunters and wages, though this was primarily limited to those with higher education. Perhaps most significantly, however, we found few other clear relationships between labor market outcomes and the use of other types of labor market intermediaries in either region; professional associations, community and vocational colleges, unions or nonprofit or government agencies seem to have little consistent impact on labor market outcomes, at least to the extent to which we could measure them in our survey.

Does this suggest that, aside from the impacts of private-sector intermediaries, we should conclude that LMIs ultimately have little or no impact on outcomes for workers in the labor market, and that researchers and policymakers concerned with improving opportunities for disadvantaged workers should not focus on intermediaries? Perhaps, but there are also a number of considerations that might lead us to think otherwise. First, it is possible that we simply have too few observations in each of these different groups in our survey to be able to distinguish significant outcomes. Second, the differences we found in outcomes for private-sector agencies versus other types of LMIs are significant. Our data do seem to show that the use of temporary agencies results in lower hourly wages and less access to employer-provided benefits and that temporary agencies provide fewer services and lead to less satisfaction for workers. Thus, understanding the factors that lead workers and employers to use other types of intermediaries rather than temp agencies can provide insights into ways of reducing negative outcomes, if not actually lead to broad-based improvement. We do not want to suggest that temporary agencies and other LMIs can be compared directly. Temporary agencies are private-sector agencies, and we would not expect them to provide the public goods or social support services that we would expect from publicly and philanthropically funded organizations. We do want to suggest, however, that since temporary agencies are so widespread and seem to have negative impacts on workers' wages and benefits, the development by other LMIs of services that effectively substitute for temp agencies or leverage the efficiencies and strengths provided by temp agencies while also providing more support for disadvantaged workers might lead to less negative outcomes.

From our qualitative data, it is clear that temp agencies provide at least one additional set of services to employers that few other LMIs do: serving as employer of record. By providing this service, private intermediaries absorb significant labor market and legal risks that the employer would otherwise bear. Temporary agencies presumably charge their clients for bearing this risk, but they are also able to absorb a certain amount of this risk by diversifying their placements, thus reducing their exposure to labor market fluctuations. Furthermore, since a temp agency's placements are explicitly temporary, it also avoids certain legal employment responsibilities that its clients would have to bear if they had to employ people in a permanent position. Being employer of record can also reduce administrative costs, especially for small and medium-sized employers, since the temporary agency can utilize economies of scale and gain efficiencies through specialization in the employment function. The question of why there are not more socially oriented intermediaries offering these business services to employer clients remains a topic of both research and potential policy change. Part of the explanation may lie with institutional rules, particularly with regard to avoiding competition between private-sector and public-sector intermediaries, but improving the attractiveness of such intermediaries to business might help with improving outcomes for workers.

A third factor in our research that might understate the positive impacts of at least some intermediaries is that the categories we use to distinguish between different types of intermediaries are quite broad and there is probably tremendous variation within each category in the quality of services provided. In our qualitative data, our interview respondents (both staff and LMI clients) eloquently described in great detail the factors they saw as important in shaping good placements and career opportunities, while also clearly identifying significant challenges (and variations) in reaching those "best practices." Of the LMI clients we interviewed, including many employers, few were able to identify what *type* of intermediary had helped them get a job or find an employee; they paid more attention to the specific services provided and the quality of the matches made than to the organizational characteristic of the LMI. In this context, "best practice" in LMI activity seems likely to be driven as much or more by the characteristics of individual agencies (leadership, capacities, quality of services, strength of relationships with workers/employers, and so on) than by the organizational typology we used in our survey.

A fourth factor to consider is that it was clear from our qualitative data that many intermediaries do not operate in isolation but in fact relate to other intermediaries in ways that may affect patterns of LMI use and labor market outcomes. For example, some temporary agencies explicitly recruit workers through nonprofit and government agencies, which also may provide additional training and support services, yet we do not know whether this combination of LMI assistance would provide a worker with a better outcome than simply using a stand-alone temporary agency directly. Similarly, nonprofit agencies reported placing a large number of their worker clients through temporary help agencies, yet we do not know whether such combination placements typically result in better or worse outcomes than placements made directly by the nonprofit or government agency itself. Other examples of "combination" or "network" LMI relationships include: private-sector agencies subcontracting with other private-sector agencies; community college placement agencies partnering in different ways with their own internal training programs or external (both private and nonprofit) placement services; and unions teaming up with community colleges and other training providers to facilitate incumbent worker training and career advancement opportunities. Again, this suggests that outcomes relating to specific types of intermediary use may be masked in our data.

Finally, our survey and logistic regression analysis documented ways in which intermediaries serve in many ways as a *substitute* for social networks as a job search strategy, but our qualitative data also indicated that LMIs may play an important role in helping to *build* high-quality social networks. Some LMIs, such as professional associations and unions, become an important ongoing *infrastructure* for sustaining occupational communities. Other LMIs, by either intentionally or unintentionally improving people's networking skills along with providing new contacts, build a base for more productive future job searches through social networks or internal career ladders, even if initial job placements do not result in higher wages. This conclusion is supported by a range of research that argues persuasively for the importance of social networks in building skills and increasing workers' ability not only to learn in the long term but to cope with layoffs and job loss and deal effectively with a range of other issues that shape long-term employment outcomes (Herzenberg et al. 1998; Hull 1997; Lave and Wenger 1991; Wenger 1998; Wial 1991). Again, these more subtle but important impacts of intermediaries are unlikely to be captured in our data.

Our research has: (1) provided a set of baseline measurements of the incidence of intermediary use among various categories of intermediaries and various groups of workers in two different regions; (2) provided some indicators of LMI impact on outcomes in the labor market, and suggested that differences in outcomes between some types of LMIs are not always easily discerned; and (3) provided insights into how the broad landscape of intermediaries operates in two regions, how different types of intermediaries relate to workers and employers, and why workers and employers use different types of agencies. These findings have implications for future research on intermediaries, to which we now turn.

Future Research

This study suggests two broad types of questions for future research. The first set of questions concern the incidence and impact of labor market intermediaries and could be addressed through replications or modifications of the survey methodology we used, perhaps in other regions or on a more national scale. The second set of questions unearthed by our study is related to the effectiveness of intermediaries in influencing worker outcomes; these questions are more appropriately addressed, at least initially, through in-depth qualitative research on particular aspects of intermediary activity. We address each of these research areas in turn.

One next step would be to replicate our survey in other regions or to run our survey again in future years in Silicon Valley and Milwaukee. The survey we developed was the first of which we are aware that measures the incidence of LMI use across a comprehensive set of different types of LMIs. With the work of developing, testing, revising, and administering the survey now completed, it would be relatively easy (though not inexpensive!) to administer the survey again. This would take advantage of economies of scale in intellectual production to begin to answer significant questions highlighted by our work to date. We are happy to make our survey instrument available to other researchers who are interested in replicating this work in other regions and comparing those results with our findings.

Replicating the survey in other regions would help answer important questions about variations in intermediary use across regions with different industrial structures and demographic characteristics. How does intermediary use in the more highly concentrated Latino labor markets of the Southwest, for instance, compare with what we observed in Milwaukee and Silicon Valley? What about comparisons to the more highly concentrated African American regions in the South? Are there significant differences in intermediary activity between small, medium, and large metropolitan areas? How does intermediary use in declining or only slowly growing cities, like Detroit or Pittsburgh, compare with intermediary use in rapidly growing cities, like Las Vegas or Miami?

Having a larger number of observations in the survey might also help answer important questions about particular types of intermediaries that we were not able to answer in our study, owing to the more limited number of our observations. Is it possible, for example, to identify more effective intermediaries within our broad categories of nonprofit and membership-based intermediaries? If so, what are the characteristics of these intermediaries and what kinds of services do they provide? What types of employees do they work with and who are their business clients?

There are undoubtedly aspects of the comparative regional analysis in our own data that could be explored further, especially in comparisons with other regions. Replicating the survey in Silicon Valley and Milwaukee in future years would also give us new insights. How is intermediary use changing over time? What factors are leading to increased or decreased intermediary use? How do patterns of intermediary use relate to changing patterns of volatility and labor market fluctuations?

To be most cost-effective and instructive, however, any replication of this study in other regions would benefit from some modifications of the survey itself. The components of our survey designed to measure the incidence of intermediary use were effective and could be productively and quite easily replicated in other regions. Indeed, it would be possible to administer a somewhat shorter and less expensive version of the survey that is simply focused on incidence of use rather than on labor market outcomes.

Other new questions that have emerged from this research could be effectively addressed through more in-depth qualitative research or more targeted surveys of subsets of intermediaries and intermediary users. These potential research topics include:

- *Temporary Agencies, Other LMIs, and Labor Market Outcomes:* Both our qualitative and quantitative research documented the significant differences between private-sector LMIs and all other types of LMIs. Not only are temporary agencies the largest type of LMIs used, but they also provide services, particularly being employer of record, that are almost unique to private-sector intermediaries. At the same time, our data show that temporary agencies are associated with poorer labor market outcomes than other types of LMIs. This raises important questions about whether it is possible to improve temporary help agencies or to find alternatives to temporary help agencies. Are labor market outcomes better with some types of temp agencies than with others? If so, what factors help explain those outcomes? Is it possible to develop alternatives to temporary agencies (such as socially oriented professional employer organizations)[2] that would provide better outcomes for workers but still provide the services that employers are searching for?

- *Racial Differences in LMI Use:* Our research clearly uncovered significant differences in how different racial groups use intermediaries and how these patterns vary across different regions. Particularly striking was Hispanics' high temporary agency use in Milwaukee and low temporary agency use in Silicon Valley. Jamie Peck and Nik Theodore (Theodore 2003; Theodore and Peck 2001) have documented temporary help agencies in Chicago targeting Latino neighborhoods for their work, and this seems to be the case in Milwaukee as well. Has this not emerged in Silicon Valley, or is there some relationship between, say, the size of a Latino community and the density of the social networks that are an alternative to intermediary use? How widespread are temporary help agencies in other areas with significant concentrations of Latinos? What are the implications of these different patterns for labor market outcomes for Latinos? Are these patterns significantly different for recent immigrants versus longer-term residents? For documented versus undocumented workers?

- *Social Networks, LMI Use, and Labor Market Outcomes:* The questions around race and LMI use also intersect closely with a set of questions around social networks and LMI use. Many social networks are heavily structured along racial lines, and our data clearly show that the strength of social connectedness is connected to LMI use and that the nature of these relationships differs in low-income neighborhoods. Social networks get constructed in different ways—through work, through neighborhood activity, through extended family networks, through school environments, through leisure activities, and so on. Do particular types of social networks lead to the use of different types of LMIs? How do these patterns differ across racial groups and in different regions and neighborhoods? To what extent are intermediaries helping to build social networks for their worker clients, such as by acting as the organizational infrastructure for maintaining occupational networks or by providing specific social networking training or opportunities for building stronger networks? Do these different patterns of social network and LMI relationships lead to different labor market outcomes?

- *"Best Practice" Across LMIs:* Our quantitative data show that there are differences in practices by different organizational types of LMIs. As we discussed in our introductory chapter, however, our review of the literature and our qualitative data also led us to develop an analytical framework for developing typologies of LMIs based on strength of ties with both sides of the labor market and the extent to which the LMIs serve particular interests (worker, employer, community). We hypothesized that the use of LMIs that have strong ties with both workers and employers and explicitly try to address workers' needs is more likely to result in positive outcomes for disadvantaged workers. This hypothesis was supported by our qualitative data, but it was impossible to measure directly these features of LMIs (such as strength of ties with employers) through a survey of workers. Our qualitative data on LMIs also revealed a set of characteristics and practices that LMIs themselves identified for us as important to their effectiveness. To what extent do different LMIs within a regional economy engage in these practices? Do they in fact result in better outcomes for workers?

- *Steering and Networking of LMIs in the Labor Market:* Our research on different LMIs across regional labor markets highlights that building on "best practice" in LMI activity may not simply involve improving the characteristics of good programs but may also involve understanding the factors that steer people to different LMIs and allow for networking between different LMIs. To what extent are workers aware of a range of options in LMI use? How do they find out about different types of LMIs? How does this differ by race, income, gender, and geography? How do LMIs communicate with each other, especially private-sector agencies with nonprofit agencies? When this happens, why does it happen? When it is absent, why is that the case?

- *The Placement Success of LMIs:* The measurements of intermediary use that we found in our study are actually incidences of *successful* intermediary placements. In other words, someone was identified as a user of an intermediary only if he or she got a job through the intermediary. We had no way of measuring the extent of *unsuccessful* intermediary use—cases in which an individual had contact with an LMI in the hopes of getting a job, but the LMI was unsuccessful in placing that person. Patterns of unsuccessful intermediary use are likely to be quite different depending on the type of LMI, and they are likely to add not insignificantly to the overall incidence rate of intermediary contact in the labor market. How do LMIs fail in providing placements for different workers? Why do they fail? To what extent is such failure shaped by the personal characteristics of the job-seeker? To what extent is it shaped by the particular characteristics of the LMI's employer clients? To what extent is it simply rooted in a mismatch of skills and interests and job requirements? How do these patterns differ by different types of intermediaries?

The issues identified here are only a portion of the overall set of research questions that are relevant for understanding LMIs and that emerged from this research project. Many other researchers are focusing on other questions, such as more targeted documentation of best practices within particular types of intermediaries and the impacts of globalization on temporary help firms. Regardless of the specific questions addressed, the scale of LMI usage demonstrated in our data indicates that an LMI is a major component of the experience of many Americans in the labor market. As a result, we think LMIs warrant significantly more research. We also believe there are opportunities for public policy to have an impact on LMI activities in ways that can improve labor market opportunities for disadvantaged workers. It remains for policymakers to flesh out the details, but we do want to provide some indicators of what we see as the most important implications of our findings for policy considerations.

Policy Implications

The level of incidence of LMI use that we document demonstrates that intermediaries have a widespread presence in two U.S. regional labor markets. Furthermore, the fact that the LMI presence in the older manufacturing region of Milwaukee and the information technology–dominated region of Silicon Valley had so much in common suggests that intermediaries are similarly represented across many different regional labor markets in the United States. We think this widespread presence justifies significant policy attention to intermediaries. Clearly significant policy attention has already been given to particular *types* of intermediaries—the restructuring of public-sector workforce development programs through the Workforce Investment Act, for example, or state-led initiatives to improve community college activities. Our research suggests, however, that attention could usefully be paid to the important role of *intermediation* in labor markets, with the recognition that this function is performed by a range of different types of institutions and that it probably plays an important role in shaping the efficiency and adaptability of labor markets as a whole, as well as outcomes for workers and employers in the labor market (Benner 2003b).

A second major policy implication that emerges from this research is that best practices in intermediary activity are not necessarily determined simply by *type of intermediary*. There is undoubtedly variation within different types of intermediaries, including within temporary help agencies. It is possible to identify and support best practices within different types of intermediaries. Indeed, a significant amount of policy work to date has been focused on the goal of supporting best practice within particular types of intermediaries. Our research, however, suggests two additional dimensions of the best-practice perspective. First, encouraging best practice might involve promoting the further development of one type of intermediary rather than another. For instance, to the extent that nonprofit or membership-based intermediaries could be encouraged to act as employer of record, this might lead to a shift of some workers away from temporary agencies toward other intermediaries that provide better outcomes. Second, since different intermediaries have different strengths and weaknesses, encouraging best practice might involve promoting networking between intermediaries, including between different types of intermediaries. This might include, for example, leveraging the capacity of temporary agencies to relate to employers and serve as employer of record, while leveraging training assistance from community colleges and wraparound support services from nonprofit or government agencies. Such intermediary partnerships are already emerging in a range of places across the country (Fitzgerald 2004; Giloth 2004), and our qualitative research supports the benefits of such networking activity.

Going beyond simply encouraging networking between intermediaries, our research on the landscape of intermediary activity in each region also made clear that there is significant fragmentation of activities and duplication of services. To a broad extent this fragmentation of services has been recognized, at least within the workforce development system. Indeed, one of the explicit goals of the Workforce Investment Act was to promote alignment between various government and nonprofit workforce development services through the creation of one-stop career centers and workforce investment boards. Our research suggests that it is important in such streamlining efforts to also take into account the activities of private-sector intermediaries and membership-based organizations, both unions and professional associations. The notion of "intermediating the intermediaries" may be excessively cumbersome, but it certainly captures the essence of a function that policy could help to encourage. Even simple policy designed to increase the information available to job-seekers and employers about the range of options available and the range of services provided, along with any performance measurements that different agencies may collect, could go one step further in steering people and employers toward more effective intermediaries.

Another major implication emerging from our research is the importance of social networks in shaping job access and experience with labor market intermediaries. Our research shows that social networks are important in leading people directly to jobs, but that when people do use intermediaries, social networks may also lead them to use better ones. Furthermore, our qualitative research suggests that at least some intermediaries can play an important role in supporting social networks. Other research is now emerging that evaluates specific programmatic efforts to promote social networking skills among disadvantaged (Spaulding 2005). Thus, policy efforts to encourage intermediaries to focus on building the social networks of the workers they serve seems strongly warranted.

Finally, our research does suggest the importance of paying particular attention to the intermediary role of temporary help agencies. Partly because of their ubiquity, there has been a mushrooming of research on temporary help agencies in the past decade. Some researchers have concluded that temp agencies play a valued role and the market should be left to operate on its own, but various other policy proposals have emerged that propose to regulate this industry in different ways, such as limiting the length of time someone can be employed in a "temporary" job or clarifying "joint employer" status. We believe that such agencies do play an important role in labor markets, often have employer trust, and are responding to market incentives. But the evidence also suggests that such agencies should be both pushed and steered into providing better long-term outcomes.

A full policy package would strike a balance of market-meeting and market-making activities within the full range of intermediaries. It would recognize the important role that intermediaries play in securing employment in a changing economy, and it would enhance their ability to add to the long-term success of job-seekers and incumbent but sometimes insecure employees. In a world in which navigating the shores of a constantly shifting labor market may itself become common practice for workers, intermediaries are not just a feature of the economy but an important set of institutions worthy of more study and more action. Encouraging their "best practices" to become common practice could yield significant social benefits.

Appendix

Data and Methods

The research presented in this book was centered on three types of data, collected using both qualitative and quantitative methodologies. Taken together, they provide for a far-reaching overview of the role of labor market intermediaries in the regional economies studied. First, in the summer and fall of 2000, we conducted a qualitative study of LMIs in Silicon Valley and Milwaukee. Second, to garner background information on the volatility of labor market conditions in both locations, we conducted an analysis of the employment patterns evidenced in unemployment insurance wage record data for California and Wisconsin for the years 1992 through 1999. Finally, between August 2001 and June 2002, we conducted a phone survey of workers to gather information on the labor market experiences of those who did use labor market intermediaries to find work and those who did not. In this appendix, we discuss each of these research strategies and the accompanying methodological issues. We conclude with a detailed discussion of the social capital measure and the tests we employed to ascertain robustness.

Intermediary Profiles

Case study research was conducted in tandem across the two regions, using the same methods in both places. From the outset, our focus was on intermediaries that primarily serve workers without college degrees. We began with a series of focus groups with representatives from a wide range of intermediaries. Our goal was twofold: to get a broad overview of the landscape of intermediaries in each region, and to get about thirty nominations for typical (as opposed to exemplary) case studies. For in-depth study, we then selected at least two cases from each of the following categories: temporary agencies, community-based or nonprofit organizations, community or technical colleges, membership-based organizations (such as unions and professional associations), and public agencies (such as welfare-to-work agencies and private industry councils). We conducted in-depth, one- to two-hour interviews with the staff of each intermediary, typically two to three people. We also interviewed the staff of at least two employers that were connected to the intermediary and two workers who had received training or placement from the intermediary. We conducted a total of 146 interviews, profiling 23 different intermediaries.

These profiles served two purposes. First, by allowing us to describe the landscape of LMIs, they provide useful information to researchers and policymakers regarding LMI strategies in the context of regional economic opportunities and constraints. Second, they informed the design of the questions in our worker survey about the types of LMIs that workers may have interacted with, as well as the types and effectiveness of the services received from them. We developed standardized, semistructured interview protocols separately for the intermediaries, employers, and workers. The content of the interviews was straightforward. We asked intermediaries about the services they provided and for whom, the barriers and challenges they encountered, their funding sources, and their relationships to employers, workers, and other intermediaries. As much as possible, we tried to gather "hard" data (for example, placement rates, average placement wages). We asked employers about their reasons for using the intermediary and about their business strategy, workplace organization, and wages and career paths. We asked workers about their employment history, how and why they contacted the intermediary, the services they received, and the jobs they ultimately found.

We should emphasize that we conducted much of our qualitative research in a period of extraordinarily tight labor markets. Both the focus groups and the detailed interviews suggested that throughout the calendar year 2000 intermediaries in both regions were scrambling to maintain worker supply; some employers expressed concern over worker quality even as many workers experienced rising wages, declines in the wait period for health insurance, and other improvements in their conditions. Thus, we were able to observe intermediaries in some of the most favorable conditions for success, since employers were especially eager for workers and therefore more willing to enter into relationships with a wider range of intermediaries. At the same time, our qualitative findings may not apply to more "normal" economic conditions, under which there might be fewer incentives for employers to engage with intermediaries that are trying to set higher standards in the labor market.

Unemployment Insurance Data

A second component of our research strategy was to analyze unemployment insurance wage record data for both states in order to better understand the regional labor markets in which labor market intermediaries are operating. The wage record data supply a complete record of the quarterly earnings of all workers who are covered by unemployment insurance in a state.[1] Available data include a record of individual workers' quarterly earnings, a unique employer identification code, the employer's geographic location, and the employer's industry. For use on this project, we obtained a 5 percent sample of all work records for the state of Wisconsin and a 10 percent sample of work records from California for the years 1992 through 1999. Thus, we are able to compare the trends in earnings and employment volatility in both states and regions over this time period. We focus this analysis on overall state and regional averages and aggregate industry averages but also look at more detailed industries that are particularly connected with employment through LMIs, such as the temporary help service industry and industries that our survey identified as the top employment destinations for workers who obtained employment through an LMI.

A key issue in analyzing these data is the handling of geographic information and its relationship to single-site and multi-site employers. At the beginning of 1999, in California and Wisconsin, respectively, 96 and 94 percent of employers were single-site establishments, but they comprised only 61 and 62 percent of jobs (with multi-site establishments being disproportionately large employers). When an employer is a single-site establishment, the location information reported typically corresponds to the actual work site and can be used to make a geographic determination of the location of employment. Thus, for employees of single-site establishments, we can identify the specific counties in which they work, and we can make regional comparisons between the Milwaukee metropolitan area (Milwaukee, Waukesha, Ozaukee, and Washington counties) and the Silicon Valley area (defined here as Santa Clara County). For employers with multiple work sites, however, the location reported with their UI data corresponds to only one of their locations (generally a headquarters location) and does not necessarily identify the work location of individual employees. For these workers, we can analyze employment patterns at the statewide level only.

These limitations allow us to examine statewide patterns for all workers in Wisconsin and California and for workers at single-site establishments only in Santa Clara County and in the four-county Milwaukee metropolitan area. To judge the representativeness of the workers identified at single-site establishments in the two regions, we conducted a comparison of single- and multi-site establishment workers statewide and compared these groups to the single-site establishment workers in each region. On the basis of this comparison, we concluded that while there are some differences between single- and multi-establishment workers (particularly in California), the single-site data for the two regions still provide a reasonable representation of the labor market patterns in those regions. This is especially true for data disaggregated at the industry level, since much of the difference between single- and multi-site establishments lies in their different industrial compositions.

Tables A.1 and A.2 present data for single- and multi-site establishments statewide in the two states, as well as for the single-site establishments alone in each of the two regions. These tables show the percentage of workers in disaggregated industries as well as two of our calculated measures of labor market volatility—job stability and the percentage of jobs with earnings increases.[2] Industry disaggregations are provided for all one-digit major industry categories, as well as for the temporary help services industry (SIC 7363) and the five two-digit industries that were most prominently represented among the jobs obtained through LMIs by LMI users in the two regions sampled in our survey of LMI use.[3]

In both states, the industry composition of single-site and multi-site employers varies, but the differences are most distinct in California. It is clear that the single-site employer data for Silicon Valley overrepresent some industries (agriculture, construction, manufacturing) and underrepresent others (transportation, communication and utilities, services, public administration). There are similar differences in Wisconsin, but their magnitude is considerably less. However, because the measures of job stability and earnings growth also vary by industry, the net effect on the regionwide averages of these measures should be mitigated. It is also important to note that within industries the characteristics of jobs with single- and multi-site employers differ from one another. In both states, jobs with single-site employers are, on average, less

(*text continues on page 245*)

Table A.1 First-Quarter 1999 Jobs That Continue and Have Earnings Increases in the Second Quarter of 1999 Among Single-Site and Multi-Site California Establishments, by Industry of First-Quarter 1999 Employer

| | California | | | | | | Santa Clara County | | |
| | Single-Site Only | | | Multi-Site Only | | | Single-Site Only | | |
	Percentage of Jobs	Percentage of Jobs Continued	Percentage of Jobs with Earnings Increases	Percentage of Jobs	Percentage of Jobs Continued	Percentage of Jobs with Earnings Increases	Percentage of Jobs	Percentage of Jobs Continued	Percentage of Jobs with Earnings Increases
All industries		0.80	0.57		0.84	0.56		0.83	0.57
One-digit industries									
Agricultural production—crops	0.06	0.61	0.63	0.01	0.80	0.67	0.02	0.78	0.66
Mining	0.00	0.81	0.54	0.00	0.93	0.46	0.00	0.67	1.00
Construction	0.08	0.73	0.62	0.01	0.81	0.61	0.08	0.77	0.64
Manufacturing	0.15	0.86	0.63	0.11	0.86	0.56	0.26	0.90	0.60
Transportation and public utilities	0.04	0.83	0.58	0.07	0.88	0.53	0.02	0.85	0.57
Wholesale trade	0.07	0.85	0.57	0.04	0.88	0.59	0.07	0.88	0.57
Retail trade	0.13	0.77	0.56	0.24	0.80	0.61	0.12	0.77	0.56
Finance, insurance, and real estate	0.05	0.84	0.48	0.07	0.89	0.46	0.03	0.86	0.50
Services	0.41	0.80	0.55	0.37	0.82	0.53	0.40	0.81	0.54
Public administration	0.01	0.90	0.60	0.08	0.93	0.61	0.00	0.86	0.65

(continued)

Table A.1 First-Quarter 1999 Jobs That Continue and Have Earnings Increases in the Second Quarter of 1999 Among Single-Site and Multi-Site California Establishments, by Industry of First-Quarter 1999 Employer

| | California | | | | | | Santa Clara County | | |
| | Single-Site Only | | | Multi-Site Only | | | Single-Site Only | | |
	Percentage of Jobs	Percentage of Jobs Continued	Percentage of Jobs with Earnings Increases	Percentage of Jobs	Percentage of Jobs Continued	Percentage of Jobs with Earnings Increases	Percentage of Jobs	Percentage of Jobs Continued	Percentage of Jobs with Earnings Increases
Environmental quality and housing	0.00	0.91	0.66	0.00	0.93	0.42	0.00	0.90	0.53
Unclassified establishments	0.00	0.25	0.57	0.00	0.31	0.47	0.00	1.00	1.00
Selected two-digit industries									
Construction (SIC 152–179)	0.08	0.73	0.62	0.01	0.81	0.61	0.08	0.77	0.64
Machinery and computing equipment (SIC 351–359)	0.02	0.88	0.62	0.01	0.93	0.44	0.07	0.91	0.64
Electrical machinery, equipment, and supplies (SIC 361–369)	0.02	0.90	0.62	0.01	0.94	0.47	0.10	0.91	0.58
Communications (SIC 481–489)	0.01	0.81	0.54	0.02	0.82	0.43	0.01	0.90	0.57
Computer and data processing services (SIC 737)	0.02	0.87	0.55	0.01	0.90	0.49	0.10	0.88	0.53
Temporary services industry (SIC 7363)	0.02	0.57	0.57	0.07	0.59	0.56	0.02	0.52	0.60

Source: Authors' compilation.

Table A.2 First-Quarter 1997 Jobs That Continue and Have Earnings Increases in the Second Quarter of 1997 Among Single-Site and Multi-Site Wisconsin Establishments, by Industry of First-Quarter 1997 Employer

| | Wisconsin | | | | | | Milwaukee, Waukesha, Ozaukee, and Washington Counties | | |
| | Single-Site Only[a] | | | Multi-Site Only[b] | | | Single-Site Only[c] | | |
	Percentage of Jobs	Percentage of Jobs Continued	Percentage of Jobs with Earnings Increases	Percentage of Jobs	Percentage of Jobs Continued	Percentage of Jobs with Earnings Increases	Percentage of Jobs	Percentage of Jobs Continued	Percentage of Jobs with Earnings Increases
All industries		0.86	0.54		0.88	0.52		0.84	0.55
One-digit industries									
Agricultural production—crops	0.01	0.83	0.61	0.00	0.88	0.71	0.01	0.80	0.67
Mining	0.00	0.89	0.74	0.00	1.00	0.36	0.00	0.73	0.75
Construction	0.06	0.85	0.65	0.01	0.86	0.58	0.05	0.85	0.64
Manufacturing	0.22	0.91	0.54	0.23	0.94	0.52	0.21	0.89	0.55
Transportation and public utilities	0.05	0.88	0.52	0.05	0.93	0.50	0.04	0.85	0.49
Wholesale trade	0.05	0.90	0.51	0.05	0.89	0.55	0.07	0.90	0.51
Retail trade	0.17	0.82	0.54	0.21	0.82	0.55	0.15	0.80	0.54
Finance, insurance, and real estate	0.04	0.91	0.46	0.06	0.93	0.47	0.06	0.91	0.49
Services	0.33	0.82	0.52	0.34	0.86	0.55	0.37	0.79	0.55
Public administration	0.05	0.92	0.56	0.04	0.95	0.22	0.04	0.95	0.70

(continued)

Table A.2 First-Quarter 1997 Jobs That Continue and Have Earnings Increases in the Second Quarter of 1997 Among Single-Site and Multi-Site Wisconsin Establishments, by Industry of First-Quarter 1997 Employer (*Continued*)

| | Wisconsin | | | | | | Milwaukee, Waukesha, Ozaukee, and Washington Counties | | |
| | Single-Site Only[a] | | | Multi-Site Only[b] | | | Single-Site Only[c] | | |
	Percentage of Jobs	Percentage of Jobs Continued	Percentage of Jobs with Earnings Increases	Percentage of Jobs	Percentage of Jobs Continued	Percentage of Jobs with Earnings Increases	Percentage of Jobs	Percentage of Jobs Continued	Percentage of Jobs with Earnings Increases
Environmental quality and housing	0.00	0.95	0.40	0.01	0.96	0.13	0.00	0.91	0.90
Unclassified establishments	0.01	0.57	0.45	0.00	0.79	0.74	0.00	0.00	0.00
Selected two-digit industries									
Construction (SIC 152–179)	0.06	0.85	0.65	0.01	0.86	0.58	0.05	0.86	0.65
Metal industry (SIC 331–349)	0.04	0.92	0.56	0.02	0.93	0.66	0.04	0.91	0.56
Machinery and computing equipment (SIC 351–359)	0.04	0.94	0.54	0.03	0.95	0.42	0.05	0.93	0.57
Transportation (SIC 401–478)	0.04	0.87	0.54	0.03	0.90	0.57	0.03	0.86	0.51
Temporary services industry (SIC 7363)	0.03	0.47	0.50	0.04	0.54	0.58	0.05	0.47	0.51
Hospitals (SIC 806)	0.03	0.95	0.59	0.04	0.94	0.42	0.04	0.94	0.77

Source: Authors' compilation.

[a] In the first quarter of 1997, total number of jobs: 88,209 (0.62); total number of employers: 24,473 (0.94).

[b] In the first quarter of 1997, total number of jobs: 53,685 (0.38); total number of employers: 1,428 (0.06).

[c] In the first quarter of 1997, total number of jobs: 29,290; total number of employers: 6,428.

stable, but they are also associated with slightly higher rates of earnings increase. Thus, we conclude that using only the single-site data to represent the two regional economies is likely to lead to small underestimates of job stability and slight overestimates of the occurrence of earnings growth in both places. These differences, while larger in California than in Wisconsin, are likely to be small, especially when the data are disaggregated by industry.

The Survey of LMI Use

The third stage of this research project involved the development and fielding of a survey of workers in both Silicon Valley and Milwaukee, investigating their use of LMIs.[4] To our knowledge, this is the first research effort to collect a broad base of quantitative information on LMI use and incidence across the whole range of types of intermediaries. The data collected allowed us to document comprehensively the role and impact of LMIs and to place them in the broader context of the labor markets in which they operate. The survey explored whether or not intermediaries serve as substitutes for or complements to the use of social networks for low-income workers, and it also gathered worker perspectives on their relationship with different intermediaries.

Although the intermediary is becoming more ubiquitous in our economic landscape, it is not yet a well-defined concept in the popular consciousness. Through repeated drafting and testing, we found that individuals were most able to give accurate accounts of their experiences with LMIs if those experiences were connected to a job they had held. We found it difficult to elicit information from random respondents about other experiences they had had with LMIs. To perfect the wording in key introductory sections that inquire about the use of LMIs, we conducted focus groups to review and test the instrument, and we pretested and piloted it prior to going into full production. On the basis of these preliminary tests, we attempted to maximize the accuracy of the answers we received by limiting our inquiry to jobs that were held (although not necessarily obtained) in the three years prior to the interview and to the LMIs that were used to obtain those jobs. As a result, the contact with the intermediary itself could have occurred at any time, and by necessity we are not reporting on intermediary experiences that did not result in employment. A full copy of the survey instrument is available from the authors.

The survey was fielded between August 2001 and June 2002 as a random-digit-dialing phone survey of workers in the Silicon Valley region of northern California and the Milwaukee, Wisconsin, metropolitan area. The sample of phone numbers drawn included both listed and unlisted numbers.[5] We collected survey responses from 1,348 individuals (659 in Milwaukee and 689 in Silicon Valley) between the ages of twenty-five and sixty-five who had worked sometime in the past three years. The age limitation was designed to curtail our observation of the early labor market experiences and job churning among the youngest members of the labor market as they are getting a foothold in the workforce, thus enabling us to focus our analysis on the labor market experiences of established workers. The average survey was conducted in twenty-two minutes and the resulting dataset contains over four hundred pieces of information. To collect detailed information on LMI use, we oversampled those who had used some kind of LMI to obtain a job that they had held in the last three years; a total of 739 observations (373 in Milwaukee and 366 in Silicon Valley) are from individuals who fall in this category. By collecting comparable information from both LMI and non-LMI users, we were able to compare the characteristics and outcomes of the two groups. Low-income phone prefixes were oversampled to ensure adequate representation of low-income individuals in the sample.[6] The survey was conducted in both English and Spanish as needed; a total of eighty-five interviews were completed in Spanish. To reduce nonresponse bias, the survey protocol included fifteen callback attempts to each unanswered phone number and repeated attempts to convert eligible respondents who might have been initially unwilling to participate in the survey.[7] The overall survey response rate was 39.9 percent.

In the survey, we identified and categorized the intermediaries used by workers into five groupings: temporary placement agencies and headhunters; unions; community-based, nonprofit, and governmental organizations and agencies; community and technical colleges and private vocational schools; and membership-based professional associations. In an effort to focus the discussion on organizations that make job matching and vocationally oriented training their primary focus, we did not include the job placement functions of regular academic institutions such as high schools and four-year colleges and universities.

We made a number of efforts to ensure that the LMIs reported were appropriately classified. First, in our initial questions regarding LMI use we provided a description of the distinguishing characteristics of each LMI type. Second, if respondents had trouble responding to a question regarding a particular type of LMI, they were asked the name of the LMI and interviewers looked up the agency or organization on reference lists of all known LMIs in each region, classified by type. Third, following the initial set of questions regarding LMI type, we included a set of backup questions asking individuals about how they obtained their most recent job, and we followed up on any relationship between their answer and possible LMI use. (For example, if they said that they obtained a job through a referral from a friend or relative, we inquired whether that friend or relative had referred them to any type of agency or organization.) Furthermore, when non-LMI users were queried later in the survey about their method of job finding, there was a similar follow-up of any answers that might have pointed to LMI use. Finally, when LMI users reported on the specifics of the LMI they used, we asked for the name of the agency and a description of the types of services the agency provided and the clientele it served. After receiving the data from the survey, we checked every LMI classification against these names and descriptions and against our lists of known organizations in each region, and we reclassified them as appropriate.[8]

We did other data cleaning to ensure data accuracy. Many questions allowed for categorical answers or for the respondent to answer "other" and provide a verbatim explanation. All of these "other" explanations were examined and, if appropriate, reclassified into one of the preexisting data categories. In some cases, new data categories were added if the "other" answers revealed a common answer that we had not initially allowed for.[9] We also checked the accuracy and consistency of particular values; variables such as earnings, hourly wages, and hours worked per week were matched to information on occupation and checked for plausibility. In a small number of cases, values were recoded if coding errors and inconsistencies were obvious (or values were set to "missing" if answers were completely incongruous). In a few cases, the number of years that individuals reported receiving assistance from a particular LMI or obtaining a GED degree was top-coded to fifteen years.

This survey involved a complex sampling strategy that allowed for the over-sampling of both LMI users and the low-income population. The result was a procedure that allowed for two separate calculations of the incidence of LMI use. For one set of randomly selected phone numbers, all eligible and willing respondents were interviewed, regardless of their LMI status. The proportions of LMI use in this sample give us one measure of LMI incidence. For a second set of randomly selected phone numbers, only eligible LMI users were interviewed. Our final incidence measures, reported and discussed in chapter 3, were constructed by combining the two samples and applying respondent weights (which reflected the probability of an individual's phone number being drawn for selection into either sample).[10] Both methods resulted in comparable LMI incidence measures. Consistent with our use of survey sampling and weighting procedures, the analysis is derived from statistical routines designed explicitly to account for the data variability introduced by survey sampling.

One final issue that merits further explanation is the differentiation between respondents who had used temporary agencies from those who used permanent placement agencies or headhunters within the overall LMI category of private agencies. As noted in chapter 4, the survey respondents specified whether they had used permanent placement agencies and temp agencies or other LMIs in answering a question designated this way because we found in focus groups and pretesting that distinguishing agencies was a challenge, and so we hoped to use other characteristics of their answers to draw the finer distinction between permanent and temporary placements. Thus, we had to sort through the data to determine which of the LMIs placed in the private agency category were temps and which were not. The task was complex, as can be seen later in this appendix, and thus we created both a "broad" and "narrow" categorization of temporary agencies and a corresponding "narrow" and "broad" categorization of permanent placement agencies and headhunters.

First, to determine the cases for which the available information was insufficient or inconsistent in pointing to either a temp agency or a permanent placement agency, we constructed two variables. The first was initially set to zero for all respondents in the "temporary placement agency and headhunter" group and was then recoded to one if the respondent reported either being recruited by the agency in question or holding no temporary or temporary-to-permanent jobs that were obtained through the agency—either answer probably indicating that it was not a temp agency that was used but rather a placement agency. The second variable was also initially set to zero for the entire group and was recoded to one only if the respondent reported that the job they obtained through the agency in question was "not temporary." These two measures were then cross-tabulated, resulting in four groups of cases: one for which both measures were consistent in suggesting that a permanent placement agency was used (1,1); one for which both measures suggested that a temp agency was used (0,0); and the remaining two for which the measures were inconsistent (1,0 and 0,1).

Our broad definition of temps assumed that virtually all of the ambiguous or inconsistent cases were temporary agencies; there were a few that were reclassified as permanent upon further investigation of the full open-ended answers (described later). Our narrow definition sought to determine more exactly which of these cases were actually temps. We thus used both the information noted earlier as well as the total number of LMI jobs held by the respondent in the three-year period, the number of these that were temporary, the number that were permanent, the number that were temporary-to-permanent, an open-ended description of the agency, and an open-ended description of how the respondent found out about the agency. We were aided in this classification task by our qualitative work identifying the agencies in each regional labor market: thus, we could classify an agency as generally offering temp positions or not based on whether sufficient information could be found about it on the Internet, or because it was familiar to one of the research team, or because the open-ended responses clearly pointed one way or the other. We tried to err on the side of caution—if the agency name was that of a well-known temporary agency but there was evidence from the open-ended answer that the placement was permanent, we did not classify the agency as a temp under the narrow definition.

Thus, the broad definition of "temp" included all those respondents who definitely used a temp as well as those who probably used a temp, and the narrow definition included respondents who definitely used a temp and who "almost definitely" used a temp; calculations on incidence using this measure were nearly identical to the temporary agency share of employment that emerged from traditional labor market data. As we note, the wage and benefits results were nearly identical whether we used the broad or narrow definition of temps; small differences between results for the broad and narrow definitions in terms of the earnings regressions are duly noted in the text. Distinguishing the temps and nontemps, however, was critical: the results on wage and benefit outcomes would have been very different if we had run the regressions with a variable that was equal to one for all private placement (temporary and permanent) LMIs, primarily because one has positive effects and the other has negative effects.

Data Issues Related to Measuring Social Capital

The Construction and Robustness of the Social Capital Variable

Our social connectedness measure is a composite that took the value of one when the respondent reported that he or she: had attended at least three different types of meetings in the past year; talked to friends or relatives at least once per week; had at least one to two friends or relatives that they would feel comfortable asking for help finding a job; and had access to the Internet. The basic method of construction involved starting with one component and adding others, as described here, checking along the way for robustness.

The meeting component of the measure was derived from a survey question that asked respondents whether they had attended different types of meetings in the past year. The types of meeting included business/professional, labor union, political, neighborhood, PTA, religious, cultural, and sport/social meetings. Attending meetings such as these would seem to increase a person's social contacts, perhaps making him or her less likely to need an intermediary. In general, we found that the greater the number of these meetings a person had attended in the last year, the less likely that person was to be an LMI user. We created one simple measure of social capital, a dummy variable called "many_meet" that was set to one for people who attended at least three meetings in the past year, which seemed a reasonable standard. This was found to have a significant effect on the probability of LMI use in a multivariate regression and was also significantly associated with choosing away from a temporary agency, squaring with our initial suppositions. However, as a measure of social capital, we felt that this measure was relatively limited, depending as it did on only one possible dimension of social connection.

We therefore added Internet access to our definition of social capital and created a second dummy variable called "soc_connected_many" that took the people considered "socially connected" under the first definition and kept only those with Internet access. With rapidly increasing Internet use throughout the country, it is likely that more and more people are turning to the web as a means of communication with others, making Internet access a viable candidate to include in our measure of social capital.[11] With the addition of Internet access, our social capital measure had a greater effect on LMI use, with a greater difference in LMI use from our first measure between those considered "socially connected" and those "not connected" by this definition.

We then decided to add two measures that would be more typical of social networks literature and would further constrain who might fall within the boundaries of a social capital dummy variable: the regularity of communication with intimates, and the number of friends or relatives the respondent reported might be used in a job search. Specifically, the survey asked respondents how often they talked on the phone or visited with any close friends or relatives and how many friends or relatives they had whom they felt they could ask for help in finding a job. We assumed not only that an increased level of communication would be associated with more social connectedness but that having more friends the respondent identified as potentially helpful in a job search would be indicative of social connectedness as well.[12] For our third measure of social capital, "soc_connected_many_version2," we maintained the meetings and Internet components of "soc_connected_many" and kept only those who communicated with any close friends or relatives at least weekly and who had at least three to five friends they could ask for help in finding a job.

Although any single one of the components of "soc_connected_many_version2" only kept around 20 percent of the sample out of the exclusive "socially connected" group—except for the meetings restriction, which was operative for only one-third of the sample—when combined under "soc_connected_many_version2," they allow only about 22 percent of the sample to be designated as "socially connected." Satisfied with the breadth of characteristics included in our third measure, our final alteration was to loosen the number-of-friends restriction by one category in order to pick up a bit more of the sample. The final measure is called "s_connected," and it captures about one-quarter of the sample; we felt that this was a large enough subgroup to test for meaningful effects, and it is the measure utilized in the text.

Although we found this specification of social connectedness to be the most theoretically pleasing (given the available answers in the survey), at least two of the components—Internet access and the number of friends and relatives who could help respondents find a job if they needed one—could give cause for concern. As noted earlier, Internet access could have a direct effect on job search and is also associated with wealth. The former issue applies to the interpretation of the effect of our social capital measure on the probability of using an LMI, and the latter could distort the effect of a good social network in two ways. First, people with greater wealth are more likely to have steady employment and thus less likely to turn to an LMI. Second, given that the "better" LMIs are associated with higher wages, LMI users with Internet access could be more likely to have used one of the "better" LMIs.

The number of friends and relatives who could help a respondent find a job if he or she needed one is problematic in that its relationship to LMI use could be construed as definitional: if a respondent had a friend or relative who could help in a job search, then what use would the respondent have had for an intermediary? However, being able to identify friends and relatives who could help does not necessarily mean that the respondent in fact used these friends and relatives, and as we discuss later, the relationship between having used a friend and being able to identify a hypothetical friend for job search purposes is not clear. In any case, the survey question is useful in that it revealed something of how close the respondent was to his or her friends and relatives, with specific reference to whether that closeness was relevant (from the respondent's view) to job hunting.

Recognizing the potential problems in our multicomponent measure, we also ran our battery of regressions with three stripped-down versions: one that dropped the Internet access restriction only; one that dropped the restriction on having one to two friends or relatives who could help find a job only; and one that dropped both of these restrictions. Although we were not particularly concerned about the frequency-of-communication component, we also ran the battery of regressions with a social capital measure based just on Internet access and meeting attendance and one based just on meeting attendance alone. For all five alternative specifications, we found the pattern results to be very similar to those obtained when using our preferred and theoretically more satisfying measure: being "socially connected" was significant in steering people both away from LMIs in general and, if an LMI user, toward the nontemp LMIs.[13] A series of other robustness tests, discussed in the next section, also gave us confidence in the measure.

Checking the Measure Against Other Measures

Several survey questions helped describe the quality of a respondent's social network more thoroughly than those that we included in our measure of social capital. However, because the survey was focused on LMI use—not to mention financial constraints—these questions were asked only of those who had no experience with LMIs and therefore had more "open time" in the interview window. In addressing our primary question about whether and to what degree social connectedness tended to provide an alternative to LMI use when people were in need of employment, we were thus restricted in the questions we could use to construct our measure of social capital to those that were asked of the entire sample; thus, we could not make use of what might have been better indicators of respondents' social networks as provided by the survey questions that were not included in that measure.

However, we could utilize these questions as an instrument for cross-checking our measure by examining the relationship between the responses given by non-LMI users to these questions and their social connectedness under our measure. The results of our investigation into this relationship turned out to be quite supportive of our measure. It should be stressed that this cross-checking exercise was based on relatively small samples of respondents, and so any particular correlation should not be given much weight. What we are attempting to show is the general pattern of answers to these questions in terms of our social capital measure.

In asking respondents about the most recent job they had held in the last three years, the survey asked them, if it was not obtained through an LMI, how the job was obtained and gave them four possible categorical responses: (1) through friends, acquaintances, coworkers, or relatives; (2) through an Internet website; (3) in answer to a newspaper ad, help-wanted sign, or e-mail notice or through contacting an employer directly; and (4) through an agency or organization. If the response fell into the first category, then the respondent was asked a series of questions that attempted to gauge the socioeconomic status of the person through whom they gained employment and to determine whether the job they got made them better off under several different measures. Depending on the particular question, between 148 and 189 respondents gave answers, and this was the first set of questions we were able to cross-check our social capital measure against, a set that we refer to as the "real-person" questions, since the answers were based on actual people who helped the respondent find a job.

Non-LMI users who did not report having obtained a job that was held in the last three years through a friend, acquaintance, coworker, or relative were later asked whether they felt that there was someone who could help them find a job if they needed one, and then asked a set of follow-up questions about that person's background. There were 229 non-LMI users who could think of one specific person whom they could ask for help in finding a job, and between 165 and 189 of these gave answers to questions about this person depending on the particular question. This was the other set of questions for which we inspected correlations with our social capital measure, and we refer to them as the "hypothetical-person" questions—this person did not actually help the respondent, but the respondent believed that he or she might be useful in future searches.

Clearly, these two sets of questions afford us a look into the quality of the respondent's social network, whether they actually used someone they knew to get a job or not. Those with a strong social network may have been more likely to have used someone to help them find a job—or perhaps more appropriately, more likely to be able to think of such a person—more likely to have used or thought of someone at least as well-off as themselves, and more likely to have seen improvement in their work situation through the use of such a contact. Here we test how well our measure of social capital squares with these notions of a strong social network with respect to the particular questions that were asked of non-LMI respondents.

All of these questions can be placed into two groups: those that revealed whether the respondent had a social network at all and those that revealed more about the quality of the social network. The two questions as to whether respondents had ever obtained a job through someone they knew and whether they felt that there was someone who could help them find a job fall in the "does the respondent have a social network at all" group, while the other questions that ask specifically about the person who did or could help them fall into the "quality of social network" group.

In dealing with the first group of questions, we found that while being socially connected under our measure had nothing to do with whether or not the respondent reported having obtained a job through someone they knew, there was a highly significant relationship between our measure and the respondent's feeling that there was someone he or she could go to for help in finding a job: 95 percent of those considered by our measure to be socially connected felt that there was someone they could go to for help, as compared to only 71 percent of those considered not connected. Initially we had expected to see a positive relationship between social connectedness and actually having used contacts to get a job, as we did with the corresponding hypothetical-person question, but in retrospect the data make sense: while not all of those who could be considered to have had a strong social network were placed in a situation in which they needed to utilize that network to get a job, we would expect them to have enough different contacts so that if they did find themselves in need of a job, at least one person would come to mind who could help them.

However, there is an issue worthy of investigation concerning the highly significant correlation between our social capital measure and respondents' feeling that there was someone who could help them find a job, and it is one of identification: having at least one or two friends or relatives whom one could call on to help find a job was embedded in our social capital measure, so of course being socially connected would lead one to feel that there was someone who could help. To get at this issue, we created a version of our social capital measure that did not include as one component the number of friends or relatives the respondent could call on to help find a job, and then once again we tested the relationship between being identified as socially connected and feeling that there was someone who could aid in job search. The result was a similar spread, though not quite as large: 89 percent of the socially connected believed that they could get someone's help, as opposed to 73 percent of those who were not connected. There was a highly significant correlation between being socially connected under this definition and feeling that there was someone to go to for help finding a job, with a Pearson correlation coefficient of 0.17, significant at better than the 0.01 level (0.0029). This indicates that our measure, even if stripped down to avoid any identification problems, is still consistent with this other, perhaps better, measure of whether the respondent had a viable social network for employment purposes.[14]

Now that we have moved beyond the question of whether our social capital measure is a worthy indicator of the existence of a respondent's social network, the remainder of this cross-check asked whether our measure captured those with a higher-quality social network among those who appeared to have at least some kind of a network. Again, the survey questions we looked to in examining this were those that were asked about the person from whom a non-LMI respondent had received help in finding a job, or if the respondent had not received help, about a specific person the respondent could ask for help if he or she needed a job. Information obtained through these questions included the closeness of relationship between the person and the respondent, the marital status of the person, his or her level of education, his or her employment status, whether he or she was on welfare, and, for the real-person questions only, information about how the person helped the respondent find a job and whether or not that job made the respondent better off as judged by several different measures of job satisfaction.

To get an idea of the relationship between our measure of social capital and these various indicators of network quality, we took simple weighted averages for all non-LMI respondents considered to be socially connected under our measure and compared them to the corresponding mean values for those we considered to be not connected. Given the relatively small sample of respondents answering these questions, not all of the social network indicator variables could be expected to show a distinct relationship to our social capital measure. However, several did, so we subsequently estimated the significance of the relationships through a set of simple bivariate correlations, the results of which are reported in table A.3, along with the comparative means.

Table A.3 Average Characteristics of Person Who Helped or Could Help Respondent Find a Job, Broken Down by Social Connectedness with Correlations

	Number of Cases	Mean Value by Whether Respondent Is Socially Connected		Correlation with Social Capital Measure	
		Socially Connected	Not Connected	Coefficient	Significance
Person who helped has high school graduate level of education or less	144	0.32	0.37	−0.04	0.61
Person who could help has high school graduate level of education or less	163	**0.13**	**0.29**	**−0.19**	**0.02**
Person who helped has college graduate level of education or higher	144	**0.60**	**0.42**	**0.16**	**0.06**
Person who could help has college graduate level of education or higher	163	**0.72**	**0.62**	**0.10**	**0.18**
Person's help led to higher wages	180	0.33	0.34	−0.01	0.93
Person's help led to more stable job	180	0.39	0.41	−0.02	0.81
Person's help led to a better schedule	181	0.37	0.36	0.01	0.85
Person's help led to better medical coverage or pension plan	180	0.36	0.26	0.09	0.21
Person's help led to better career opportunities	180	**0.59**	**0.46**	**0.11**	**0.13**
Person's help led to better child care situation	150	0.13	0.10	0.04	0.64
Person's help led to better commute	180	**0.26**	**0.14**	**0.14**	**0.07**
Person's help led to better working conditions	177	0.73	0.65	0.07	0.33
Person's help led to other improvements in job	181	0.12	0.10	0.03	0.72

Source: Authors' compilation.
Bold = significant at the .20 level or better.

As can be seen in table A.3, those who were socially connected tended to have personal contacts who were better educated, evidenced both by the lower percentage of these contacts who had a high school diploma or GED as their highest level of education and the higher percentage of those who had a BA degree or better. If we put some raw numbers in place of the averaged values to further illustrate the relationship, we find that among the 32 respondents considered to be socially connected out of a total of 148 who obtained a job with the help of a friend, only three were assisted by a friend of lesser education, while the remaining 29 got help from someone of equal or higher education. For those respondents who did not get a job through a friend and were therefore asked if they could think of a person who could help them find a job if they needed one, among the 60 considered to be socially connected out of 165 total, only four thought of someone with a lower level of education, while the remaining 56 thought of someone with the same or higher level of education. For both of these examples, the not-connected respondents had a pronounced tendency to identify "helpful" friends with lower levels of education than their own.

Given the finding that the socially connected were more likely to have contacts with the same or higher level of education, we examined the relationship of our socially connected measure and contact level of education in low-income areas to see whether social capital worked the same way in these more burdened neighborhoods. As roughly demarcated by telephone prefixes, we looked at the education levels of people who could help or did help respondents find a job in these areas, and we found an even higher tendency among those respondents considered to be socially connected under our measure to have friends or other contacts with the same or higher levels of education than the respondents themselves. This is modest evidence that in more impoverished areas social capital can play an important role in connecting a person with people who may be able to help given their higher level of human capital, at least judging by the relative education levels.

The remaining indicators of network quality that described the outcome of a job that the respondent obtained with the help of someone he or she knew showed a less stable positive relationship to our social capital measure. Gaining better career opportunities and a better commute were significantly correlated with being socially connected, and gaining better medical coverage and/or an improved pension plan was close to significant, but the rest of the indicators were not significant, at least not for the entire sample. However, when we broke the sample down by region, we found that only three of the nine indicators had no significant correlation to our social capital measure in any one region, pointing to the differing rewards in the workplace by region that personal contacts can yield. For example, while being socially connected was not significantly correlated with getting higher wages or better career opportunities in Silicon Valley, in Milwaukee the relationship was significant. And while in Milwaukee being socially connected was not significantly correlated with "other improvements in job," it was in Silicon Valley.

Another interesting aspect of our measure of social capital involves the race of those identified by the respondent as potential allies in finding a job. We would suspect that being socially connected would make respondents of color more able to cross over the societal barriers and come up with a white person when asked to think of someone who could help them find a job, or even more likely to have actually been helped by a white person in getting a job. We found that this theory held up in the data to some degree when we ran a t-test comparing the rate of socially connected persons of color who had identified a white person who *did* help them find a job and the rate for socially connected persons of color who had identified a white person who *could* help them find a job to the same rates for persons of color considered to be not connected under our measure. The difference in the rates at which persons of color identified a white person who *did* help them was insignificant, but we found that the higher rate at which socially connected persons of color identified a white person who *could* help them to be significantly different from the lower rate among those considered not connected, at the .20 level. This is reasonable given the very small sample size.

We conclude that our indirect social capital measure, for all its imperfections, is robust across specifications and would have been well related to a richer measure of social connectedness had we been able to afford to ask the full battery of connectedness questions of the full sample.

Notes

Chapter 1

1. Data obtained from www.bls.gov, with temporary help measured by North American Industry Classification System (NAICS) code 56132 (temporary help services).

2. One example of such data inconsistency: using data from the Current Population Survey (CPS), Kenneth Swinnerton and Howard Wial (1995) find evidence of a secular decline in job stability, whereas Francis Diebold, David Neumark, and Daniel Polsky (1994) and Henry Farber (1996) do not. This difference is due in part to changes in the wording of the CPS tenure questions after 1981, in part to how researchers treat the self-employed, and in part to how they treat other non-respondents. For a good review of the evidence on job stability, see Neumark (2000) and Bernhardt and Marcotte (2000).

3. This is a slightly different boundary around LMIs than that offered by Osterman (1999, 134), who distinguishes between passive intermediaries, aggressive intermediaries that customize programs, provide training, and so on, and those intermediaries that seek to change "the terms of trade in the labor market." However, his third category seems to include mostly organizations of macro scale—such as community-based groups pressing corporations for concessions, living wage campaigns, and unions in general—with no apparent requirement that these actors also be performing the basic role of job matching associated with LMIs.

4. As we will see later in the data discussion, this emphasis also leads us to focus on certain occupations within the LMI universe, such as clericals in the service sector and machine operators in the manufacturing sector. For comparison purposes, we do include LMIs that serve craft positions, such as plumbers in the high-tech

industry and even a few professional occupations; however, we study these sectors to garner lessons for the lower end of the labor market.

5. This is a well-known problem in the labor process. See Bowles (1985) and Shapiro and Stiglitz (1984).

6. For more on Internet use in job search, see Kuhn and Skuterud (2000), who note that Internet use is not necessarily at odds with the use of other intermediaries, such as public employment agencies, and indeed, that those using one form of search mechanism may be more likely to use another.

7. These three sets of intermediary activities are very similar to the categorization offered by Richard Kazis (1998), who distinguishes between efforts to improve the efficiency of the job-matching process, efforts to improve supply-side work-force development institutions, and efforts to change the employer demand for labor. One distinction in our framework is that we assume that market making can include workforce development institutions. Moreover, we explicitly inter-sect this framework with interests. While Kazis also discusses interests or intended beneficiaries of LMIs, he assumes that the purpose of focusing on LMIs and labor demand is to reduce inequality; clearly, however, some LMIs alter labor markets without having as a goal the reduction of inequality.

Chapter 2

1. Because of Wisconsin's change in industry coding schemes in 1998, the analysis of Wisconsin data for the years 1998 and 1999 is limited to some aggregate cal-culations only. As discussed in the appendix, UI data identify the geographic loca-tions of individual jobs only for employers who operate single-site establishments.

2. This is measured only in aggregate for each state, because job changing can involve changing geographic locations within a state as well as changing industries.

3. These figures were based on a sample of individuals in Milwaukee and Silicon Valley who had worked during that period. It is plausible that these figures are lower and of reversed magnitudes (as compared with those calculated from UI data) because (1) the survey was less likely to measure multiple job holding than the UI data, (2) dynamics at the regional level are different than at the state level, or (3) there were underlying differences in labor market conditions in the two regions between the 1995 to 1997 and 1999 to 2001 periods.

4. Industry detail for these calculations, not shown here, is available from the authors.

5. Job durations differ significantly when measured prospectively and retrospec-tively. This reflects the underlying dynamics of job holding: many of the jobs begun in any one quarter are short-lived; thus, prospective job duration measures

are quite short. On the other hand, most currently held jobs are still held precisely because they have persisted. Thus, they have longer durations. There are analogies in other dynamic processes, such as the length of hospital stays and the duration of welfare spells (see, for example, Bane and Ellwood 1994).

6. These programs were initially brought together in 1973 under the Comprehensive Employment and Training Act (CETA), which was superseded in 1983 by the Joint Training Partnership Act (JTPA), and again in 1998 by the Workforce Investment Act (WIA). WIA went into effect on July 1, 2000.

7. These BLS statistics include everyone who is on the payroll of the firm, including both permanent staff and everyone who is placed on temporary assignments, regardless of how many hours they work. These average figures thus hide tremendous variation in earnings.

8. Reliable data on unionization rates are not separately available for the San Jose MSA.

Chapter 3

1. This informality obviously leaves open the possibility that LMIs reinforce cultural stereotypes about appropriate firm-worker matches, which clearly happens in some cases.

2. This approach is in sharp contrast to the response of much of the software industry to its skill shortages, which has been focused on recruiting people from outside the United States through expanding the H-1B program, rather than prioritizing the development of training programs in the United States.

3. Interview, September 13, 2000.

4. Indeed, as we show in chapter 6, stronger networks tend to dissuade workers from using temporary agencies.

5. Currently, if a worker affiliated with a temporary agency turns down employment because of poor wages or working conditions, he or she is ineligible for unemployment insurance. This condition ties workers to their temp agency and forces them to accept any offer, no matter how inadequate from the point of view of career-building.

Chapter 4

1. We limited the survey coverage to this age group in order to focus on the experiences of established adult workers.

2. Our analysis focuses on organizations that concentrate on job matching and vocationally oriented training and therefore does not include the job placement

functions of regular academic institutions, such as high schools and four-year colleges and universities.

3. Because we are missing data on current job status for a few survey respondents, we can calculate either an upper or lower bound for this measure. The figures presented here are a lower bound; the upper-bound figures are only slightly higher— 22.3 percent in Milwaukee and 15.8 percent in Silicon Valley.

4. Measured by a t-test at the standard .05 level of statistical significance.

5. These cases account for between 7.6 and 34.4 percent of private agency observations, depending on which LMI incidence measure is being considered.

6. It should be noted, however, that these latter figures were lower-bound estimates for our "current jobs" measure. The corresponding upper-bound estimate (not shown) is 4.2 percent in both regions.

7. For LMI users, the reference job is the last job they held during the last three years that was obtained through an LMI. For the non-LMI sample, the reference job is the current or most recent job held.

8. Furthermore, in the multivariate analysis explaining wages and benefits presented in chapter 5, we include job tenure as an explanatory variable, thus helping to account for different temporal distributions of reference jobs.

9. Annual household income cutoffs of $35,000 and $50,000 were used for the Milwaukee area and the Silicon Valley area, respectively.

Chapter 5

1. David Autor and Susan Houseman (2005a) report a similar concentration of temporary agency placements in production and manual labor occupations relative to direct-hire job placements. The lack of clerical jobs among temp workers in their sample can be attributed to its limitation to workers with relatively low skill levels.

2. These results are consistent with findings by others who report lower earnings in temporary agency placements in the general population (DiNatale 2001; GAO 2000; Segal and Sullivan 1997a), but stand in contrast with findings by Autor and Houseman (2005b) of higher raw wages among temp agency users. However, the latter result probably reflects their limited population of welfare recipients, among whom the relatively more-skilled individuals obtain temporary agency work.

3. Wage models are estimated using OLS regression. The benefits models are estimated using logistic regression. All models are estimated with procedures allowing for robust errors, minimizing the variance associated with survey sampling procedures.

4. We also experimented with the inclusion of the social connectedness variable discussed in chapter 6. However, we found that, with one exception, it does not enter any of these equations significantly. Social connectedness is positively related to the receipt of employer-provided health insurance benefits in Silicon Valley only in table 5.3, but its inclusion has little effect on the estimated coefficients on the LMI variables of interest.

5. We investigate the differential sorting of workers to different types of LMIs more fully in chapter 6. To the extent that unobservable characteristics are correlated with variables included in the equation, their effects should be largely accounted for.

6. The odds (or odds ratio) that a particular group will have a benefit available to them can be represented as $p/(1 - p)$ where p is the probability of having the benefit plan. When exponentiated, the coefficient on a binary variable representing a particular group represents the ratio of the odds for that group relative to the odds of the baseline group. For example, the exponentiated coefficient for "used temp agency" can be interpreted as $[p/(1 - p)]/[pb/(1 - pb)]$, where p is the probability that a temp agency user has the benefit and pb is the probability that a member of the baseline group has the benefit. Thus, estimated ratios of less than one would indicate that temp agency users have lower odds of having the benefit than the baseline group, and an estimate of greater than one would suggest the opposite.

7. This estimate of the relationship between current unemployment and the probability of unemployment is based on an examination of data from the 1999 March CPS (the year our own survey was conducted) covering California and Wisconsin (the two states included in our survey). We compared the rate of experiencing any unemployment (any positive number of weeks looking for work or on layoff) during the year prior to the survey to the rate of unemployment for all persons age twenty-five to sixty-four who were or had been in the labor force, that is, were either currently in the labor force at the time of the survey or who had spent any (positive) number of weeks looking for work or on layoff during the year prior to the survey. We found that the rate of experiencing any unemployment was about two times as high as the unemployment rate—13 percent as compared to 7 percent, respectively.

8. While this might seem high, recall that these are individuals in low-income prefixes; the employment rates for the whole sample are closer to the employment rates reported for the two regions being studied.

9. It also makes intuitive sense that respondents who offered hourly and weekly pay levels might have been less used to projecting continuity at the job than those who immediately thought of monthly and annual pay levels. Another alternative is to exclude the hourly and weekly employees; this yields similar results but severely restricts the sample size.

10. Although we find similar results using both our "broad" and "narrow" temp agency measures, we present only the findings for the narrow measure here; these make the closest match to the temp agency experiences that Autor and Houseman's sample probably had.

11. The resulting coefficient on this dummy variable, depicted in table 5.8, indicates a positive effect on earnings of close to 40 percent, a marginal effect that is strikingly close to the 45 percent reported for the full-quarter dummy in the regression most similar to ours, the fourth column of table 5.8 in Andersson, Holzer, and Lane 2005.

12. We focus here on the results in column 4 of table 5.10 in Andersson et al. (2005, 101), in which they consider temp agency use in the three years prior to the earning period under consideration. More generally, they find that the effects of temp agency use in the three-year period at the beginning of their nine-year sample yield a 6 to 10 percent improvement in earnings, with the effect more or less disappearing when firm effects are entered. Interestingly, when studying the more recent temp effect (which is positive), they find a negative effect of earlier temp use on earnings that is significant at the 0.20 level.

Chapter 6

1. This understates the role of friends and neighbors, since such contacts are also used to locate appropriate labor market intermediaries, a feature we will take up in future research.

2. Here and elsewhere in the chapter, the term "permanent placement agency"—or more simply, "placement agency"—includes all permanent placement agencies and headhunter LMIs.

3. We were not able to ask as full a range of questions as in those previous surveys, mostly because the LMI survey was already quite long, but also because we deployed the resources available to us within the short interview time we had with each respondent primarily to gather as wide a range of data as possible on LMI use and services. We should also note that the responses from the battery of traditional social connection questions are as of the time of the survey, while the job obtained through an LMI could have been held sometime in the past

and with a differing level of social capital. This is a problem inherent in this survey, but since the findings here are so dramatic, they evidence a degree of robustness to the basic model. Moreover, our concerns about timing and sequencing are alleviated by the likelihood that social capital is a rather slow-changing variable.

4. Among all respondents with Internet access who answered the question about how they got their last job, the percentage who reported getting it through the Internet was about twice as high among the group considered not to be socially connected under our measure than it was among those considered socially connected (8 percent as compared to 4 percent, respectively).

5. Work experience and squared work experience are sometimes common in the literature. However, we were concerned that the decision to use an LMI seems to be more a function of age than work experience per se, particularly for those in the later years of their working life.

6. We should note that the specific educational categories that are collapsed into the "above high school education (no BA)" variable include associate's degrees and certificates earned by those with more than twelve years of schooling.

7. Here we are using the term "degree" loosely to mean the successful completion of any gradual step in one's education, including the completion of primary school, high school, an associate's degree, a bachelor's degree, a master's degree, a PhD, or any professional degree or certification.

8. It is an imperfect measure—someone may have had a volatile experience well before the sample period and still be in an LMI-secured job in the current period—but we do not have the optimal measure: the full history of a respondent's work experience.

9. We should note that there were twenty-four observations that could have been included in the logit that excludes our social capital measure mentioned here (as well as in the multinomial logit that excludes social capital as reported later). These observations were excluded because they have missing values for the social capital measure and therefore are not included in the regression that controls for social capital; we wanted the exact same observations to be included in both of these regressions for the sake of consistency in comparisons made between them. All regressions were implemented in STATA, using its survey procedures, to account for the weighting and standard error corrections discussed in the text.

10. These include appropriate weights and special procedures to correct for the standard error distortion that can be created when weighting survey observations. Such corrections were made for all subsamples as well.

11. The formula used to calculate the marginal effect is P(1 − P)B; where P is the percentage of respondents taking a value of one for the response variable and B is the reported coefficient from the logistic regression. The estimated marginal effects reported here and their significance levels were all generated using the *mfx* procedure in STATA.

12. The fact that the estimated effect of "socially connected" is larger when we control for other explanatory factors than in the simple comparison of figure 6.1—13 percent compared to 11 percent—is interesting. Normally when there is a large gap between two groups of people for some observed characteristic, the coefficient on a dummy variable that splits the groups entered alone is the simple difference given by a means comparison. Subsequent inclusion of various explanatory factors generally reduces the coefficient on the dummy variable; the other explanatory variables on the right-hand side are allowed to pick up some of the explanation, whereas in a comparison of the means all the explanation is assigned to the difference in, say, race, because that is the only dimension by which another variable—say, income—is being contrasted. In this case, when we consider all the other important characteristics that we have measures for, such as race, gender, education, marital status, English fluency, job turnover, and someone in the house on welfare, social capital is even more important than we would expect through looking at the difference in means mentioned earlier.

13. This figure, along with the rest concerning temp agencies and placement agencies reported in this chapter, is based on the "narrow" definition of temp agencies, which implies the "broad" definition of placement agencies. See chapter 4 for a description of the difference between the broad and narrow definitions of temps and placement agencies. This measure was found to come closest to SIC data on the incidence of temp agencies among all nonfarm employment for the areas under study; moreover, by restricting the definition to its most narrow, we are setting the bar higher for finding significance in our hypotheses.

14. However, before running this model and the simplified version of it that follows, we needed to test each model when applied to the full sample and to each subgroup considered to be sure that the assumption of the independence of irrelevant alternatives (IIA) was valid; we did this via Hausman tests implemented in STATA. This is an assumption made in the multinomial logistic framework that, in this case, the relative probability of choosing, for example, a temp agency over no LMI is unaffected by the exclusion of, for example, the union-type LMI group. The IIA was found to hold for all multinomial regressions presented here, obviating the need to conduct a more complex probit analysis.

15. There were six fewer observations in this regression than in the logit that modeled the probability of LMI use because the six respondents who held jobs in the three years prior to the survey obtained them through more than one LMI type.

16. For a thorough review of the literature on social networks and job search, including the function of social networks in low-income areas, see Ioannides and Loury (2004).

17. We should note here that, while it is not the case in other regression specifications reported, for this particular regression there is a large difference in the effect of social capital on the probability of using a placement agency depending on whether the "broad" or "narrow" definition of temp agency is used. More specifically, the negative impact of social capital on the probability of using a permanent placement agency turns out to be insignificant when the broad definition is used, and concurrently the significance of social capital for the use of temp agencies rises. The reason seems to be that utilizing the narrow definition of temps—an approach that intentionally errs on the side of allocating temps to perms when there is ambiguity—has a stronger impact on the incidence rate for temps in the low-income prefixes. Thus, the strong negative effect of social capital on the probability of using a placement agency in the low-income prefixes may be at least partly a product of the negative relationship between social capital and temp use, if properly measured. However, to be consistent with the rest of the chapter, we chose to use the narrow definition of temps rather than the broad one.

18. This particular wage regression was run without the survey weights. This allowed the oversampled LMI users to have more weight in the regression (each observation was now equally weighted), which is important when looking for a difference between such small populations—the socially connected and the not socially connected users of nonprofit LMIs who lived only in the low-income prefixes in our sample. However, this is another reason to interpret these results cautiously.

Chapter 7

1. For example, one hypothesis is that the Silicon Valley Hispanic population is much larger and can therefore make use of denser social networks, obviating the need to utilize temporary agencies. However, this is not easily testable given the small sample of Hispanics in Milwaukee.

2. The Wisconsin Regional Training Partnership, for example, has been working with the Service Employees International Union (SEIU) to develop a professional employer organization (PEO) for small and medium-sized employers in the child care and home health care industries; see Zabin (2006) and Weisul (2003).

Appendix

1. Self-employed persons are excluded from coverage in both states, and these administrative data do not reflect any "informal" employment that is not recorded for tax purposes. In California, coverage includes virtually all businesses with one or more employees paying $100 or more per quarter in wages. In Wisconsin, employers are subject to UI tax liability if they pay $1,500 or more in wages in any calendar quarter or have full or part-time employees working for them in twenty weeks or more during a calendar year. In Wisconsin, family workers of sole proprietors are excluded from coverage, and special provisions apply to agricultural employers and to 501(c)(3) nonprofit organizations.

2. These measures were reviewed in greater length in chapter 2. The job stability measure is calculated as the percentage of jobs held during a given quarter that continue on in the next quarter. For these purposes, a job is defined as positive quarterly earnings for a given individual with a given employer. The percentage of jobs with earnings increases is calculated as the percentage of jobs for which earnings were higher in the next quarter than the current quarter. Of course, quarter-to-quarter earnings increases can result from variation in the number of days or hours worked in a quarter as well as from pay raises.

3. In Silicon Valley, these industries were construction, machinery and computing equipment manufacturing, electrical machinery equipment and supplies manufacturing, communications, and computer and data processing services. In Milwaukee, these industries were construction, machinery and computing equipment manufacturing, metalworking, transportation, and hotels.

4. For these purposes, Silicon Valley was defined as phone prefix ranges that encompass all of Santa Clara County as well as bordering areas of San Mateo County, Alameda County, and Santa Cruz County. The Milwaukee metropolitan area is defined as Milwaukee, Ozaukee, Washington, and Waukesha counties.

5. According to the U.S. Census data, 98.5 percent of California households and 98.4 percent of Wisconsin households had a telephone.

6. Low-income prefixes were defined as those in which average household income was in the lower 30 percent of the distribution specific to each region. These criteria led to an income cutoff of $30,000 in the Milwaukee area and $50,000 in Silicon Valley.

7. To increase overall response rates, a monetary incentive of $10 for each participating respondent was added midway through the field period.

8. Sometimes we moved respondents from the LMI sample to the non-LMI sample when it was clear that they had not obtained their job through an organization we would consider to be an LMI (for example, individuals reporting that they obtained a job with a city government by checking the job listings at the city personnel office). Respondents who reported four-year colleges or universities as their "LMI" were recoded as non-LMI users.

9. For example, in a question that asked why the respondent had been looking for a job at the time that he or she sought assistance from the LMI, the interviewer was to listen to the respondent's answer and select one from a list of possibilities, such as "had been laid off," "moved," and "finished school." A review of the "other" explanations led us to create additional categories of answers such as "needed a second job" and "needed a better-paying job."

10. The probability of being selected into the sample was also adjusted for oversampling of low-income phone prefixes.

11. See also chapter 6 for the references that relate Internet access to social capital; in particular, see Dutta-Bergman (2005) and Shah et al. (2001).

12. Interestingly, having very high levels of frequency of communication and very high numbers of potential friends for job search was associated with higher rates of LMI use in the raw data. However, there may be other associated characteristics of these individuals that are controlled for in the multivariate analysis.

13. As we note in the chapter text, our preferred measure was also the most robust across all the specifications with subsamples; still, the basic point here is that a series of reasonable alternative specifications performed similarly.

14. This is also consistent with the tests of the stripped-down measures of social capital in the logit regressions discussed earlier, in which we obtained a similar pattern of results over different specifications of social capital.

References

AFL-CIO Working for America Institute. 2000. *High Road Partnerships Report: Innovations in Building Good Jobs and Strong Communities.* Washington, D.C.: AFL-CIO Working for American Institute.

Albelda, Randy. 2001. "Fallacies of Welfare-to-Work Policies." *Annals of the American Academy of Political and Social Sciences* 577: 66–79.

Allard, Scott, and Sheldon Danziger. 2003. "Proximity and Opportunity: How Residence and Race Affect the Employment of Welfare Recipients." *Housing Policy Debate* 13: 4.

Anderson, Steven, Anthony Halter, and Brian Gryzlak. 2004. "Difficulties After Leaving TANF: Inner-City Women Talk About Reasons for Returning to Welfare." *Social Work* 49(2): 185–94.

Andersson, Fredrik, Harry Holzer, and Julia Lane. 2005. *Moving Up or Moving On: Who Advances in the Low-Wage Labor Market?* New York: Russell Sage Foundation.

Aspen Institute. 2002. *Working with Value: Industry-Specific Approaches to Workforce Development: A Summary of Findings.* Washington, D.C.: Aspen Institute.

Autor, David H. 1999. "Why Do Temporary Help Firms Provide Free General Skills Training?" Cambridge, Mass.: Massachusetts Institute of Technology, Economics Department.

———. 2001. "Wiring the Labor Market." *Journal of Economic Perspectives* 15: 1.

———. 2003. "Outsourcing at Will: Unjust Dismissal Doctrine and the Growth of Temporary Help Employment." *Journal of Labor Economics* 21(1): 1–42.

Autor, David, and Susan N. Houseman. 2005a. "Do Temporary Help Jobs Improve Labor Market Outcomes for Low-Skilled Workers? Evidence from Random Assignments." Working paper 05-124. Kalamazoo, Mich.: W. E. Upjohn Institute for Employment Research (October).

———. 2005b. "Temporary Agency Employment as a Way Out of Poverty?" Working paper 05-123. Kalamazoo, Mich.: W. E. Upjohn Institute for Employment Research (May).

Autor, David H., Frank Levy, and Richard Murnane. 1999. "Skills Training in the Temporary Help Sector: Employer Motivations and Worker Impacts." Washington: U.S. Department of Labor, Employment and Training Administration (September).

Bane, Mary Jo, and David T. Ellwood. 1994. *Welfare Realities: From Rhetoric to Reform.* Cambridge, Mass.: Harvard University Press.

Bania, Neil, Laura Leete, and Claudia Coulton. 2001. "The Effect of Job Accessibility and Neighborhood Characteristics on Employment Stability of Welfare Leavers in an Urban Labor Market." Washington: U.S. Department of Health and Human Services, Office of Assistant Secretary of Planning and Evaluation.

Barley, Stephen, and Gideon Kunda. 2004. *Gurus, Hired Guns, and Warm Bodies: Itinerant Experts in a Knowledge Economy.* Princeton, N.J.: Princeton University Press.

Barnow, Burt S., and Christopher T. King. 2005. *The Workforce Investment Act in Eight States: State Reports from a Field Network Study.* Washington: Rockefeller Institute of Government and U.S. Department of Labor, Employment and Training Administration (February).

Bartik, Timothy J. 2001. *Jobs for the Poor: Can Labor Demand Policies Help?* New York: Russell Sage Foundation.

Benner, Chris. 2002. *Work in the New Economy: Flexible Labor Markets in Silicon Valley.* Oxford: Blackwell Press.

———. 2003a. " 'Computers in the Wild': Guilds and Next Generation Unionism in the Information Revolution." *International Review of Social History* 48: S11.

———. 2003b. "Labor Flexibility and Regional Development: The Role of Labor Market Intermediaries." *Regional Studies* 37(6 and 7): 621–33.

———. 2003c. "Learning Communities in a Learning Region: The Soft Infrastructure of Cross-Firm Learning Networks in Silicon Valley." *Environment and Planning A* 35(10): 1809–30.

Bernhardt, Annette, and Dave Marcotte. 2000. "Is 'Standard Employment' Still What It Used to Be?" In *Nonstandard Work: The Nature and Challenges of Changing Employment Arrangements,* vol. 2000 (annual research volume), edited by Françoise Carré, Marianne Ferber, Lonnie Golden, and Stephen Herzenberg. Champaign, Ill.: Industrial Relations Research Association.

Bernhardt, Annette, Martina Morris, Mark Handcock, and Marc Scott. 2001. *Divergent Paths: Economic Mobility in the New American Labor Market.* New York: Russell Sage Foundation.

Bloom, H. S., L. L. Orr, S. H. Bell, G. Cave, F. Doolittle, W. Lin, and J. M. Bos. 1997. "The Benefits and Costs of JTPA Title II-A Programs: Key Findings from the National Job Training Partnership Act Study." *Journal of Human Resources* 32(3): 549–76.

Bluestone, Barry, and Bennett Harrison 1988. "The Growth of Low-Wage Employment: 1963–1986." *American Economic Review* 78(2): 124–28.

Bok, Marcia, and Louise Simmons. 2002. "Postwelfare Reform, Low-Income Families, and the Dissolution of the Safety Net." *Journal of Family and Economic Issues* 23(3): 217.

Bowles, Samuel. 1985. "The Production Process in a Competitive Economy: Walrasian, Marxian, and Neo-Hobbesian Models." *American Economic Review* 76(1): 16–36.

Bridges, William. 1994. *JobShift: How to Prosper in a Workplace Without Jobs.* Reading, Mass.: Addison-Wesley.

Briggs, Xavier de Souza. 1998. "Brown Kids in White Suburbs: Housing Mobility and the Many Faces of Social Capital." *Housing Policy Debate* 9(1): 177–211.

Brownstein, Bob. 2000. "Working Partnerships: A New Political Strategy for Creating Living Wage Jobs." *Working USA* 4(1): 35–48.

Cappelli, Peter. 1999. *The New Deal at Work: Managing the Market-Driven Workforce.* Boston: Harvard Business School Press.

Carnevale, Anthony P., and Donna M. Desrochers. 2004. "The Political Economy of Labor Market Mediation in the United States." In *Workforce Intermediaries for the Twenty-first Century,* edited by Robert P. Giloth. Philadelphia: Temple University Press.

Carré, Françoise, Joaquín Herranz Jr., Dorie Seavey, Carlha Vickers, Ashley Aull, and Rebecca Keegan. 2003. "Alternative Job Brokering: Addressing Labor Market Disadvantages, Improving the Temp Experience, and Enhancing Job Opportunities." Cambridge, Mass.: Radcliffe Institute for Advanced Study.

Center on Wisconsin Strategy. 2002. "Milwaukee, Ozaukee, Washington, and Waukesha Counties: An Economic, Environmental, and Political Snapshot." Madison: University of Wisconsin, Center on Wisconsin Strategy (March).

Christopherson, Susan, and Michael Storper. 1989. "The Effects of Flexible Specialization on Industrial Politics and the Labor Market: The Motion Picture Industry." *Industrial and Labor Relations Review* 42(3): 331–47.

Crispin, Gerry, and Mark Mehler. 1999. *Career Xroads: The 1999 Directory to the 500 Best Job, Résumé, and Career Management Sites on the World Wide Web,* 4th ed., Kendall Park, N.J.: MMC Group.

Diebold, Francis X., David Neumark, and Daniel Polsky. 1994. "Job Stability in the United States." NBER Working Paper No. 4859.

DiNatale, Marisa. 2001. "Characteristics and Preference for Alternative Work Arrangements, 1999." *Monthly Labor Review* 124(3): 28–49.

Dutta-Bergman, Mohan J. 2005. "Access to the Internet in the Context of Community Participation and Community Satisfaction." *New Media and Society* 7(1): 89–109.

Elliot, Mark, Anne Roder, Elisabeth King, and Joseph Stillman. 2001. "Gearing Up: An Interim Report on the Sectoral Employment Initiative." Philadelphia: P/PV.

Erickcek, George, and Susan Houseman. 1997. *Temporary, Part-time, and Contract Employment in the United States: A Report on the W. E. Upjohn Institute's Employer Survey on Flexible Staffing Policies.* Kalamazoo, Mich.: W. E. Upjohn Institute for Employment Research (June).

Falcón, Luis. 1995. "Social Networks and Employment for Latinos, Blacks, and Whites." *New England Journal of Public Policy* 11: 17–28.

Farber, Henry. 1996. "Are Lifetime Jobs Disappearing? Job Duration in the United States, 1973–1993." In *Labor Statistics Measurement Issues,* edited by John Haltiwanger, Marilyn Manser, and Robert Topel. Chicago: University of Chicago Press.

Ferber, Marianne A., and Jane Waldfogel. 1998. "The Long-Term Consequences of Nontraditional Employment." *Monthly Labor Review* 121(5): 3–12.

Fernandez, Roberto M., and Nancy Weinberg. 1997. "Sifting and Sorting: Personal Contacts and Hiring in a Retail Bank." *American Sociological Review* 62(6): 883–902.

Fick, Barbara. 1987. "Political Abuse of Hiring Halls: Comparative Treatment Under the NLRA and the LMRDA." *Industrial Relations Law Review* 9(3): 339–410.

Fischer, David. 2005. "Workforce Intermediaries: Powering Regional Economies in the New Century." New York: Center for an Urban Future (May).

Fitzgerald, Joan. 2004. "Moving the Workforce Intermediary Agenda Forward." *Economic Development Quarterly* 18(1): 3–9.

———. 2006. *Moving Up in the New Economy: Career Ladders for U.S. Workers.* Ithaca, N.Y.: ILR Press.

Freedman, Audrey. 1996. "Contingent Work and the Role of Labor Market Intermediaries." In *Of Heart and Mind: Social Policy Essays in Honor of Sar A. Levitan,* edited by Garth Mangum and Stephen Mangum. Kalamazoo, Mich.: W. E. Upjohn Institute for Employment Research.

Freeman, Richard B., and James L. Medoff. 1984. *What Do Unions Do?* New York: Basic Books.

Friedman, Sheldon, ed. 1994. *Restoring the Promise of American Labor Law.* Ithaca, N.Y.: ILR Press.

General Accounting Office (GAO). 1994. "Multiple Employment Training Programs: Most Federal Agencies Do Not Know If Their Programs Are Working Effectively." Washington: General Accounting Office.

———. 2000. "Contingent Workers: Incomes and Benefits Lag Behind the Rest of the Workforce." Washington: General Accounting Office (June).

Giloth, Robert, ed. 2004. *Workforce Intermediaries for the Twenty-first Century.* Philadelphia: Temple University Press.

Gonos, George. 1997. "The Contest over 'Employer' Status in the Postwar United States: The Case of Temporary Help Firms." *Law and Society* 31(1): 81–110.

Gordon, David M. 1996. *Fat and Mean: The Corporate Squeeze of Working Americans and the Myth of Managerial "Downsizing."* New York: Martin Kessler Books.

Granovetter, Mark. 1995. *Getting a Job: A Study of Contacts and Careers.* Chicago: University of Chicago Press.

Gray, Lois, and Ronald Seeber, eds. 1996. *Under the Stars: Essays on Labor Relations in Arts and Entertainment.* Ithaca, N.Y.: ILR Press.

Grubb, W. Norton. 1995. *Evaluating Job Training Programs in the United States: Evidence and Explanations.* Berkeley, Calif.: National Center for Research in Vocational Education.

———. 1996. *Learning to Work: The Case for Reintegrating Job Training and Education.* New York: Russell Sage Foundation.

Grubb, W. Norton, Norena Badway, Denise Bell, Debra Bragg, and Maxine Russman. 1997. "Workforce, Economic, and Community Development: The Changing Landscape of the Entrepreneurial Community College." Mission Viejo, Calif.: League for Innovation in the Community College.

Grubb, W. Norton, Norena Badway, Denise Bell, and Eileen Kraskouskas. 1996. "Community College Innovations in Workforce Preparation: Curriculum Integration and Tech-Prep." Mission Viejo, Calif.: League for Innovation in the Community College.

Harrison, Bennett, and Marcus S. Weiss. 1998. *Workforce Development Networks: Community-Based Organizations and Regional Alliances.* Thousand Oaks, Calif.: Sage Publications.

Heckscher, Charles. 1996. *The New Unionism: Employee Involvement in the Changing Corporation.* Ithaca, N.Y.: ILR Press.

Heinrich, Carolyn J., Peter R. Mueser, and Kenneth R. Troske. 2005. "Welfare to Temporary Work: Implications for Labor Market Outcomes." *Review of Economics and Statistics* 87(1): 154–73.

Herzenberg, Stephen, John Alic, and Howard Wial. 1998. *New Rules for a New Economy: Employment and Opportunity in Postindustrial America.* Ithaca, N.Y.: ILR Press.

Hipple, Steven. 2001. "Contingent Work in the Late 1990s." *Monthly Labor Review* (March): 3–27.

Houseman, Susan N., Arne L. Kalleberg, and George A. Erickcek. 2001. "The Role of Temporary Help Employment in Tight Labor Markets." Working paper 01-73. Kalamazoo, Mich.: W. E. Upjohn Institute for Employment Research (June).

Hull, Glynda A. 1997. *Changing Work, Changing Workers: Critical Perspectives on Language, Literacy, and Skills.* Albany: State University of New York Press.

Indergaard, Michael. 1997. "Community-Based Restructuring? Institution Building in the Industrial Midwest." *Urban Affairs Review* 32(5): 662–82.

Ioannides, Yannis, and Linda Datcher Loury. 2004. "Job Information Networks, Neighborhood Effects, and Inequality." *Journal of Economic Literature* 42(4): 1056–93.

Jargowsky, Paul. 1997. *Poverty and Place: Ghettos, Barrios, and the American City.* New York: Russell Sage Foundation.

Johnson, James H., Elisa Jayne Bienenstock, and Walter C. Farrell. 1999. "Bridging Social Networks and Female Labor-Force Participation in a Multiethnic Metropolis." *Urban Geography* 20(1): 3–30.

Johnson, James H., Melvin L. Oliver, and Lawrence D. Bobo. 1994. "Understanding the Contours of Deepening Urban Inequality: Theoretical Underpinnings and Research Design of a Multi-City Study." *Urban Geography* 15: 77–89.

Kalleberg, Arne. 2000. "Nonstandard Employment Relations: Part-time, Temporary, and Contract Work." *Annual Review of Sociology* 26: 341–65.

Kazis, Richard. 1998. "New Labor Market Intermediaries: What's Driving Them? Where Are They Headed?" Cambridge, Mass.: Massachusetts Institute of Technology, Sloan School of Management (September).

Kenney, Martin, ed. 2000. *Understanding Silicon Valley: The Anatomy of an Entrepreneurial Region.* Palo Alto, Calif.: Stanford University Press.

Kuhn, Peter, and Mikai Skuterud. 2000. "Job Search Methods: Internet Versus Traditional." *Monthly Labor Review* 123(10): 3–11.

Lafer, Gordon. 1994. "The Politics of Job Training: Urban Poverty and the False Promise of JTPA." *Politics and Society* 22(3): 349–88.

Lane, Julia, Kelly S. Mikelson, Pat Sharkey, and Doug Wissoker. 2003. "Pathways to Work for Low-Income Workers: The Effect of Work in the Temporary Help Industry." *Journal of Policy Analysis and Management* 22(4): 581–98.

Lave, Jean, and Etienne Wenger. 1991. *Situated Learning: Legitimate Peripheral Participation.* Cambridge: Cambridge University Press.

Lee, Chong-Moon, William Miller, Marguerite Gong Hancock, and Henry Rowen, eds. 2000. *The Silicon Valley Edge: A Habitat for Innovation and Entrepreneurship,* Palo Alto, Calif.: Stanford University Press.

Leete-Guy, Laura, and Juliet Schor. 1994. "Assessing the Time-Squeeze: Hours Worked in the U.S., 1969–1989." *Industrial Relations Law Review* 33(1): 25–43.

Lichter, Michael, and Melvin Oliver. 2000. "Racial Differences in Labor Force Participation Among Less Education Men." In *Prismatic Metropolis: Race, Segregation, and the Dynamics of Inequality in Los Angeles,* edited by Lawrence D. Bobo, Melvin L. Oliver, James H. Johnson, and Abel Valenzuela Jr. New York: Russell Sage Foundation.

Marcelli, Enrico, and David Heer. 1997. "Unauthorized Mexican Workers in the 1990 Los Angeles County Labor Force." *International Migration* 35(1): 59–83.

Massey, Douglas, and Kumiko Shibuya. 1995. "Unraveling the Tangle of Pathology: The Effect of Spatially Concentrated Joblessness on the Well-being of African Americans." *Social Science Research* 24(4): 352–66.

Melendez, Edwin, and Luis M. Falcón. (1999) "Closing the Social Mismatch: Lessons from the Latino Experience," In *Moving Up the Economic Ladder: Latino Workers and the Nation's Future Prosperity,* edited by Sonia M. Perez. Washington, D.C.: National Council of La Raza.

Melendez, Edwin, and Bennett Harrison. 1998. "Matching the Disadvantaged to Job Opportunities: Structural Explanations for the Past Successes of the Center for Employment Training." *Economic Development Quarterly* 12(1): 3–11.

Montgomery, James D. 1991. "Social Networks and Labor Market Outcomes: Towards an Economic Analysis." *American Economic Review* 81(5): 1408–18.

Neuenfeldt, Phil, and Eric Parker. 1996. *Wisconsin Regional Training Partnership: Building the Infrastructure for Workplace Change and Skill Development.* Washington, D.C.: AFL-CIO Human Resources Development Institute.

Neumark, David. 2000. "Changes in Job Stability and Job Security: A Collective Effort to Untangle, Reconcile, and Interpret the Evidence." Working paper 7472. Cambridge, Mass.: National Bureau of Economic Research.

Neuwirth, Esther. 2004. "Permanent Strategies: Staffing Agencies and Temporary Workers in the New Millennium." PhD diss., University of California at Davis.

O'Regan, Katherine M. 1993. "The Effects of Social Networks and Concentrated Poverty on Black Youth Employment." *Annals of Regional Science* 27(4): 327–42.

Osterman, Paul. 1999. *Securing Prosperity: The American Labor Market: How It Has Changed and What to Do About It.* Princeton, N.J.: Princeton University Press.

———. 2004. "Labor Market Intermediaries in the Modern Labor Market." In *Workforce Intermediaries for the Twenty-first Century,* edited by Robert Giloth. Philadelphia: Temple University Press.

Osterman, Paul, and Brenda Lautsch. 1996. "Project Quest: A Report to the Ford Foundation." Cambridge, Mass.: Massachusetts Institute of Technology, Sloan School of Management.

Parker, Eric, and Joel Rogers. 2001. "Building the High Road in Metro Areas: Sectoral Training and Employment Projects." In *Rekindling the Movement: Labor's Quest for Relevance in the Twenty-first Century,* edited by Lowell Turner, Harry Katz, and Richard Hurd. Ithaca, N.Y.: ILR Press.

Parker, Robert E. 1994. *Flesh Peddlers and Warm Bodies: The Temporary Help Industry and Its Workers.* New Brunswick, N.J.: Rutgers University Press.

Partnership for Employer-Employee Responsive Systems (PEERS). 2003. "Workforce Intermediaries: Generating Benefits for Employers and Workers." New York: PEERS.

Pastor, Manuel, and Ana Robinson Adams. 1996. "Keeping Down with the Jones: Neighbors, Networks, and Wages." *Review of Regional Studies* 26(2): 115–45.

Pastor, Manuel, Peter Dreier, Eugene Grigsby, and Marta Lopez-Garza. 2000. *Regions That Work: How Cities and Suburbs Can Grow Together.* Minneapolis: University of Minnesota Press.

Pastor, Manuel, and Enrico Marcelli. 2000. "Men 'n the Hood: Skill, Spatial, and Social Mismatch Among Male Workers in Los Angeles County." *Urban Geography* 21(6): 474–96.

Peck, Jamie, Nik Theodore, and Kevin Ward. 2005. "Constructing Markets for Temporary Labor: Employment Liberalization and the Internationalization of the Staffing Industry." *Global Networks* 5(1): 3–26.

Pindus, Nancy, Carolyn O'Brien, Maureen Conway, Conaway Haskins, and Ida Rademacher. 2004. *Evaluation of the Sectoral Employment Demonstration Program.* Washington, D.C.: Urban Institute.

Putnam, Robert D. 2000. *Bowling Alone: The Collapse and Revival of American Community.* New York: Simon & Schuster.

Reimers, Cordelia W. 1985. "A Comparative Analysis of the Wages of Hispanics, Blacks, and Non-Hispanic Whites." In *Hispanics in the U.S. Economy,* edited by George J. Borjas and Marta Tienda. New York: Academic Press.

Rogers, Jackie Krasas. 2000. *Temps: The Many Faces of the Changing Workplace.* Ithaca, N.Y.: Cornell University Press.

Rousseau, Denise. 1995. *Psychological Contracts in Organizations: Understanding Written and Unwritten Agreements.* Thousand Oaks, Calif.: Sage Publications.

Sadd, James, Manuel Pastor, Tom Boer, and Lori Snyder. 1999. " 'Every Breath You Take . . . ': The Demographics of Toxic Air Releases in Southern California." *Economic Development Quarterly* 13(2): 107–23.

Sampson, Robert J., and W. Byron Groves. 1989. "Community Structure and Crime: Testing Social-Disorganization Theory." *American Journal of Sociology* 94(4): 774–802.

Saxenian, AnnaLee. 1994. *Regional Advantage: Culture and Competition in Silicon Valley and Route 128.* Cambridge, Mass.: Harvard University Press.

Scott, Allen John. 1998. *Regions and the World Economy: The Coming Shape of Global Production, Competition, and Political Order.* Oxford: Oxford University Press.

Segal, Lewis M., and Daniel G. Sullivan. 1997a. "The Growth of Temporary Services Work." *Journal of Economic Perspectives* 11: 117–36.

———. 1997b. *Temporary Services Employment Durations: Evidence from State UI Data.* Chicago: Federal Reserve Bank of Chicago.

Shah, Dhavan V., Nojin Kwak, and R. Lance Holbert. 2001. " 'Connecting' and 'Disconnecting' with Civic Life: Patterns of Internet Use and the Production of Social Capital." *Political Communication* 18(2): 141–62.

Shapiro, Carl, and Joseph Stiglitz. 1984. "Equilibrium Unemployment as a Worker Discipline Device." *American Economic Review* 74(3): 433–44.

Spaulding, Shayne. 2005. "Getting Connected: Strategies for Expanding the Employment Networks of Low-Income People." Philadelphia: Public/Private Ventures.

Swinnerton, Kenneth, and Howard Wial. 1995. "Is Job Stability Declining in the U.S. Economy?" *Industrial and Labor Relations Review* 48(2): 293–304.

Theodore, Nik. 2003. "Political Economies of Day Labor: Regulation and Restructuring of Chicago's Contingent Labor Markets." *Urban Studies* 40(9): 1811–27.

Theodore, Nik, and Jamie Peck. 2001. "Contingent Chicago: Restructuring the Spaces of Temporary Labor." *International Journal of Urban and Regional Research* 25(3): 471–96.

Thieblot, Armand J. 2002. "Technology and Labor Relations in the Construction Industry." *Journal of Labor Research* 23(4): 559–74.

Trejo, Stephen. 1997. "Why Do Mexican Americans Earn Low Wages?" *Journal of Political Economy* 105: 1235–68.

Turner, Lowell, Harry Katz, and Richard Hurd, eds. 2001. *Rekindling the Movement: Labor's Quest for Relevance in the Twenty-first Century.* Ithaca, N.Y.: ILR Press.

U.S. Department of Labor. 1995. *What's Working (and What's Not): A Summary of Research in the Economic Impacts of Employment Training Programs.* Washington: U.S. Department of Labor.

Weisul, Kimberly. 2003. "A Health Union of Convenience." *Business Week,* November 14.

Well, David. 2005. "The Contemporary Industrial Relations System in Construction: Analysis, Observation, and Speculations." *Labor History* 46(4): 447.

Wenger, Etienne. 1998. *Communities of Practice: Learning, Meaning, and Identity.* Cambridge: Cambridge University Press.

Wial, Howard. 1991. "Getting a Good Job: Mobility in a Segmented Labor Market." *Industrial Relations* 30(3): 396–416.

Wilson, William Julius. 1996. *When Work Disappears: The World of the New Urban Poor.* New York: Alfred A. Knopf.

Wolf-Powers, Laura. 2003. "The Role of Labor Market Intermediaries in Promoting Employment Access and Mobility: A Supply- and Demand-Side Approach." PhD diss., Rutgers University.

Zabin, Carol. 2006. *Quality Services and Quality Jobs for Supporting Californians with Developmental Disabilities.* Berkeley: California Policy Research Center.

Index

Boldface numbers refer to figures and tables.

mobility, career: for-profit LMIs' lack of focus on, 92; market molding by LMIs, 21, 61, 72–80; public-sector LMIs inability to focus on, 93; workers' and employers' perspectives, 96

nonprofit LMIs: and advocacy for job quality, 81; demographic factors in use of, **109–10,** 111; and disadvantaged workers, 65, 92–93, 118, **119**; and earnings outcomes, **161**; incidence of use, **101–2,** 105, **107**; and job outcomes, **134–35,** 138; market molding by, 72, 74–75; on-the-job assistance, 69; outreach challenges for, 64; reasons for use, **112–13**; regional market overview, 47–48; satisfaction levels, 116, **117**; and social networks, 80, 173, **191,** 192–93, **195, 197, 199, 201,** 203, **217,** 220; soft-skill training by, 73; supplementary services from, 114, **115**; and wage outcomes, **146–47, 167**
North Valley (NOVA) PIC/WIB, 47
number of jobs held variable, 43, **44–45,** 46

Occupational Training Institute, 75
occupations: and LMIs' focus, 259–60n4; and LMIs' impact on job outcomes, 126, **127, 129,** 131, **132**; and wages in regional markets, 35, **37–38,** 39
one-stop career centers, 47, 71, 235
on-site temporary agencies, 68, 77–78, 88, 90
on-the-job assistance by LMIs, 69–70

opportunity, economic: LMIs complex impact on, 13; market molding by LMIs, 21, 61, 72–80; and volatility of labor market, 4. *See also* market making
outreach to workers and employers, 63–67

Peck, Jamie, 231
pension plans, 140–42
permanent placement agencies: and benefits outcomes, **150, 152**; and changing labor market, 7; demographic factors in use of, **109–10,** 111; incidence of use, **101–2** 105, **107**; and job outcomes, **134–35,** 138; reasons for use, 111, **112–13**; regional market comparison, 124, 225; and social networks, 172, 190–93, **194, 196, 198, 200,** 202, **204–19**; supplementary services from, 114, **115**; and wage outcomes, 131, **148–49, 167,** 226
PICs (private industry councils), 47, 48, 50
placement firms. *See* permanent placement agencies; temporary employment agencies
policy implications, 3, 133–34, 221, 227, 234–36
power relationship, employer-employee, 15
pre-employment training, 73–74
private industry councils (PICs), 47, 48, 50
private-sector LMIs: demographic factors in use of, **109–10,** 111; and dis-

advantaged workers, 64, 91–95; employer relationships, 77–78; incidence of use, **101–2,** 104–5; and job outcomes, 138–39; marketing flexibility of, 64–65; networking with public-sector LMIs, 227–28, 235; on-the-job assistance, 70; reasons for use, **112–13**; regional market overview, 50–51, **52,** 53, **54**; response to changing labor market, 7; supplementary services from, 114, **115**. *See also* membership-based LMIs; permanent placement agencies; temporary employment agencies

production occupations, 35. *See also* manufacturing industries

professional associations: and benefits outcomes, **152**; demographic factors in use of, **109–10**; and disadvantaged workers, **119**; and earnings outcomes, **161**; incidence of use, **101–2**; and industry knowledge base, 78–79; and job outcomes, **134–35**; and mentoring relationships, 70; reasons for use, **112–13**; regional market overview, 56, 225; satisfaction levels, 116, **117**; and social networks, 80, **191,** 192, **195, 197, 199, 201, 217**; supplementary services from, 114, **115**

Professional Employer Organization, 90

public-sector LMIs: and changing labor market, 7; demographic factors in use of, **109–10,** 111; and disadvantaged workers, 92–93, 118, **119**; and earnings outcomes, **161**; and federal workforce development programs, 7–8, 46, 47, 75, 81; funding restric-

tions, 75–76; growth of, 9; incidence of use, **101–2** 105, **107**; and job outcomes, **134–35,** 138; marketing challenges for, 64–65; market molding by, 72; networking with private-sector LMIs, 227–28, 235; one-stop career centers, 47, 71, 235; on-the-job assistance, 69; outreach challenges for, 64; private industry councils, 47, 48, 50; reasons for use, **112–13**; regional market overview, 46–50; and social networks, 80, 173, **191, 192–93, 195, 197, 199, 201,** 203, **217**; supplementary services from, 70–72, 73, 114, **115**; and wage outcomes, **167**; welfare-to-work services, 46, 114. *See also* community colleges; nonprofit LMIs; technical colleges

quality, job. *See* market making

race and ethnicity: and benefits outcomes, **150, 152, 154–55**; and earnings outcomes, **161, 165**; future research considerations, 231; and intensity of contact with LMIs, **122–23**; and LMIs' influence on job outcomes, **136–39**; regional market comparison, **26,** 27, **28**; and social networks, **179,** 181, 182, **183–87,** 188–90, **194–95, 198–99,** 202, **204–5, 208–17**; usage patterns for LMIs, 108, **109–10,** 118, **119,** 225–26; and wage outcomes, **146–47, 167**

reasons for using LMIs: employers, 9, 64, 92; workers, 111, **112–13,** 118, 120–21, 224

stability, job: duration of jobs, 43, **44–45,** 46, 107–8, 260–61*n*5; and earnings outcomes, **161, 165;** regional market comparison, 39–43, **44–45,** 46; and wage outcomes, **167,** 169. *See also* tenure, job

staffing agencies, private, 68. *See also* private-sector LMIs

state-funded workforce development programs, 46, 47

supplementary support services: for disadvantaged workers, 70–72; and usage patterns for LMIs, 111, 114, **115,** 116, 121

switching, job: and LMIs' growth, 14; and social networks, **179,** 181, **184, 187,** 192, **194–95, 198–99,** 202, **204–5, 208–9, 212–13, 216–17**

technical colleges: advancement opportunities in, 94; incidence of use, **101–2,** 104, 105; influence on internal job training, 83; market making by, 66; market molding by, 74–75; regional market overview, 48, 50

technology-based industries: employer-LMI relationship, 65; lack of unionization in, 56; and LMIs' growth, 14; need for vocational training, 74–75; professional associations' role in, 56, 225; recruitment of labor from outside U.S., 225, 261*n*2; regional market comparison, 35

temporary employment agencies: and advocacy for job quality, 81; and benefits outcomes, 138–40, 141, 142, **150, 152;** definitional issues,

266*n*13, 267*n*17; demographic factors in use of, 108, **109–10,** 111; and disadvantaged workers, 88, 91–92, 118, **119,** 162–69, 261*n*5; and earnings outcomes, 126, 159–69, 170, 226, 264*n*12; as employer of record, 88–91, 227; future research considerations, 231; and hours of work, 131; and imperfect information, 14; incidence of use, **101–2,** 104, 105, 106, **107;** increase in, 4, 7; job stability in, 41–42; links to public-sector agencies, 228; and occupation-industry job outcomes, **127–30;** on-site, 68, 77–78, 88, 90; on-the-job assistance, 70; policy implications, 235–36; reasons for use, **112–13;** regional market overview, 50–51, **52, 54;** relationship with employers, 68; satisfaction levels, 116, **117,** 121, 227; and social networks, 79–80, 172, 190–93, **194, 196, 198, 200,** 202, **204–19;** supplementary services from, 114, **115;** and wage outcomes, 131–33, **134–35, 146–47,** 226; and welfare reform programs, 50–51, 53

Temporary Workers Employment Project, 56

tenure, job: and benefits outcomes, **151, 153;** and earnings outcomes, **161, 165;** and labor market volatility, 4–6; and wage outcomes, **146–47, 167**

tight labor markets, 64, 72, 92

training: employers' internal, 82–83, **151;** job training by LMIs, 47–48, 50, 69, 72–76, 114, 116, 131,

134–35. *See also* community colleges; technical colleges

unemployment status, 27–28, **29,** 111, **112–13,** 261*n*5
unions: advancement opportunities in, 94–95; and advocacy for job quality, 81; and benefits outcomes, 143, **151, 153, 155–56;** and changing labor market, 8–9; demographic factors in use of, **109–10;** and disadvantaged workers, **119;** hiring hall system, 9, 84–86; incidence of use, **101–2,** 105; and industry knowledge levels, 76, 78–79; influence on internal job training, 83; and job outcomes, **134–35;** market making by, 83–88; market molding by, 72; public sector unionization rates, 53; reasons for use, **112–13;** regional market comparison, 53, 55–56; satisfaction levels, 116, **117;** and social networks, 80, **191,** 192, 193, **194, 196, 198, 200, 217;** supplementary services from, **115**

vocational ESL (VESL) training, 73
vocational training, 74–76. *See also* technical colleges
volatility, labor market: impact on LMI usage, 224–25; and job tenure, 4–6; methods and data, 240, **241–44;** regional market comparison, 39–46; and social networks, 178, **179,** 181, **184, 187,** 192, **194–95, 198–99,** 202, **204–5, 208–9, 212–13, 216–17**

wages: LMIs' influence on job outcomes, 131–33, **134–37,** 137–40, **146–49,** 158–66, **167–68,** 169, 170, 226, 264*n*12; regional market comparison, 31, 35, **36–38,** 39; and social networks in low-income areas, 220. *See also* hourly wages
Waukesha County Technical College, 50
Web-based job searches, 7, 103, 175, 225, 260*n*6, 265*n*4
welfare programs, 7, 50, 71–72
welfare-to-work services, 46, 114
WIBs (workforce investment boards), 47, 235
Wisconsin Regional Training Partnership (WRTP), 50, 55, 66, 70, 83, 86–87, 90
Wisconsin Works (W2), 50, 71
women. *See* gender
work, shifts in nature and organization of, 3–10
work experience variable, **161, 165, 167,** 265*n*5
workforce development system, 7–8, 11–12, 46, 47, 75, 81, 235
Workforce Investment Act (1998), 7, 47, 50, 75, 235
workforce investment boards (WIBs), 47, 235
Working Partnership, 82, 90
workplace environment, 1–2, 50, 73–74
WRTP (Wisconsin Regional Training Partnership), 50, 55, 66, 70, 83, 86–87, 90